The Structure of English
for Readers, Writers, and Teachers

by Mary M. Clark

College Publishing books are printed on acid-free paper.

ISBN 0-9679121-4-8
Library of Congress Control Number 2002108900

College Publishing
12309 Lynwood Drive, Glen Allen, Virginia 23059
T (804) 364-8410 F (804) 364-8408
collegepub@mindspring.com

The Structure of English
for Readers, Writers, and Teachers

by Mary M. Clark

College Publishing
Glen Allen, Virginia

TABLE OF CONTENTS

ACKNOWLEDGEMENTS

I gratefully acknowledge the support of the College of Liberal Arts, University of New Hampshire, who provided financial assistance for the preparation of this manuscript. I owe a special debt of gratitude to the students in my English Grammar class at the University of New Hampshire, who tested every part of this text and gave me their honest opinions as I constructed it, gradually, over the years. The following reviewers made helpful comments on a draft version of the manuscript: Jeanette K. Gundel, University of Minnesota; Susan Smith, University of Oregon; Madelyn J. Kissock, Oakland University; and Gregory K. Iverson, University of Wisconsin-Milwaukee. Special thanks to Susannah Clark and Joshua Wilson, who helped prepare the exercises, and to Julia Curl, who provided the sample of three-year-old speech in the Appendix. Finally, thanks to Bernie, who was a good sport about sailing alone during the summer of 2001.

CHAPTER 1

INTRODUCTION

The teaching of formal grammar has a negligible or, because it usually displaces some instruction and practice in actual composition, even a harmful effect on the improvement of writing.

—Richard Braddock, Richard Lloyd-Jones,
and Lowell Schoer, 1963

... what was stopped [in the schools] was not just bad *teaching of grammar, but* all *teaching of grammar. In retrospect this is a clear case of an important baby being thrown out with some rather dirty bathwater.*

—Richard Hudson, 1992

The best reason for studying grammar is that grammar is interesting.

—Paul Roberts, 1958

1.1 What Is Grammar?

Since this is a book about English grammar, I should begin by saying what I mean by that term and why it is a subject worthy of study. In this text, I will use the term *grammar* to refer to the system we follow, whether consciously or unconsciously, in creating well-formed phrases and sentences. By *well-formed*, I mean well-formed within a particular language variety; for example, sentences that are well-formed in British English may not be well-formed in American English; sentences that are well-formed in conversational English may not be well-formed in formal writing; sentences that are well-formed in African-American Vernacular may not be well-formed in Standard American English (and vice versa). The goal of this text is not to pare English down to a single approved variety (formal written English), but to look at the various forms that English takes, with some attention to the question of which forms are appropriate under which circumstances.

1.2 Why Study Grammar?

As you can see from the quotations at the beginning of this chapter, people have very different opinions about the study of grammar. (Some of these differences probably derive from a difference in how the term is defined.) Those who believe in the study of grammar usually base that belief on one or more of the following arguments:

1. A knowledge of grammar can help with some aspects of writing. For example, the following sentences contain constructions that are unacceptable in formal speech or writing. Try to identify the problem in each sentence:

Industries now tend to use more machines and less people.
Jane looked awfully well in her dress.
You are the person whom I think would do the best job.

A writer who understands grammar will be less likely to stumble into questionable constructions like these. A strong sense of grammatical structure is also helpful at the editing stage of composition when we are considering how to eliminate redundancies, reorder information within a sentence, break up long, awkward sentences, or combine short, choppy sentences into longer, smoother ones.

2. Teachers who work with student writers need a conscious awareness of sentence structure in order to monitor their students' progress. For example, the writers below are starting to use structures that are normally found only in written English, not in conversation:

> *The sounds, <u>although totally disconnected</u>, seemed to form a weird symphony which was going somewhere.*
> (Twelve-year-old, cited in Perera 1984, 236)
> *He is just a ghost <u>to whom I pay no attention at all</u>.* (Thirteen-year-old, cited in Perera, 237)
> *One [of them] was getting very intelligent, like plucking at moving things. <u>This one</u> we called Charlie.*
> (Thirteen-year-old, cited in Perera, 250)

These students are acquiring written English structures in the same way they acquired their spoken language—by assimilating, intuitively, the forms they hear and see. They do not need a formal grammatical analysis of these structures. However, the parents and teachers of these students will be able to provide more intelligent assistance if they have a conscious understanding of the structures the children are using and of the stages the children will go through on their way to becoming proficient adult writers.

3. A third reason for studying grammar is to develop the vocabulary and concepts to talk about language. One student told me that her literature professor had asked the class to watch for changes of tense in a short story by James Baldwin, but because she had never taken a course in grammar, she did not understand the assignment. A course in the structure of English would have helped her to address this assignment with confidence, along with other topics such as the following:

> the language of a two-year-old who is just learning to talk
> the spelling of a first-grader who is just learning to read
> the sentence structure of a fourth-grader who is beginning to write more fluently
> the written English of a college freshman who is acquiring the register of academic discourse
> the language of a poem or story
> the language of another era (that of Shakespeare, for example, or of Jane Austen), and how it differs from our own
> the language of another dialect (the speech of a presidential candidate from Texas,

for example, or of African Americans in the inner city)

the varieties of English that are used by one individual speaker in different places and circumstances

the shared language of a sports team or a group of friends

the differences between English and other languages such as French, Spanish, or Japanese

the problems of students who are learning English as a second language

the differences between male and female language

the language we use to handle awkward social situations such as making excuses or ending conversations

the language of the characters in a story

4. Finally, as stated by Paul Roberts (1958) in the quote that appears at the beginning of this chapter, grammar is worth studying because it is interesting. The system we use to create phrases and sentences in English and other languages is astonishingly complex. For example, consider the construction called the "tag question," which is illustrated in the examples below. Native speakers of English have no difficulty in creating these tags; you were able to form them by the time you were about four years old. But if you look at this construction carefully, you will see that it is a great deal more intricate than you first realized. First, ascertain that you know how to form tag questions by filling in the missing tags below. Then, try to figure out the system you follow in creating these tags. (*Hint:* Each set of four sentences requires a further elaboration of the rule.)

You can go, can't you?
He should know, _____?
They are leaving, _____?
We've done a good job, _____?

Sue can go, _____?
Bill should know, _____?
Bill and Sue are leaving, _____?
You and I have done a good job, _____?

Sue can't go, _____?
Bill shouldn't know, _____?
Bill and Sue aren't leaving, _____?
You and I haven't done a very good job, _____?

She knows, _____?
They always finish on time, _____?
We enjoy ourselves, _____?
They left, _____?

Figuring out the rules for tag questions will not help you speak or write better English, but it should give you a new appreciation of the linguistic system you use every day, even when you think you are following no rules at all. As observed by Noam Chomsky, the MIT linguist who founded transformational generative grammar,

> *Few students are aware of the fact that in their normal, everyday life they are constantly creating new linguistic structures that are immediately understood, despite their novelty, by those to whom they speak or write. They are never brought to the realization of how amazing an accomplishment this is, and of how limited is our comprehension of what makes it possible. Nor do they acquire any insight into the remarkable intricacy of the grammar that they use unconsciously, even insofar as this system is understood and can be explicitly presented. . . . [S]ome way [should] be found to introduce students to the tantalizing problems that language has always posed for those who are puzzled and intrigued by the mysteries of human intelligence (Noam Chomsky, 1969, 12).*

1.3 The Purpose of This Text

This text is designed for students who want to learn something about the English language as preparation for teaching, or for studying literature or foreign languages, or because they are trying to become better writers. Linguists traditionally distinguish between *prescriptive* grammars, which tell people how they should speak or write, and *descriptive* grammars, which describe the language we actually use. Insofar as it deals with the improvement of writing, the present text will contain some prescriptive elements, with an emphasis on improving the overall structure of sentences rather than avoiding grammatical "errors." However, the primary approach of this text will be descriptive, with a focus on the third goal discussed earlier: learning to observe and talk about language. Topics such as dialect variation, the historical development of our vocabulary, and the acquisition of language by children are worth studying for their own sake and should be especially interesting to those who want to read, write, or teach English.

1.4 The Organization of Language

Human languages have a particular organization, which is set out in figure 1.4. All human languages are based on meaningful units called words, which we learn over the course of a lifetime by hearing or reading them in context. Complex words such as *disapproval* can be broken into parts called *morphemes*—in this case, a prefix (*dis-*), a root (*approve*) and a suffix (*-al*); we use our knowledge of morphemes to invent and interpret new words. By the age of about five years, we have mastered not only the basic vocabulary of our language, but also the system for organizing words into phrases, sentences, and conversations (*discourses*).

At a more basic level, words and morphemes are made up of consonant and vowel sounds (in spoken language) or of letters (in written language). The sounds and letters have no meanings of their own—meanings are attached only to the words and morphemes that the sounds or letters represent. The expressive power of human language derives from this hierarchical structure. If all we had were the *sounds* of English, then we would be able to make only about forty-four different utterances (depending on the number of consonant and vowel sounds in our particular dialect). Similarly, if all we had were the words, then we could express some 75,000 notions, which is the approximate number of words that an average speaker commands. However, because words are made up of *sequences* of sounds or letters, we can create as many words as we like, and because we have a system for combining words into meaningful phrases and sentences, the number of ideas we can express is unlimited. Speakers of human languages can, in principle, produce an infinite number of words and phrases, each with its own unique meaning.

1.5 The Organization of This Text

This text will begin at the midpoint of the linguistic hierarchy, with the structure of words, in chapter 2. Chapter 3 will set out the grammatical categories ("parts of speech"); the grammatical category of a word determines where it can be placed in a sentence. Chapter 4 will look briefly at the sound system of English, using the pronunciation symbols that are commonly used in Ameri-

> **Discourse**

> **Sentences:** *A murmur of disapproval filled the classroom.*
> *Why did you open the window?*

> **Phrases:** *a murmur of disapproval, of disapproval, filled the classroom,*
> *the classroom*

> **Words:** *a, murmur, of, disapproval, filled, the, classroom*

> **Morphemes (=prefixes, suffixes, and roots):** *a, murmur, of, dis-, approve*
> *(ad + prove), -al, fill, -ed, the, class, room*

> **Phonemes (Sounds):** [ă], [ā], [ô], [o͞o], [ə], [h], [hw], [sh], [th], [*th*], [k], etc.
> or
> **Letters:** <a>, <d>, <i>, <s>, <p>, <r>, <o>, <v>, <e>, <n>, etc.

Figure 1.4 Chart of the hierarchical structure of a human language.

can dictionaries, followed by an overview of our spelling system and how it works (or does not work). Chapter 5 is concerned with the dictionary and the information that is given there.

Chapters 6 and 7 begin the grammar "proper," with an overview of the structure of statements and the basic types of phrases: noun phrases, verb phrases, adjective phrases, adverb phrases, and prepositional phrases. Chapter 8, on semantics, is concerned with the *meaning* of a statement and how that meaning is determined from the words the sentence contains and the way they are structured. Chapters 9 and 10 discuss the English tense system and the formation of interrogative, exclamative, and imperative sentences.

Chapter 11 provides a short respite from the grammatical analysis, by applying the concepts that have been developed so far to the study of variation—variation in the language of individual speakers, as well as variation in dialect among geographical regions and social groups. Chapter 12 introduces the grammar of sentences that contain more than one clause. Finally, chapters 13, 14, and 15 are "application" chapters which apply the grammatical analysis to questions regarding punctuation, especially commas (chapter 13), the presentation of information in connected discourse (chapter 14) and the acquisition of spoken and written language by children (chapter 15).

No one can learn grammar simply from reading about it; you will have to make use of what you have learned. Thus, this book is filled with exercises, and the exercises are interspersed with the text. I urge you to at least try the exercises in each section before going on. Each concept builds on previous ones, and you will need a reasonably solid understanding of one concept in order to understand the next one.

1.6 Some Things to Do

Please turn now to the Appendix and skim over the samples of written and spoken English that you will be asked to observe and think about while reading this book. Some of the samples are excerpts from short stories, and you may want to read the entire story if you have not done so already. You are also asked to provide some samples of your own—a sample of your writing, and a short conversation that you have recorded and transcribed.

1.7 Dictionaries

As you work through this text, you will need a good, up-to-date college dictionary (not an abridged paperback version). Any of the following would be a good choice:

Merriam Webster's Collegiate Dictionary, 10th ed. Springfield, MA: Merriam-Webster, 1993.

Random House Webster's College Dictionary. New York: Random House, 1995.

The American Heritage College Dictionary, 4th ed. Boston: Houghton Mifflin, 2000.

The Concise Oxford Dictionary, 9th ed. Oxford: Clarendon Press, 1995.

Webster's New World College Dictionary, 3rd ed. New York: MacMillan, 1996.

Chapter 2
The Vocabulary of English

If you think about the construction of [an anthill] by a colony of a million ants, each one working ceaselessly and compulsively [on] his region of the structure without having the faintest notion of what is being constructed elsewhere . . . there is only one human activity that is like this, and it is language. . . . We can never let up; we scramble our way through one civilization after another, metamorphosing, sprouting tools and cities everywhere, and all the time new words keep tumbling out . . . each one perfectly designed for its use.

—Lewis Thomas, 1978

2.1 Introduction

Part of what characterizes a particular piece of discourse in English is the words that are used—whether they are formal (*catharsis*), informal (*chow*), or neutral (*table*); whether they are nouns (*clarity*) or adjectives (*clear*); whether they have subjective meanings (*dismal*) or (at least potentially) objective meanings (*dark*).

English has a very large number of words to choose from—unabridged dictionaries contain some 500,000-600,000 lexical entries, each with a number of subentries. Of course, no individual speaker knows all of these words (you probably know fifteen to twenty percent of them), but each word in the dictionary is known and used by English speakers somewhere—otherwise it wouldn't be listed in the dictionary.

Exercise 1. Estimate the size of your own vocabulary, using the following technique:

(1) Choose ten pages at random from a good college dictionary.

(2) On each page, make a tick beside every word you know. If there are additional words at the end of an entry (for example, *anarchistic* at the end of the entry for *anarchist*; *catch on*, *catch up* and *catch it* at the end of the entry for *catch*), then count those as well, if you know them.

(3) Count the total number of ticks and divide by ten. This gives you the number of words that you know, on average, on each page of the dictionary.

(4) Multiply this number by the total number of pages in the dictionary; this gives you an estimated number for the size of your vocabulary.

Caution: The Merriam Webster's Collegiate Dictionary lists each part of speech as a separate word; for example, the word *measure* is listed twice—first as a noun and then as a verb. Other dictionaries list *measure* only once, with the noun and verb meanings included under one large entry. Thus, your vocabulary will appear larger if you use *Merriam Webster* for this exercise than if you use another dictionary. Do you see any other problems with this method of estimating vocabulary size?

EXERCISE 2. This exercise will ask you to talk about the *content* of your vocabulary, and how it resembles or differs from that of other English speakers.

There is a core vocabulary that is known by all English speakers: If you don't know the words *house, car, water,* and *foot,* then you don't know how to speak English! However, many of the words you know depend on who you are, where you live, and what you are interested in: If you call a refrigerator an *icebox,* then you are probably a member of the older generation; if you call a milk shake a *frappe,* then you are probably from eastern New England; if you know the word *morpheme,* then you have probably taken a course in linguistics; if you are not interested in cooking, then you probably don't know the word *parboil.*

Write a 500 word essay describing your vocabulary and explaining how it derives from who and what you are. Be sure to give examples. Include some of the vocabulary that you share with all English speakers, as well as the special words that you know because of your age, geographical location, education, job, hobbies, or other interests. If you can, find one or two words that are in your vocabulary but which are not listed in the dictionary; these might be "family" words that you use at home or slang words that you use with a group of friends.

Caution: When a word is used as a word, it must be italicized, underlined, or surrounded with quotation marks; for example,

I never heard the expression *wicked good* until I moved to New England.

or

I never heard the expression <u>wicked good</u> until I moved to New England.

or

I never heard the expression "wicked good" until I moved to New England.

2.2 Where Do Our Words Come From?

In order to understand the vocabulary of English, you will need to know something about its historical development.

English is a European language, brought to America by settlers from England, Scotland, and Ireland. Like most European languages, it is a member of the Indo-European language family. Languages in this family are descended from an ancient language called Proto-Indo-European, which is believed to have been spoken near the border of Europe and Asia somewhere around 4500 B.C. (the exact date is controversial). The linguistic descendants of the Proto-Indo-Europeans spread out in two directions: northwest into Europe, and southeast into Iran, Pakistan, and northern India, as shown in figure 2.2a. Since writing had not yet been invented in 4500 B.C., there are no written records of Proto-Indo-European; everything we know about this ancient language is obtained by studying the languages that are descended from it and then reasoning backwards to determine what the parent language must have been like.

EXERCISE 3. Many descendants of Proto-Indo-European (PIE) words can be recognized in Modern English. Use the sound and meaning of the PIE roots below to find their Modern English offspring:

ad-	'at'	*dheu-*	'to flow'	*er-*	'earth'		
agro-	'field'	*dhīgᵂ-*	'to stick'	*gel-*	'to freeze'		
angh-	'painful'	*dhreg-*	'drink'	*gembh-*	'to comb'		
ant-	'front'	*dhughəter*	'daughter'	*genu-*	'knee'		
ayer	'day'	*dō*	'give'	*ghabh-*	'to give'		
awl	'bird'	*dwo-*	'two'	*ghrebh-*	'to seize'		
bhardh-	'beard'	*ed-*	'to eat'	*kan-*	'to sing'		
bher-	'carry'	*eg-*	'I'	*kand-*	'to shine'		
bhergh-	'high'	*eghs-*	'out'	*kwetwer-*	'four'		
bhrāter	'brother'	*el-*	'elbow'	*man-*	'hand'		
dekm̩	'ten'	*en*	'in'	*mē̆*	'me'		
deru-	'steadfast'	*epi-*	'also'	*medhyo-*	'middle'		

As Indo-European spread over a larger and larger geographical area, the speakers of the language became isolated from one another, and sub families developed, as shown in the "family tree" in figure 2.2b. English belongs to the Western branch of the Germanic subfamily of Indo-European; its immediate ancestors were the languages spoken by three Germanic tribes—the Angles, the Saxons, and the Jutes, who lived in what is now northern Germany and Denmark. Our closest linguistic relatives are the four other West Germanic languages: Dutch, German, Frisian, and Yiddish.

2.3 The History of English

English belongs to the Germanic branch of the Indo-European language family. It originated as a dialect of Proto-Germanic, spoken by three Germanic tribes—the Angles, the Saxons, and the Jutes—who lived in northern Europe, in what is now part of Germany and Denmark. Britain, at that time, was inhabited by the Celts (the ancestors of the modern Irish, Scots, and Welsh), under the rule of the Romans. When the Romans withdrew in 410 A.D., the Angles, Saxons, and Jutes invaded England and pushed the Celts back into what is now Scotland and Wales. The name "English" comes from the name "Angles"; the language they spoke was called *Angl-isc*. In its basic

GEOGRAPHICAL DISTRIBUTION OF THE INDO-EUROPEAN FAMILY OF LANGUAGES

Table 2.2 Some Other Language Families

Uralic:	Finnish, Hungarian, . . .
Altaic:	Turkish, Mongolian, Korean, Japanese, . . .
Sino-Tibetan:	Chinese, Tibetan, . . .
Niger-Congo:	Swahili, Zulu, Igbo, . . .
Khoisan:	!Kung, Nama, Sandawe, . . .
Austronesian:	Hawaiian, Maori, Samoan, Tagalog, . . .
Semitic:	Arabic, Hebrew, . . .
Na-Dene:	Navaho, Apache, Salish, . . .
Amerind:	Algonquian, Mayan, Aztec (Nahuatl), Quechua, . . .
Eskimo-Aleut:	Inuit, Yupik, . . .
Australian:	Tiwi, Warlpiri, . . .

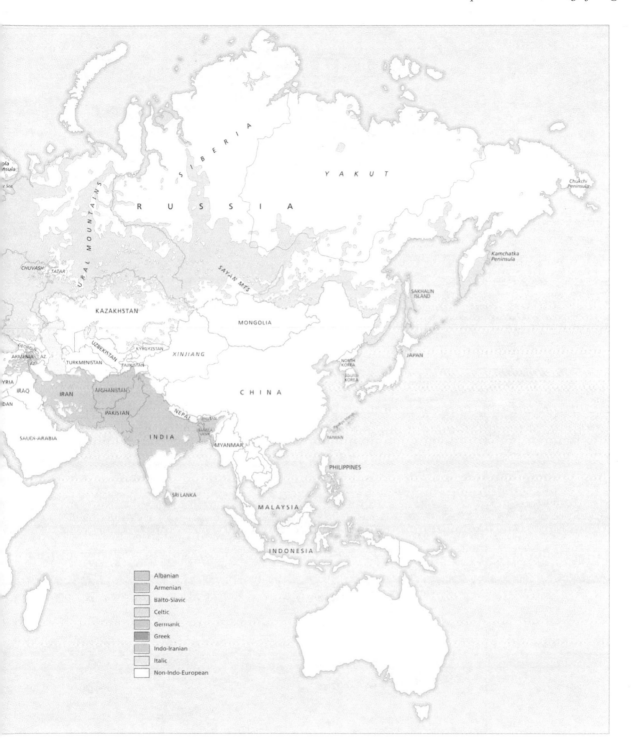

Figure 2.2a Geographical distribution of the Indo-European family of languages. Reprinted with the permission of Cambridge University Press.

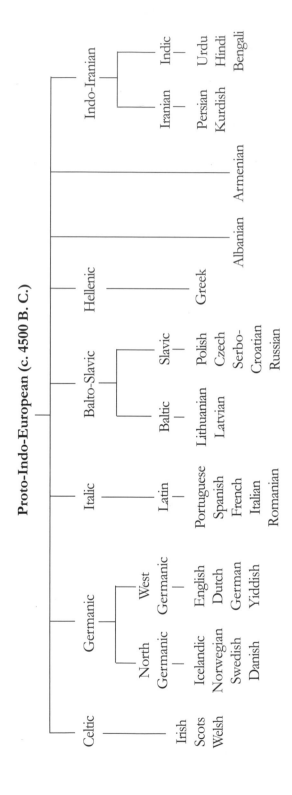

Figure 2.2b Indo-European family tree.

structure—its grammar, its core vocabulary, and its pronunciation—English still shows its Germanic origins. However, as we will see later in this section, English, more than most languages, has borrowed vocabulary from foreign sources.

The history of English is divided into three periods: the Anglo-Saxon or Old English period (449–1100), the Middle English period (1100–1500), and the Modern English period (1500–present).

Old English (449–100)

Students are often surprised to learn that the language of Shakespeare and the *King James Bible* is not Old English, but Early Modern English. Old English was spoken long before Shakespeare's time and is so different from Modern English that it seems like a foreign language. Here is a sample of Old English; see if you can figure out what it says:

1 Fæder ure þu ðe eart on heofonum si þin nama gehalgod. Tobecume þin
2 rice. Gewurðe þin willa on eorðan swa swa on heofonum. Urne
3 gedæghwamlican hlaf syle us to dæg. And forgyf us ure gyltas swa swa
4 we forgyfaþ urum gyltendum. and ne gelæd þu us on costnunge ac alys
5 us of yfcle. Soðlice.

—From Paul Roberts (1958, 37)

The grammar of Old English was like that of Modern German, with an elaborate system of suffixes to indicate tense, person (first, second, third), number, gender, and case (which indicates the grammatical function of a noun within a sentence). Suffixes that provide this sort of information are called "inflectional suffixes." The order of the words within the sentence was also different from Modern English, and less rigid.

The Old English vocabulary was almost entirely Germanic as well, and much of our conversational vocabulary still derives from this source; words like *man, child, house, strong, eat, drink,* and *fight* are all Germanic in origin. However, the vocabulary also contained a small number of words that had been borrowed from Latin, as a result of contact with the Romans either in England or while the Angles, Saxons, and Jutes were still living on the continent of Europe. Some Latin words that entered English in this way are *cheese, wine, butter, angel, school* and *street.*

A more important source of borrowing into Old English was Old Norse. During the eighth century, the Vikings, who spoke Old Norse, began a series of raids against the English coast, and in the ninth and tenth centuries they established permanent settlements in the northeastern part of England. These invaders eventually intermarried with the English, and many words from Old Norse entered the English language. A few examples are *sky, skirt, egg, fellow, freckle, sister, dirt, die, rake, scowl,* and *take*—plus our third person plural pronouns *they, their,* and *them.* Because Old Norse and Old English were closely related languages, and because the Old Norse borrowings entered our ordinary conversational vocabulary, it is difficult for a speaker of Modern English to determine, by ear, which words came from which source. To determine the origin of any individual word that was already present in Old English, you will have to consult a dictionary.

13

Middle English (1100–1500)

Middle English originated with the Norman Conquest of 1066—the invasion of England by the Normans, who came from France, under William the Conqueror. The Norman invaders took control of the great estates of England, as well as assuming important positions in the government and in the church, and for several generations—until they became thoroughly assimilated to British society—they continued to speak French. Thus, for the next three hundred years, French (or Old French, as the French of that time is called) was the predominant language of the English aristocracy. By the fourteenth century, when English reemerged as the dominant language, thousands of French words had been borrowed into English—words having to do with government (*parliament, treaty, tax*), with the church (*religion, baptism, faith*), with the law (*sentence, fine, prison*), with food (*salmon, oyster, pork, bacon, beef*) and with fashionable life (*curtain, chair, music, dalliance*, and *conversation*). Perhaps the best known example of Middle English is Chaucer's *Prologue to the Canterbury Tales* (1971), the first few lines of which are quoted below:

Whan that Aprill with his shoures soote	*1*
The droghte of March hath perced to the roote,	*2*
And bathed every veyne in swich licour	*3*
Of which vertu engendred is the flour;	*4*
Whan Zephirus eek with his sweete breeth	*5*
Inspired hath in every holt and heeth	*6*
The tendre croppes, and the yonge sonne	*7*
Hath in the Ram his halve cours yronne	*8*
And smale foweles maken melodye,	*9*
That slepen all the nyght with open ye	*10*
(So priketh hem nature in his corages);	*11*
Thanne longen folk to goon on pilgrimages . . .	*12*

This selection, though still strange to our ears, is far more accessible than the Old English passage of the previous section. First, the grammar of Middle English had become more like that of Modern English. Most of the inflectional suffixes that we saw in Old English had been lost; Middle English, like Modern English, relied primarily on word order and structural words (auxiliaries, prepositions, and so forth) to establish grammatical relationships within the sentence. However, the chief characteristic that makes this passage more accessible to us is its lexicon; Chaucer was using the French words that make up so much of our vocabulary today. Words like *perced* 'pierced', *veyne* 'vine', *licour* 'liquor' (='liquid'), *vertu* 'virtue', *engendred* 'engendered', *flour* 'flower', *inspired* 'inspired', *tendre* 'tender', *cours* 'course', *melodie* 'melody', *corages* 'courage' (='emotions'), and *pilgrimages* 'pilgrimages' were borrowed from French during Middle English times and are still in use today, though sometimes with a slightly different spelling and meaning.

Modern English (1500–present)

The Modern English period was ushered in by the invention of the printing press, which was introduced to England by William Caxton in 1475. Books suddenly became more common, and many people learned to read and write. To satisfy the public demand for learning, classical works were translated into English from Latin, Greek, and French, and this brought a further augmentation to our vocabulary. When a translator came across a Latin or Greek word that could not easily be rendered into English, he often simply appropriated the original term, sometimes with a slight change in spelling. It was in this way that English acquired such words as *pedestrian, bonus, insurgent, palliate, paradox, philanthropy, cosmos,* and *amphibious.* Note that these words were borrowed from written texts rather than from spoken conversation, and even today they retain their character as primarily *written*, rather than spoken, words.

Early Modern English (1500–1700)

The most familiar example of Early Modern English (aside from the *King James Bible*) is Shakespeare. Here is a brief excerpt from the first act of *Hamlet*, which is found immediately after the appearance of the ghost:

Marcellus. 'Tis gone!	1
We do it wrong being so majestical	2
To offer it the show of violence,	3
For it is as the air, invulnerable,	4
And our vain blows malicious mockery.	5
Bernardo. It was about to speak when the cock crew.	6
Horatio. And then it started like a guilty thing,	7
Upon a fearful summons; I have heard	8
The cock that is the trumpet to the morn	9
Doth with his lofty and shrill-sounding throat	10
Awake the god of day, and at his warning	11
Whether in sea or fire, in earth or air,	12
Th'extravagant and erring spirit hies	13
To his confine, and of the truth herein	14
This present object made probation.	15

Shakespeare is not easy to read. (It helps if you read along with a recorded performance of the play, so that you have the benefit of both the spoken and the written word.) His grammar is sometimes different from ours — for example, he uses some inflectional forms that we no longer use (the third person singular form *doth* 'does' and the past tense form *crew* 'crowed'). And some words have different meanings (for example, *erring* in line 13 is used to mean 'wandering'). However, the words themselves are, for the most part, familiar to us; Shakespeare's vocabulary, like ours, contains native English words (*wrong, god, fearful,* and such), Norman French words (*guilty, vain, violence,* and so forth), and also words like *invulnerable* and *object,* which were borrowed into English from Latin texts.

Late Modern English (1700–present)

In Late Modern times, English has become a world language. It is the national language not just of England, but also of the United States, Canada, Australia, and New Zealand. In dozens of other countries—India, Nigeria, Ghana, and Singapore, to name just a few—English is an official "second" language, used for official business and for education.

In this global environment, English has taken in words from many different languages; the examples below are a very small sampling:

French: *chic, savoir faire, hors d'oevres, mousse, fatigue, fiancé*

Italian: *pizza, opera, piazza, fortissimo, spaghetti, ciao*

Spanish: *adobe, lasso, hombre, marijuana, tomato, coyote, cafeteria, bonanza, peon, patio, tornado, savvy, pronto*

Dutch: *Santa Claus, cookie, caboose, sloop, cole slaw, waffle, boss, sleigh, poppycock*

American Indian languages: *wigwam, moccasin, teepee, toboggan, moose, raccoon, skunk, powwow, totem,* and many American place names

African languages: *okra, gumbo, voodoo, chimpanzee, tsetse fly, banana, jazz,* and possibly *o.k.*

Hindi: *bangle, Brahman, bungalow, dinghy, jungle, nirvana, pariah, thug, toddy, verandah*

Japanese: *futon, hibachi, sushi, honcho, kimono, daikon*

Chinese: *chop suey, kowtow, chow*

Yiddish: *mensch, schnozz, chutzpah, glitch, schlep, schlemiel, schmuck*

Late Modern English has also, for first time, undergone efforts to regulate and control the language. The first English dictionaries were published in the eighteenth century, and the nineteenth and twentieth centuries have seen the rise of usage handbooks and school grammars which attempt to distinguish between "correct" and "incorrect" usages.

2.4 Using a Dictionary to Find the Origin of a Word

The words of Modern English have entered the language in three ways: Some are *native* (i.e., present in the language from the time of the Anglo-Saxons), some were *borrowed* from other languages during the course of our history, and some were *invented* by English speakers. As we saw in our brief historical survey of English, our borrowed vocabulary has come from five main sources. Thus, if we ignore, for a moment, the category of invented words, then the vocabulary of English can be classified, historically, as follows:

1. Native vocabulary

2. Borrowed vocabulary

    a. From (spoken) Latin into Old English

    b. From Old Norse into Old English and Middle English

    c. From Old French into Middle English in the aftermath of the Norman invasion

    d. From the classical languages Latin and Greek into Middle English and Modern English

    e. From modern spoken languages into Modern English

In some cases, you will be able to guess the historical origin of an English word from its internal structure and its level of formality. (For example, words that are borrowed from Latin often have prefixes and/or suffixes and seem formal in register.) In other cases, you will have to look in the dictionary. The origin or *etymology* of the word is given in square brackets either at the beginning or, in some dictionaries, at the end of the entry.

Illustrations are given below for the six major historical sources of English words. These etymologies follow the format of the *American Heritage Dictionary*; other college dictionaries may use *fr.* 'from' instead of "<". The *Merriam Webster's Collegiate Dictionary* lists, in addition to the etymology, the earliest date at which the word is known to have occurred in English. Dictionaries may also list related words from other languages (*akin to* ...); for example, if a word has been borrowed into English from French, then there will probably be kindred words in other Romance languages, such as Spanish, Portuguese, and Italian.

1. Native vocabulary

child [ME < OE *cild*]

This etymology indicates that the word *child* was present in Middle English (ME) and that it was derived from the Old English (OE) word *cild*. Since no further information is given, we can conclude that the word was not borrowed from any other language, but has been present in English as far back as can be traced. Thus it is part of our native vocabulary.

2a. Borrowings from Latin into Old English

aloe [ME < OE *aluwe* < Lat. *aloe* < Gk.]

According to this etymology, the word *aloe* was present in Middle English (ME) and Old English (OE), where it was spelled *aluwe*. OE borrowed it from Latin, (Lat.); thus, *aloe* is not a *native* English word, but a borrowing from Latin into OE (while Latin was still a spoken language). The entry also tells us that Latin borrowed the word from Greek (Gk.), but that is outside our sphere of interest; we are not asking where the word came from *originally*, but how it came into English.

2b. Borrowings from ON into OE and ME

skin [ME < ON *skinn*]

The etymology tell us that this word was borrowed from Old Norse (ON) during the ME period.

2c. Borrowings from Old French into Middle English as a result of the Norman invasion

chair [ME *chaiere* < OFr. < Lat. *cathedra,* chair < Gk. *kathedra*]

The etymology tells us that *chair* was borrowed from Old French (OFr.) during the Middle English (ME) period.

2d. Borrowings from the classical languages (Latin and Greek) into written English during the Middle English and early Modern English periods

anatomy [ME *anatomie* < LLat. *anatomia* < Gk. *anatome,* dissection]

The etymology tells us that the word *anatomy* was borrowed into Middle English (ME) from Late

Latin (LLat.). By that time, Latin was no longer a spoken language; *anatomy* was borrowed into written English from a written Latin text.

> *pedestrian* [Lat. *pedester,* going on foot]

The word *pedestrian* was borrowed into Modern English (it was not present in Middle English) from (written) Latin.

> *archaic* [Gk. *arkhaikos,* old-fashioned < *arkhaios,* ancient]

The word *archaic* was borrowed into Modern English from Greek.

In the etymologies above, we are also told that Latin borrowed the word *anatomia* from Greek and that the Greek word *arkhaikos* was derived from an earlier word, *arkhaios*; however, this information is irrelevant to the question we are concerned with here, which is how these words came into English.

2e. Borrowings into Modern English from modern spoken languages

> *naive* [Fr. *naive,* fem. of *naif* < OFr, natural, native < Lat. *nativus,* rustic]

The word *naive* was borrowed into Modern English (it was not present in Middle English) from French.

> *nabob* [Hindi *nawab, nabab* < Ar. *nuwwab,* pl. of *na'ib,* deputy]

Nabob was borrowed into Modern English from Hindi.

> *nip* 'a small amount of liquor' [Prob. short for *nipperkin,* of LGer. origin]

Nip 'a small amount of liquor' was probably borrowed into Modern English from Dutch or Low German (LGer.).

> *kangaroo* [Guugu Yimidhirr (an Aboriginal language of NE Australia)]

Kangaroo was borrowed from Guugu Yimidhirr, an Aboriginal language of northeast Australia.

EXERCISE 4. Determine the origins of the marked words on the following pages from the *American Heritage Dictionary, 2nd College Edition* in figures 2.4a and 2.4b. Try to place each word in one of the categories set out above (1, 2a, 2b, 2c, 2d, 2e). (*Caution*: If the word doesn't fit any of these categories, just say so.) Which categories seem to be most common? What is the origin of the unmarked words on these pages?

2.5 The Register of a Word and Its Relation to Historical Origin

A *register* is a variety of language that is associated with a particular social context. For example,

powders used to propel projectiles from guns, esp. a black explosive mixture of potassium nitrate, charcoal, and sulfur.

gunpowder tea *n.* A green tea whose leaves are rolled into pellets.

gun·room (gŭn'room', -room') *n.* The quarters of midshipmen and junior officers on a British warship.

gun·run·ner (gŭn'rŭn'ər) *n.* One that smuggles firearms and ammunition. —**gun'run'ning** *n.*

gun·shot (gŭn'shŏt') *n.* **1.** Shot fired from a gun. **2.** The range of a gun.

gun·shy (gŭn'shī') *adj.* **1.** Afraid of loud noise, as that made by gunfire. **2.** Extremely distrustful or wary.

gun·sling·er (gŭn'slĭng'ər) *n.* A gunman. —**gun'sling'ing** *n.*

gun·smith (gŭn'smĭth') *n.* One who makes or repairs firearms.

gun·stock (gŭn'stŏk') *n.* A handle on a gun; stock.

Gun·ter's chain (gŭn'tərz) *n.* A chain (sense 9). [After Edmund *Gunter* (1581–1626).]

Gun·ther (gŏon'tər) *n.* In the *Nibelungenlied*, a king of Burgundy and husband of Brunhild. [G.]

gun·wale also **gun·nel** (gŭn'əl) *n.* The upper edge of a ship's side.

Guo·yu (kwô'yoo') *n.* Mandarin (sense 3). [Chin.; *guo²*, nation + *yu*, language.]

gup·py (gŭp'ē) *n., pl.* **-pies.** A small, brightly colored freshwater fish, *Poecilia reticulata* or *Lebistes reticulatus*, of northern South America and adjacent islands of the West Indies, that is popular in home aquariums. [After R.J.L. *Guppy* (1836–1916).]

gur·gi·ta·tion (gûr'jĭ-tā'shən) *n.* A whirling motion; ebullition. [< LLat. *gurgitare*, to engulf < *gurges*, whirlpool.]

gur·gle (gûr'gəl) *v.* **-gled, -gling, -gles.** —*intr.* **1.** To flow in a broken, uneven current making intermittent low sounds. **2.** To make a gurgling sound. —*tr.* To express or pronounce with a gurgling sound. —*n.* The act or sound of gurgling. [Prob. imit.] —**gur'gling·ly** *adv.*

Gur·kha (gŏor'kə) *n.* **1.** A member of a Rajput ethnic group predominant in Nepal. **2.** A soldier from Nepal serving in the British or Indian armies.

gur·nard (gûr'nərd) *n., pl.* **-nards** or **gurnard. 1.** Any of various marine fishes of the family Triglidae, and esp. of the Old World genus *Trigla*, having large, fanlike pectoral fins. **2.** The flying gurnard. [ME < OFr. *gornart*.]

gur·ney (gûr'nē) *n., pl.* **-neys.** A wheeled stretcher or litter.

gu·ru (gŏor'oo, gŏo-roo') *n.* **1.** *Hinduism.* A personal spiritual teacher. **2. a.** A recognized leader or guide. **b.** An acknowledged advocate, as of a movement or idea. [Hindi *gurū* < Skt. *guru*, venerable.]

gush (gŭsh) *v.* **gushed, gush·ing, gush·es.** —*intr.* **1.** To flow forth suddenly and violently. **2.** To issue or emit an abundant flow. **3.** To make an excessive display of sentiment or enthusiasm. —*tr.* To emit abundantly. —*n.* **1.** A sudden, violent, or copious outflow: *a gush of tears.* **2.** Something emitted by gushing. **3.** An excessive display of sentiment. [ME *gushen*, prob. of Scand. orig.]

gush·er (gŭsh'ər) *n.* **1.** One that gushes. **2.** A gas or oil well with an abundant natural flow.

gush·y (gŭsh'ē) *adj.* **-i·er, -i·est.** Characterized by excessive displays of sentiment or enthusiasm. —**gush'i·ly** *adv.* —**gush'i·ness** *n.*

gus·set (gŭs'ĭt) *n.* A triangular insert, as in a garment, for strengthening or enlarging. [ME < OFr. *gosset.*]

gus·sy (gŭs'ē) *tr.v.* **-sied, -sy·ing, -sies.** To dress up; decorate: *all gussied up in sequins and feathers.* [Orig. unknown.]

gust¹ (gŭst) *n.* **1.** A violent, abrupt rush of wind. **2.** An abrupt or sudden outburst. —*intr.v.* **gust·ed, gust·ing, gusts.** To blow in gusts. [Prob. < ON *gustr*.] —**gust'i·ly** *adv.* —**gust'i·ness** *n.* —**gust'y** *adj.*

gust² (gŭst) *n.* **1.** *Archaic.* Relish; gusto. **2.** *Obs.* Personal taste or inclination; liking. [ME *guste*, taste < Lat. *gustus.*]

gus·ta·tion (gŭ-stā'shən) *n.* The act or faculty of tasting. [Lat. *gustatio*, a tasting < *gustare*, to taste < *gustus*, taste.]

gus·ta·tive (gŭs'tə-tĭv) *adj.* Gustatory.

gus·ta·to·ry (gŭs'tə-tôr'ē, -tōr'ē) *adj.* Of or pertaining to the sense of taste. —**gus'ta·to'ri·ly** *adv.*

gus·to (gŭs'tō) *n., pl.* **-toes. 1.** A specialized or individual taste. **2.** Vigorous enjoyment; zest. **3.** *Archaic.* Artistic style. [Ital. < Lat. *gustus*, taste.]

gut (gŭt) *n.* **1.** The alimentary canal or a portion thereof, esp. the intestine or stomach. **2. guts.** The bowels; entrails. **3. guts.** The essential contents of something: *the guts of an old television set.* **4.** The intestines of some animals used as strings for musical instruments or in surgical sutures. **5. guts.** *Slang.* Courage; fortitude. **6.** A narrow passage or channel. **7.** Fibrous material taken from the silk gland of a silkworm before it spins a cocoon, used for fishing tackle. —*tr.v.* **gut·ted, gut·ting, guts. 1.** To remove the intestines or entrails of; eviscerate. **2.** To destroy the interior of: *gut a house.* —*adj. Slang.* **1.** Arousing or involving basic emotions; visceral: *a gut issue; a gut response.* **2.** Easy: *gut courses.* [< ME *guttes*, entrails < OE *guttas.*] —**gut'ty** *adj.*

Guth·run (gŏoth'rŏon'). *n.* Variant of **Gudrun.**

gut·less (gŭt'lĭs) *adj.* Lacking courage. —**gut'less·ness** *n.*

guts·y (gŭt'sē) *adj.* **-i·er, -i·est.** *Slang.* Full of courage; plucky. —**guts'i·ly** *adv.* —**guts'i·ness** *n.*

gut·ta (gŭt'ə) *n., pl.* **gut·tae** (gŭt'ē'). **1.** *Archit.* One of a group

of small, droplike ornaments on a Doric entablature. **2.** *Med.* A drop. [Lat., drop.]

gut·ta-per·cha (gŭt'ə-pûr'chə) *n.* A rubbery substance derived from the latex of any of several tropical trees of the genera *Palaquium* and *Payena* and used as electrical insulation and for waterproofing. [Malay *gětah percha* : *gětah*, sap + *percha*, strip of cloth.]

gut·tate (gŭt'āt') also **gut·tat·ed** (-ā'tĭd) *adj.* **1. a.** In the form of drops. **b.** Having drops. **2.** Spotted as if by drops. [Lat. *guttatus*, speckled < *gutta*, drop.]

gut·ter (gŭt'ər) *n.* **1.** A channel for draining off water at the edge of a street or road. **2.** A pipe or trough for draining off water under the border of a roof. **3.** A furrow or groove formed by running water. **4.** The trough on either side of a bowling alley. **5.** *Printing.* The white space between the facing pages of a book. **6.** The lowest class or state of human existence. —*v.* **-tered, -ter·ing, -ters.** —*tr.* To form gutters or furrows in. —*intr.* **1.** To flow in channels or rivulets. **2.** To melt away through the channel in the side of the hollow formed by a burning wick. Used of a candle. **3.** To burn with a low flame; flicker. [ME *goter* < OFr. *gotier* < VLat. *guttarie < Lat. *gutta*, drop.]

gut·ter·snipe (gŭt'ər-snīp') *n.* **1.** A street urchin. **2.** A person of the lowest class.

gut·tur·al (gŭt'ər-əl) *adj.* **1.** Of or pertaining to the throat. **2.** Produced in the throat. **3.** Velar. [OFr. < Lat. *guttur*, throat.] —**gut'tur·al** *n.* —**gut'tur·al·ism** *n.* —**gut'tur·al'i·ty** (-ə-răl'ĭ-tē) *n.* —**gut'tur·al·ly** *adv.* —**gut'tur·al·ness** *n.*

gut·tur·al·ize (gŭt'ər-ə-līz') *tr.v.* **-ized, -iz·ing, -iz·es. 1.** To pronounce gutturally. **2.** To velarize. —**gut'tur·al·i·za'tion** *n.*

guy¹ (gī) *n.* A rope, cord, or cable used for steadying, guiding, or holding something. —*tr.v.* **guyed, guy·ing, guys.** To steady, guide, or hold with a guy. [Prob. of LG orig.]

guy² (gī) *n.* **1.** *Informal.* A man; fellow. **2.** *Informal.* **guys.** Persons of either sex: *What are you guys doing?* **3.** *Chiefly Brit.* A person of odd or grotesque appearance or dress. **4.** Often **Guy.** An effigy of Guy Fawkes paraded through the streets of English towns and burned on Guy Fawkes Day. —*tr.v.* **guyed, guy·ing, guys.** To make fun of; mock. [After *Guy* Fawkes (1570–1606).]

Guy Fawkes Day (gī' fôks') *n.* November 5 celebrated in commemoration of the 1605 attempt led by Guy Fawkes to assassinate the king and assembled parliament in retaliation for increasing repression of Roman Catholics in England.

guy·ot (gē'ō) *n.* A flat-topped seamount. [After Arnold H. *Guyot* (1807–1884).]

guz·zle (gŭz'əl) *v.* **-zled, -zling, -zles.** —*tr.* To drink greedily or habitually: *guzzle whisky.* —*intr.* To drink esp. alcoholic beverages greedily or habitually. [Orig. unknown.] —**guz'zler** *n.*

gybe (jīb) *v. & n.* Variant of **jibe¹.**

gym (jĭm) *n. Informal.* **1.** A gymnasium. **2.** Physical education. **3.** A frame supporting structures used in outdoor play.

gym·kha·na (jĭm-kä'nə) *n. Chiefly Brit.* A display of athletic or equestrian contests. [Prob. alteration of Hindi *gend-khānā*, racket court.]

gym·na·si·um (jĭm-nā'zē-əm) *n., pl.* **-si·ums** or **-si·a** (-zē-ə). **1.** A room or building equipped for gymnastics and sports. **2.** (gĭm-nä'zē-ŏom'). An academic high school in various European countries, esp. Germany, that prepares students for studies at a university. [Lat., school < Gk. *gumnasion* < *gumnazein*, to exercise naked < *gumnos*, naked.]

gym·nast (jĭm'năst') *n.* One skilled in gymnastic exercises. [Gk. *gumnastēs* < *gumnazein*, to exercise naked < *gumnos*, naked.]

gym·nas·tic (jĭm-năs'tĭk) *adj.* Of or pertaining to gymnastics. —**gym·nas'ti·cal·ly** *adv.*

gym·nas·tics (jĭm-năs'tĭks) *n. (used with a sing. or pl. verb).* Body-building exercises, esp. those performed with special apparatus in a gymnasium.

gym·nos·o·phist (jĭm-nŏs'ə-fĭst) *n.* One of an ancient sect of naked Hindu ascetics, as reported in classical antiquity. [Lat. *gymnosophista* < Gk. *gumnosophistēs* < *gumnos*, naked + *sophistēs*, expert. —see SOPHIST.]

gym·no·sperm (jĭm'nə-spûrm') *n.* A plant of the class Gymnospermae, which includes the coniferous trees and other plants having seeds not enclosed within an ovary. [NLat. *Gymnòspermae*, class name : Gk. *gumnos*, naked + Gk. *sperma*, seed.] —**gym'no·sper'mous** *adj.* —**gym'no·sper'my** *n.*

gyn– *pref.* Variant of **gyno-.**

gynaec– or **gynaeco–** *pref.* Variants of **gyneco-.**

gy·nan·dro·morph (jī-năn'drə-môrf', gī-) *n.* An individual having both male and female characteristics. —**gy·nan'dro·mor'phic, gy·nan'dro·mor'phous** *adj.* —**gy·nan'dro·mor'phism, gy·nan'dro·mor'phy** *n.*

gy·nan·drous (jī-năn'drəs, gī-) *adj.* **1.** Having the stamens and pistil united to form a column. **2.** Hermaphroditic.

-gyn·ar·chy (jĭn'är'kē, jī'när'-, gī'-) *n., pl.* **-chies.** Government by women. —**gyn·ar'chic** *adj.*

-gyne *suff.* Female reproductive organ: *trichogyne.* [< Gk. *gunē*, woman.]

gyneco– or **gynec–** or **gynaeco–** or **gynaec–** *pref.* Woman: *gynecology.* [Gk. *gunaiko-* < *gunē*, woman.]

gyn·e·coc·ra·cy (jĭn'ī-kŏk'rə-sē, gī'nĭ-) *n., pl.* **-cies.** Political

---

p pop / r roar / s sauce / sh ship, dish / t tight / th thin, path / *th* this, bathe / ŭ cut / ûr urge / v valve / w with / y yes / z zebra, size / zh vision / ə about, item, edible, gallop, circus / œ Fr. feu, Ger. schön / ü Fr. tu, Ger. über / KH Ger. ich, Scot. loch / N Fr. bon.

Figure 2.4a *The American Heritage Dictionary, Second College Edition*, 583. Copyright © 1991 by Houghton Mifflin Company. Reproduced by permission from *The American Heritage Dictionary, Second College Edition.*

of sheepskin and used for bookbinding. **2.** One that skives. **3.** A knife or other cutting device used in skiving.

Skiv·vies (skĭv′ēz). A trademark for underwear.

ski-wear (skē′wâr′) *n.* Clothing that is appropriate to wear for skiing.

skoal (skōl) *interj.* Used as a drinking toast. [Dan. and Norw. *skaal*, cup.]

sku·a (skyo͞o′ə) *n.* **1.** A predatory gull-like sea bird, *Catharacta skua*, of northern regions, having brownish plumage. **2.** *Chiefly Brit.* A jaeger. [NLat. < Faroese *skúvur* < ON *skúfr*.]

skul·dug·ger·y (skŭl-dŭg′ə-rē) *n.* Variant of **skullduggery**.

skulk (skŭlk) *intr.v.* **skulked, skulk·ing, skulks. 1.** To lie in hiding; lurk. **2.** To move about stealthily. **3.** To evade work or obligation; malinger. —*n.* One who skulks. **2.** A group of foxes. [ME *skulken*, of Scand. orig.] —**skulk′er** *n.*

skull (skŭl) *n.* **1.** The framework of the head of vertebrates, made up of the bones of the brain case and face. **2.** The head, esp. regarded as the seat of thought or intelligence. **3.** A death's-head. [ME *skulle*.]

skull and crossbones *n.* A representation of a human skull above two long crossed bones, a symbol of death once used by pirates and now used as a warning label on poisons.

skull-cap (skŭl′kăp′) *n.* **1. a.** A light, close-fitting, brimless cap sometimes worn indoors. **b.** A yarmulke. **2.** Any of various plants of the genus *Scutellaria*, having clusters of two-lipped flowers.

skull-dug·ger·y also **skul·dug·ger·y** (skŭl-dŭg′ə-rē) *n., pl.* **-ger·ies.** Crafty deception or trickery. [Orig. unknown.]

skunk (skŭngk) *n.* **1.** Any of several small, carnivorous New World mammals of the genus *Mephitis* and related genera, having a bushy tail and black fur with white markings and ejecting a malodorous secretion from glands near the anus. **2.** The glossy black and white fur of the skunk. **3.** *Slang.* A mean or despicable person. —*tr.v.* **skunked, skunk·ing, skunks.** *Slang.* **1.** To defeat overwhelmingly, esp. by keeping from scoring. **2. a.** To cheat. **b.** To fail to pay. [Massachuset *squnck*.]

skunk cabbage *n.* **1.** An ill-smelling swamp plant, *Symplocarpus foetidus*, of eastern North America, having minute flowers enclosed in a mottled greenish or purplish spathe. **2.** A plant, *Lysichitum americanum*, of western North America similar to skunk cabbage.

skunkweed (skŭngk′wēd) *n.* Skunk cabbage.

sky (skī) *n., pl.* **skies. 1.** The upper atmosphere, appearing as a hemisphere above the earth. **2.** The highest level or degree: *reaching for the sky.* **3.** The celestial or heavenly regions. **4.** Often **skies.** The appearance of the upper atmosphere, esp. with respect to weather: *threatening skies.* —*tr.v.* **skied, sky·ing, skies. 1.** To hit or throw (a ball, for example) high in the air. **2.** To hang (a painting, for example) high up on the wall, above the line of vision, esp. in an exhibition. [ME < ON *skȳ*, cloud.]

sky blue *n.* A light to pale blue, from a light greenish to light purplish blue.

sky-borne (skī′bôrn′, -bōrn′) *adj.* Airborne.

sky-cap (skī′kăp′) *n.* An airport employee who carries luggage. [SKY + (RED)CAP.]

sky-dive (skī′dīv′) *intr.v.* **-dived, -div·ing, -dives.** *Sports.* To jump from an airplane, performing various maneuvers before pulling the ripcord of a parachute. —**sky′div′ing** *n.*

Skye terrier (skī) *n.* A small terrier of a breed native to the Isle of Skye, having a long, low body, short legs, and shaggy hair.

sky-ey (skī′ē) *adj.* Of or resembling the sky.

sky-high (skī′hī′) *adv.* **1.** To a very high level: *garbage piled sky-high.* **2.** In a lavish or enthusiastic manner. **3.** In pieces or to pieces; apart: *blew the bridge sky-high.* —*adj.* **1.** High up in the air. **2.** Exorbitantly high: *sky-high prices.*

sky-jack (skī′jăk′) *tr.v.* **-jacked, -jack·ing, -jacks.** To hijack (an airplane, esp. one in flight) through the use or threat of force. [SKY + (HI)JACK.] —**sky′jack′er** *n.* —**sky′jack′ing** *n.*

sky-lark (skī′lärk′) *n.* An Old World bird, *Alauda arvensis*, having brownish plumage and noted for its singing while in flight. —*intr.v.* **-larked, -lark·ing, -larks.** To indulge in frolic.

sky-light (skī′līt′) *n.* An overhead window admitting daylight.

sky-line (skī′līn′) *n.* **1.** The line along which the surface of the earth and sky appear to meet; horizon. **2.** The outline of a group of buildings or a mountain range seen against the sky.

sky-lounge (skī′lounj′) *n.* A vehicle that collects passengers and then is carried by a helicopter between a downtown terminal and an airport.

sky marshal *n.* An armed federal law-enforcement officer assigned to prevent skyjackings.

sky pilot *n.* *Slang.* A clergyman; chaplain.

sky-rock·et (skī′rŏk′ĭt) *n.* A firework that ascends high into the air where it explodes in a brilliant cascade of flares and starlike sparks. —*intr. & tr.v.* **-et·ed, -et·ing, -ets.** To rise or cause to rise rapidly and suddenly, as in amount, position, or reputation.

sky-sail (skī′səl, -sāl′) *n.* A small square sail above the royal in a square-rigged vessel.

sky-scrap·er (skī′skrā′pər) *n.* A very tall building.

sky-walk (skī′wôk′) *n.* An elevated usually enclosed walkway between two buildings.

sky-ward (skī′wərd) *adj. & adv.* At or toward the sky. —**sky′wards** *adv.*

sky wave *n.* A radio wave.

sky-way (skī′wā′) *n.* **1.** An airline route; air lane. **2.** An elevated highway.

sky-writ·ing (skī′rī′tĭng) *n.* **1.** The process of writing in the sky by releasing a visible vapor from an airplane. **2.** The letters or words formed in skywriting. —**sky′writ′er** *n.*

slab¹ (slăb) *n.* **1.** A broad, flat, somewhat thick piece, as of cake, stone, or cheese. **2.** An outside piece cut from a log when squaring it for lumber. **3.** *Baseball.* The pitcher's rubber. —*tr.v.* **slabbed, slab·bing, slabs. 1.** To make or shape into a slab. **2.** To cover or pave with slabs. **3.** To dress (a log) by cutting slabs. [ME *slabbe*.]

slab² (slăb) *adj. Archaic.* Viscid. Used in the phrase *thick and slab.* [Prob. of Scand. orig.]

slab-sid·ed (slăb′sī′dĭd) *adj. Informal.* **1.** Having flat sides. **2.** Tall and slim; lanky.

slack¹ (slăk) *adj.* **1.** Not lively or moving; sluggish. **2.** Not busy; lacking in work: *a slack business season.* **3.** Not tense or taut; loose: *a slack rope.* **4.** Lacking firmness: *a slack grip.* **5.** Lacking in diligence; negligent: *a slack worker.* **6.** Flowing or blowing with little speed. Used of the wind or tide. —*v.* **slacked, slack·ing, slacks.** —*tr.* **1.** To slacken. **2.** To be remiss about. **3.** To slake (lime). —*intr.* To be or become slack. —*phrasal verb.* **slack off.** To decrease in activity or intensity; abate. —*n.* **1.** A loose or slack part or portion of something, such as a rope or sail. **2.** A lack of tension; looseness. **3.** A period of little activity; lull. **4. a.** A cessation of movement in a current of air or water. **b.** An area of still water. **5. slacks.** Separate trousers not part of a suit. —*adv.* In a slack manner: *"His mouth hung slack between laughter and surprise"* (Ivan Gold). [ME *slac* < OE *slæc*.] —**slack′ly** *adv.* —**slack′ness** *n.*

slack² (slăk) *n.* A mixture of coal fragments, coal dust, and dirt that remains after screening coal. [ME *sleck*.]

slack³ (slăk) *n. Chiefly Brit.* **1.** A small dell or hollow. **2.** A bog; morass. [ME *slak* < ON *slakki*.]

slack-baked (slăk′bākt′) *adj.* **1.** Not perfectly baked; underdone; half-baked. Used chiefly of bread. **2.** Imperfectly made.

slack·en (slăk′ən) *v.* **-ened, -en·ing, -ens.** —*tr.* **1.** To make slower; slow down: *The runners slackened their pace.* **2.** To make less vigorous, intense, firm, or severe. **3.** To reduce the tension or tautness of; loosen. —*intr.* **1.** To slow down. **2.** To become less energetic, active, firm, or strict. **3.** To become less tense or taut; loosen.

slack·er (slăk′ər) *n.* A person who shirks work or responsibility, esp. one who tries to evade military service in wartime.

slack water *n.* **1.** The period at high or low tide when there is no visible flow of water. **2.** An area in a sea or river unaffected by currents; still water.

slag (slăg) *n.* **1.** The vitreous mass left as a residue by the smelting of metallic ore. **2.** Scoria (sense 1). —*v.* **slagged, slag·ging, slags.** —*tr.* To change into slag. —*intr.* To form slag; become slaglike. [MLG *slagge*.] —**slag′gy** *adj.*

slain (slān) *v.* Past participle of **slay**.

slake (slāk) *v.* **slaked, slak·ing, slakes.** —*tr.* **1.** To quench or satisfy: *slaked her thirst.* **2.** To lessen the force or activity of; moderate: *slaking his anger.* **3.** To cool or refresh by wetting or moistening. **4.** To combine (lime) chemically with water or moist air. —*intr.* To undergo a slaking process; crumble or disintegrate, as lime. [ME *slaken*, to abate < OE *slacian* < *slæc*, slack, sluggish.]

sla·lom (slä′ləm) *n.* **1.** Skiing in a zigzag course. **2.** A race along such a course, laid out with flag-marked poles. [Norw. : *slad*, sloping + *lom*, path.] —**sla′lom** *v.* **(-lomed, -lom·ing, -loms).**

slam¹ (slăm) *v.* **slammed, slam·ming, slams.** —*tr.* **1.** To shut with force and loud noise: *slammed the door.* **2.** To put, throw, or otherwise forcefully move so as to produce a loud noise: *slammed the book on the desk.* **3.** To hit or strike with great force. **4.** *Slang.* To criticize harshly; attack verbally. —*intr.* **1.** To close or swing into place with force so as to produce a loud noise. **2.** To hit something with force; crash. —*n.* **1. a.** A forceful movement that produces a loud noise. **b.** The noise so produced. **2.** *Slang.* A harsh or devastating criticism. [Perh. of Scand. orig.]

slam² (slăm) *n.* In bridge and other whist-derived card games, the winning of all the tricks or all but one during the play of one hand. [Orig. unknown.]

slam-bang (slăm′băng′) *adv.* **1.** Swiftly and noisily. **2.** Recklessly.

slam·mer (slăm′ər) *n. Slang.* A jail: *"If he doesn't wind up in the slammer, he's likely to get a job teaching journalism"* (Nat Hentoff). [< SLAM¹.]

slan·der (slăn′dər) *n.* **1.** *Law.* The utterance of defamatory statements injurious to the reputation or well-being of a person. **2.** A malicious statement or report. —*v.* **-dered, -der·ing, -ders.** —*tr.* To utter damaging reports about. —*intr.* To utter or spread slander. [ME *slaundre* < OFr. *esclandre* < Lat. *scandalum*, scandal < Gk. *skandalon*, trap.] —**slan′der·er** *n.* —**slan′der·ous** *adj.* —**slan′der·ous·ly** *adv.*

ă pat / ā pay / âr care / ä father / b bib / ch church / d deed / ĕ pet / ē be / f fife / g gag / h hat / hw which / ĭ pit / ī pie / îr pier / j judge / k kick / l lid, needle / m mum / n no, sudden / ng thing / ŏ pot / ō toe / ô paw, for / oi noise / ou out / o͞o took / o͞o boot /

Figure 2.4b *The American Heritage Dictionary, Second College Edition,* 1148. Copyright © 1991 by Houghton Mifflin Company. Reproduced by permission from *The American Heritage Dictionary, Second College Edition.*

the expressions *fly ball* and *pop up* belong to the register of baseball, and the phrase *privileges pertaining thereunto* belongs to the legal register. The word *gigabyte* is technical in register; *bogie* is from the language of golf; *seminar* is from the academic register. The word *cute* is used by female speakers more than by males, while *take it easy* as a parting remark is more common among males. These are all observations about the register of words.

Speaking in more general terms, we can identify a given word as formal, informal, or neutral in register. *Desultory* is a formal word usually found in writing rather than in speech; in fact, some of you may recognize this word but not know how to pronounce it. Other words, such as *veggies*, are informal; they are found in conversation and in informal writing, such as in a letter to a friend. Words like *understand* are neutral in register, meaning that they can be used in either a formal or an informal setting.

The register of a word is often related to its historical origin—how it came into English. The words we learn at home as children are, for the most part, words that were already present in Old English (categories 1, 2a, and 2b above). Throughout our lives, these are the words we use in ordinary conversation and which have the strongest meaning for us; thus, they are used even in formal contexts by speakers and writers who want an emotional connection with their audience. As we noted above, classical borrowings like *anatomy* and *pedestrian* (category 2d) were taken originally from written texts, and they are found, even today, primarily in written language. These are the words that appear on vocabulary lists and on the college board exams. We learn them in school rather than at home, and we use them to display our educational level or technical expertise. They tend to be intellectual in tone rather than emotional. Words borrowed from Norman French (category 2c) have an intermediate status; some of them, such as *lesion,* are formal in register; others, like *curtain,* are neutral. Words borrowed into Modern English from modern spoken languages often retain a foreign flavor: *kimono* (from Japanese), *bidet* (from French), *tepee* (from Sioux), *lox* (from Yiddish).

EXERCISE 5. The words below are all native English words and, like most native words, are neutral in register. Find Old French or classical borrowings (categories 2c and 2d) whose meanings are similar to these words. For example, corresponding to the native English word *big*, we have the Latin and Greek derivatives *enormous* and *gigantic*; corresponding to the native English word *drink,* we have the Latin borrowing *imbibe*. In looking for classical correlates of these native English words, begin by making the best guess you can, relying on meaning and on your sense of the formality level of the words. Then check your answer with your college dictionary. The point of the exercise is for you to see that you already have a pretty good sense of the distinction between native vocabulary and Old French or classical borrowings.

big	*brotherly*	*buy*	*childish*	*die*
drink	*eat*	*farming*	*on foot*	*give*
give up	*hate*	*look at*	*lucky*	*shorten*

EXERCISE 6. The following is a selection from a speech that Winston Churchill gave at the beginning of World War II, when Britain declared war against Germany. Almost all the vocabulary of this passage is native English and Old Norse. However, there are six words that were borrowed from Old French during Middle English times. Find them, by first making the best guess you can, and then checking with your dictionary:

> *We shall go on to the end, we shall fight in France, we shall fight on the seas and oceans, we shall fight with growing confidence and growing strength in the air, we shall defend our Island, whatever the cost may be, we shall fight on the beaches, we shall fight on the landing grounds, we shall fight in the fields and in the streets, we shall fight in the hills; we shall never surrender.*

> —Winston Churchill, 1940

Why did Churchill choose mostly native and Old Norse vocabulary for this speech?

EXERCISE 7. In order to do this exercise, you will need to know the difference between **content** words [nouns, verbs (except *is*), adjectives, and adverbs] and **structural** or **function** words (words like *a, the, and, of, to, with, some, other, it,* etc.) The content words, as their name implies, provide the semantic content of the sentence; the function words are there primarily to set up the grammatical structure. Except for the third person plural pronouns *they, them,* and *their,* our function words are all derived from native English. When we borrow words, we borrow into the content (or, as they are sometimes called, "open") categories: nouns (*sauerkraut*), verbs (*denote*), adjectives (*primary*), and adverbs (*occasionally*).

a. First, pick out the content words in the following passage from the *University of New Hampshire Catalog.*

b. Except for eleven native English words and one word from Old Norse, all the content words in this passage are classical borrowings (category 2d). Your assignment is to find the content words that are *not* classical borrowings. Of course, even in this academic register, the *function* words (the words that you have *not* picked out) are native English and Old Norse.

> *The general education program is designed to emphasize the acquisition and improvement of those fundamental skills essential to advanced college work, especially the abilities to think critically, to read with discernment, to write effectively, and to understand quantitative data. It aims to acquaint the student with some of the major modes of thought necessary to understanding oneself, others, and the environment. It seeks to develop a critical appreciation of both the value and the limitations of significant methods of inquiry and analysis. Its goal, moreover, is the student's achievement of at least the minimal level of literacy in mathematics, in science and technology, in historical perspectives and the comprehension of our own and other cultures, in aesthetic sensibility, and in the diverse approaches of the humanities . . . .*

EXERCISE 8.

a. Read through the Ernest Hemingway, D. H. Lawrence, and Toni Morrison passages in Appendix Section 1. One of these passages uses mainly "core" vocabulary (native English and borrowings from Old Norse), one uses lots of classical ("Latinate") vocabulary, and one is mixed. Which is which? Support your answer with examples. How does the choice of vocabulary affect the style of the passage?

b. Look over the children's writing samples in Appendix Section 2. How much classical vocabulary (category 2d) do you see in their writing?

c. Look over your own writing sample(s) in Appendix Section 3. To what extent do you use Latinate vocabulary? (Give examples.) Does your use of Latinate vocabulary vary depending on the type of writing you are doing?

EXERCISE 9. The following words are borrowed from modern spoken languages. First try to *guess* their origins; then check your intuitions with your college dictionary:

gesundheit	ciao	ginseng	guru	hummus
chimpanzee	karate	kayak	klutz	kvetch
mambo	maestro	rouge	santé	tortilla

2.5 Invented Vocabulary

In addition to our native vocabulary and the words that we borrow from other languages, English (like other languages) contains many words that we have simply invented. Words are usually not invented arbitrarily, but are created by one of the following methods:

1. Imitation or Onomatopoeia. Words like *slurp* and *ding* are imitative words; that is, they designate a sound that is similar to the sound of the word itself. Words for animal noises are also onomatopoetic: *baa, moo, neigh, woof, cock-a-doodle-doo,* and so forth.

EXERCISE 10. Find onomatopoetic words in another language and compare them with the corresponding English words.

2. Reduplication. Reduplicated words are formed by repeating a word, usually with a change in one sound: *hodgepodge, hurly-burly, nitty-gritty, flimflam, harum-skarum, seesaw, teeter-totter, knickknack.* [1]

[1] From the National Public Radio program *Says You!* of 6/3/01: Give a double reduplication to describe a really fine train. (Answer: *a lulu choochoo*)

EXERCISE 11.

a. List ten additional reduplicated words in English.

b. Some reduplicated words are written as one word, and some are written with a hyphen. What is the rule? (*Hint:* It has to do with the number of syllables in the word.)

---

3. Compounds and Idiomatic Phrases. Compounds are created by combining two or more words to make a new word, as in the slang word *airhead* 'a silly, unintelligent person,' which is created by combining the words *air* and *head*. Compounds are written sometimes as a single word (a *slingshot*), sometimes as two words (a *fork lift*), and sometimes with a hyphen between the two parts (a *slip-on*). There is no general rule; you will have to consult a dictionary if you are uncertain (and even dictionaries are sometimes inconsistent).

What identifies a word as a compound is its pronunciation, with heaviest stress on the first element; this differs from phrasal stress, with emphasis on the *final* element. Pronounce the examples below, and notice the difference in stress:

Compound		Phrase	
a blackboard	'a chalk board'	*a black board*	'a board that is black'
the White House	'the house of the President'	*a white house*	'a house that is white'
a bigmouth	'a loud-mouthed person'	*a big mouth*	'a mouth that is big'
a roundhouse	'a building for repairing trains'	*a round house*	'a house that is round'

Compounds often have *idiomatic* (unpredictable) meanings (a *blackboard* is not necessarily black, a *clotheshorse* is not a horse, a *nest egg* is not an egg), but some compounds have *compositional* (predictable) meanings (*a grocery store, a nerve cell, a frying pan*). Phrases usually have compositional meanings (*a black board, a big mouth*), but some phrases are *idiomatic* (*a green thumb, a swelled head, hot air,* meaning 'boastful talk'). Phrases with idiomatic meanings are called *idiomatic phrases* or *lexicalized phrases*, and they are listed in the dictionary.

EXERCISE 12.

a. Pronounce each expression below, and use the stress pattern to identify it as a compound or a phrase.

animal crackers Phrase	*(a) bargain basement* Phrase	*French fries* Comp.
animal husbandry Phrase	*bargain hunting* Comp.	*French toast* Comp.
(a) bathing beauty Phrase	*(an) iron hand* Comp.	*(a) free throw* Comp.
Comp. *(a) bathing suit*	*(the) Iron Age* Comp.	*free enterprise* Phrase

b. Say whether the expression is compositional or idiomatic in meaning. (For example, *animal crackers* is a compound with a compositional meaning, in that it refers to crackers shaped like animals; *iron hand* is a phrase with an idiomatic meaning—its compositional meaning would be 'a hand made out of iron.') After you have finished the exercise, check to see if the compound or phrase is listed in the dictionary; if it is, then the editors of the dictionary have judged it to be idiomatic.

4. Affixation (Sometimes Called "Derivation"). Once a word has entered our lexicon, new words can be created from it by adding *affixes* (prefixes or suffixes). For example, to the word *plane* (created by the shortening of *airplane*), flight attendants have added the prefixes *em-* and *de-* to create *emplane* 'get on a plane' and *deplane* 'get off a plane.' Similarly, to the slang word *nerd* 'a stupid, socially inept, or unattractive person,' slang users have added the suffix *-y* to create the adjective *nerdy* and then the suffix *-ness* to create the abstract noun *nerdiness.*

EXERCISE 13. Prefixes and suffixes make up the class of *affixes*. Prefixes, suffixes, and roots are called *morphemes*. Find the morphemes in the following words, and identify each morpheme as an affix or a root. Note any problems you encounter; in some cases the answer is not clear cut.
- a. *happy, happily, unhappily*
- b. *soft, softer, soften, softened*
- c. *sand, sandy, sandbox*
- d. *work, worker, worker's, workers'*
- e. *oyster, oysters*
- f. *true, truth, untrue*
- g. *disturb, disturbed, disturbing*
- h. *inspect, inspection, respect, respective*

The structure of words formed by affixation is related to their historical origin. Words that were formed in English (even if the individual morphemes came from other languages) normally add prefixes or suffixes to a complete *word*, as in the chart in figure 2.6.

a. Affixation in Words Borrowed from Latin.

As we have seen, English has a large number of words that were borrowed from Latin (sometimes by way of French). Latin words were built from *bound roots;* that is, the root of the word was not itself a word. For example, the word *re-ject* consists of the prefix *re-* plus the bound root *ject,* meaning 'throw.' This root appears in many English words which were borrowed from Latin: *in-ject, e-ject, de-ject-ed, con-ject-ure,* and so forth. That is why words borrowed from Latin almost always have two or more syllables: every word must have a prefix or suffix in addition to the root.

PREFIX	MEANING	EXAMPLES	FROM	TO
ex-	'former . . .'	ex-president, ex-con	noun	noun
dis-	'not . . .'	dishonest, disloyal, dissatisfied	adj	adj
fore-	'. . . before'	foresee, foreshorten, foreshadow	verb	verb
in-	'not . . .'	incompetent, incomplete, intolerable	adj	adj
mid-	'in the middle of . . .'	midseason, midweek, midair	noun	noun
mis-	'. . . in a wrong manner'	mistake, misunderstand, misspell	verb	verb
re-	'. . . again'	rework, rethink, reevaluate, redo	verb	verb
un-	'not . . .'	unhappy, untrue, unsure, unconscious	adj	adj
un-	'do the opposite of . . .'	untie, unwrap, uncover, undo, unfold	verb	verb

SUFFIX	MEANING	EXAMPLES	FROM	TO
-able	'able to be . . .ed'	lovable, fixable, breakable, washable	verb	adj
-age	'the result of . . . ing)'	breakage, bondage, dosage	verb	noun
-(i)al	'pertaining to . . .'	national, musical, presidential	noun	adj
-ate	'make . . .'	activate	adj	verb
-ation	'act of . . .ing'	relaxation, meditation, realization	verb	noun
-dom	'state of being . . .'	wisdom, freedom, boredom	adj	noun
-en	'make . . .'	gladden, widen, soften, roughen, redden	adj	verb
-er	'one who . . .s'	baker, teacher, owner, wanderer	verb	noun
-ful	'full of . . .'	graceful, joyful, playful, hopeful	noun	adj
-hood	'state of being a . . .'	sisterhood, childhood, neighborhood	noun	noun
-ic	'pertaining to . . .'	organic, atmospheric	noun	adj
-ify	'make (into a). . .'	classify, objectify, solidify	noun/adj	verb
-ion	'act or result of . . .ing'	protection, compensation, reflection	verb	noun
-ish	'like a . . .'	boyish, childish, foolish, sheepish	noun	adj
-ity	'the quality of being . . .'	sanity, activity, passivity, masculinity	adj	noun
-ive	'tending to . . .'	assertive, comprehensive, reflective	verb	adj

Figure 2.6 Productive Affixes. A "productive" affix is one that is used by speakers of modern English to create new words. For example, *-ness* is a productive affix because we can use it to create words such as *dorkiness* 'the state of being dorky.' The suffix *-th* of *stealth*, by contrast, is no longer productive in English. (My thanks to my student Linda Thiel for her assistance in putting together this chart.)

SUFFIX	MEANING	EXAMPLES	FROM	TO
-ize	'make . . .'	visualize, unionize, crystallize	noun/adj	verb
-less	'without . . .'	penniless, priceless, hopeless	noun	adj
-ly	'like a . . .'	friendly, womanly, manly, cowardly	noun	adj
-ly	'in a . . . manner'	slowly, happily, hurriedly, foolishly,	adj	adv
-ment	'act or result of . . .ing'	adjournment, government, movement	verb	noun
-ness	'quality of being . . .'	happiness, firmness, kindness	adj	noun
-ous	'characterized by . . .'	famous, poisonous, rancorous	noun	adj
-ship	'state of being (a) . . .'	championship, kinship, governorship	noun	noun
-some	'characterized by . . .'	troublesome, burdensome, worrisome	noun	adj
-y	'-like . . .'	mealy, pulpy, mousy, icy, fruity, fiery	noun	adj

Figure 2.6 Productive Affixes *(continued)*

EXERCISE 14. Create as many English words as you can in ten minutes, using Latin prefixes, roots, and suffixes from the following table.

Prefixes		Roots		Suffixes
ad-,ac-,ag-,al-,ar-,as-	'to'	*ag, act*	'do, move'	*-al*
ab- ~abdominal~	'from'	*cede, ceed, cess*	'go'	*-able, -ible*
ambi-	'two'	*ceive, cept*	'take'	*-ance/-ence*
con-,col-,com-,cor-	'with, together'	*dict* ~ionary~	'speak'	*-ant/-ent*
contra- ~contradiction~	'against'	*duce, duct*	'lead'	*-(at)ion*
de-	'down, away from'	*fend, fens(e)*	'act against'	*-ile*
di-,dis-	'away, apart'	*fer*	'carry'	*-ity*
e-,ex-	'out from'	*flect, flex*	'bend'	*-ive*
inter-	'between'	*ject*	'throw'	*-ment*
in-,il-,im-,ir-	'not'	*port* ~portable~	'carry'	*-or*
in-,il-,im-,ir-	'in, into'	*pos(e)*	'put'	
inter- ~international~	'between'	*riv(e)*	'flow'	
ob-	'against'	*scend, scent*	'climb'	
pre-	'before'	*scrib(e), script*	'write'	
post-	'after'	*spic, spect*	'look'	

Prefixes		Roots		Suffixes
pro-	'for, forward'	*tain, ten(t)*	'hold'	
re-	'back'	*tend, tens(e)*	'stretch'	
sub-,suf-,sup-	'under'	*tract*	'pull'	
trans-	'across'	*vert*	'turn'	
voc	'call'			

b. Affixation (and Compounding) in Words Derived from Greek

Greek roots, like Latin roots, are "bound," meaning that the root by itself is not a word. Some Greek words, such as *chron-ic,* consist of a root plus a suffix. However, Greek words often have a compound root with a vowel (usually *-o-*) between the two parts, and followed by prefixes or suffixes, if any:

> *anthrop - o - log - y*   *gram - o - phone*   *phon - o - graph*
> *matr - i - arch - y*   *patr - i - arch - y*

EXERCISE 15. Create as many words you can create in ten minutes, using Greek prefixes, suffixes, and roots from the following table.

Prefixes		Roots		Suffixes
a-/ an-	'without'	*andr*	'male'	*-ia*
amphi-	'two'	*anthrop*	'human'	*-ic(al)*
anti-	'against'	*arche*	'rule'	*-ism*
auto- ~automated~	'self'	*audi* ~auditoryum~	'sound'	*-ist*
di-	'two'	*bibli* ~biblical~	'book'	*-ize*
dia-	'across'	*bi*	'life'	*-oid*
dys-	'faulty'	*chron*	'time'	*-ous*
eu-	good'	*ge*	'earth'	*-y*
ex-	'out'	*gene*	'birth'	
homo- ~homosexual~	'same'	*gon*	'angle'	
hyper- ~hyperbolism~	'beyond'	*gram / graph*	'writing'	
hypo-	'under'	*gyn(ec)*	'female'	
mega-	'big'	*log* ~logic~	'study'	
micro- ~microorganism~	'small'	*met(e)r*	'measurement'	

Prefixes		**Roots**		**Suffixes**
penta-	'five'	*mat(e)r*	'mother'	
poly-	'many'	*nom/nym*	'name'	
pro-	'for, forward'	*pat(e)r*	'father'	
pseudo-	'false'	*phil(e)*	'love'	
syn- or *sym-*	'together'	*phob(e)*	'fear'	
tele-	'far'	*phon(e)*	'sound'	
		phot	'light'	
		psych(e)	'mind, soul'	
		soph	'wisdom'	
		therm	'heat'	
		zo	'animal'	

EXERCISE 16. In Exercise 15, you were asked to find real English words constructed from Greek morphemes. However, English speakers also often *invent* words using these morphemes. The following words were invented by a previous class that used this text; give definitions of their words and see if you can come up with some yourself:

    a. *We have such enormous <u>sympsychia</u> that we've decided to get married.*

    b. *She's a real <u>phobophile</u>—always reading Stephen King novels.*

    c. *College is full of <u>pseudosophs</u>.*

    d. *Many couples are now choosing <u>polynyms</u> for their children to acknowledge their full family lineage.*

(Thanks to my colleague Cinthia Gannett, who suggested this exercise.)

5. Acronymy

Acronyms (words formed by combining the first letter or first part of each word of a phrase) are very common, especially in institutional settings. Acronyms may be pronounced in either of two ways: as a series of letter names, as in UNH (<u>U</u>niversity of <u>N</u>ew <u>H</u>ampshire), or as a word, as in Wasp (<u>w</u>hite <u>A</u>nglo-<u>S</u>axon <u>P</u>rotestant).

EXERCISE 17.

a. Identify the origin of the following acronyms. Indicate whether each acronym is pronounced as a word or as a sequence of letters. (Note that some of these acronyms have more than one possible interpretation.)

OD	NCTE	op-ed (page)	PBS	RBI
NATO	GI	snafu	CPR	ROTC
UNICEF	FBI	NBA	scuba	dink
ERA	CIA	NYPD	laser	NCAA

[handwritten margin notes: IEHP, FAFSA, APU, CAPS, RCC, RCRMC, CELDT, ENT, MVUSD]

b. Acronyms are commonly found in *institutional* language. List ten acronyms that are used in an organization or institution with which you are associated.

6. Shortening or "Clipping"

Words are often shortened in conversation, as when *information* is called *info.* Sometimes the original long form of the word is lost; most people do not know that *bus* is short for *omnibus,* or that *piano* is short for pianoforte.

EXERCISE 18. Give the long versions of the following shortened forms: *diss, gym, phone, math, fridge, mike, Sis, Mom, perp, perm, perk, nuke, lit, bio, psych, narc, disco, rev* (as in *"Rev up the engines."*)

---

7. Back-formation

Back-formation is a type of shortening in which the portion of a word which appears to be an affix is removed. Examples are *emote* (from *emotion*), *enthuse* (from *enthusiasm*), *liaise* (from *liaison*), *lase* (from *laser*), *couth* (from *uncouth*), and *typewrite* (from *typewriter*). The word *pea* was derived by back-formation from Middle English *pease,* which sounded like a plural. Young children can sometimes be heard making a back-formation from the word *clothes,* pronounced [klōz]: The child creates a corresponding singular form [klō] ("I can't find my clo!")

8. Blending

In blending, the beginning of one word is joined with the end of another to create a single word. An example is the word *smog,* from *smoke + fog.*

EXERCISE 19. Determine the origins of the following blends: *motel, brunch, electrocute, stagflation, Reaganomics, dancercise, Spanglish, Dixiecrat, Monicagate.*

---

9. Category Shift

Category shift is the movement of a word from one syntactic category to another, as when the noun *floor* comes to be used as a verb ("You really floored me with that announcement."). English makes very frequent use of category shift, especially the use of nouns as verbs. In fact, most common nouns can also be used as verbs, as when we *book* a flight, *table* a motion, *wall* up an opening, or *paper* something over. Verbs can also often be used as nouns, as in *a run, a jump, a laugh,* or *a cry*.

EXERCISE 20. The names of body parts are basically nouns, but many of them can also be used as verbs. Which of the following body-part names can be used as verbs? Support your answer by using the word in a sentence: *head, hair, eye, nose, mouth, ear, neck, shoulder, back, stomach, arm, hand, finger, thumb, hip, leg, elbow, knee, foot, ankle, toe.*

One special type of category shift is the use of a proper name as a common noun or verb, as when we use the trademark *Xerox* to mean "make a copy," or the word *watt* (from the name of the inventor James Watt) to refer to a unit of electricity, or create the verb *tantalize* from the name of the mythological character Tantalus. When a person's name is used in this way (as in *watt*), then the word is called an *eponym*, and the word-formation process is called *eponyomy*.

10. Semantic Extension

Perhaps the most common method of word formation is the addition of a new meaning to an already existing word. Thus, for example, when new words were needed to support the invention of photography, the words that were employed generally already existed in the language, with other meanings: *shutter, lens, film, negative, develop*. Or consider the sport of basketball: words like *basket, dribble,* and *travel* already existed in English, but were given special meanings within this sport.

EXERCISE 21. First decide on a basic meaning for each of the following words, and then find several extended meanings for each word: *heart, graft, cold, bright, sink.*

2.7 Summary Exercises

These summary exercises ask you to review all the word-formation processes that have been introduced in this section.

EXERCISE 22. Identify the word-formation processes by which the words in the left-hand column were converted into those on the right. Your choices are *imitation (onomatopoeia), compounding, formation of an idiomatic phrase, affixation, acronymy, shortening (including back-*

---

formation), blending, category shift, and *semantic extension.*

a.	television	→	televise
b.	environment	→	environmentalist
c.	happening, circumstance	→	happenstance
d.	hook, shot	→	hook shot
e.	market	→	to market (a product)
f.	a psychopath	→	(a) psycho
g.	slave	→	antislavery
h.	dance, marathon	→	danceathon
i.	day, break	→	daybreak
j.	stroll	→	stroller
k.	binary, digit	→	bit
l.	biology	→	bio
m.	short, fuse	→	(She has a) short fuse
n.	National Education Association	→	NEA
o.	(a) demonstration model	→	(a) demo

EXERCISE 23. (*Patterned after an exercise in O'Grady, Dobrovolsky, and Aronoff, 1993*) Create new words with the specified meanings, using the suggested word-formation processes:

a. Use onomatopoeia to create a word that means 'the sound of leaves blowing in the wind.'

Outside the window, we would hear a gentle _____.

b. Use reduplication to create a name for the mud that gets tracked into the house during a rainstorm.

After you've taken out the trash, please clean up the _____ from the hallway.

c. Use compounding to create a name for the artificial smile people use when they're not really happy.

Sharon _____ed when George said she didn't look half as bad as she did yesterday.

d. Use affixation to create a word for the process of knocking the outside mirror off your car:

When I drove too close to the wall, I accidentally _____ed my car.

e. Use acronymy for the gum left overnight on the bedpost. (Note: Function words need not be included in acronyms.)

The first thing I did when I woke up was reclaim my _____.

f. Use backformation to create a verb from the adjective *breathtaking*.

Mom's going to _____ when she sees how clean the kitchen is.

g. Use blending to name a child after his parents.

Samantha and Emmanuel named their son _____.

h. Use shortening to create a slang word for *adjective*.

My writing instructor said I should use more _____.

i. Use category shift for the act of playing tennis.

We golfed all morning and _____ed during the afternoon.

j. Use acronymy to create a name for the anxiety students feel during final exams.

She did yoga exercises to control her _____.

EXERCISE 24. Discuss the register of words that are formed by each of the word-formation processes described in this section: *imitation, reduplication, compounding, affixation, acronymy, shortening, blending, category shift,* and *semantic extension.* Do the words that are formed by each method tend to belong to a particular register? Are they formal or informal? Can you make any other observations about the circumstances in which each type of word is used?

Exercise 25. The *Barnhart Dictionary of New English* lists words that have come into use during the past thirty years or so. A page from the *Barnhart Dictionary* is reproduced in figure 2.7. Identify the source of each word that is listed on this page. Your choices are imitation, reduplication, compounding, affixation, acronymy, shortening, blending, category shift, semantic extension, borrowing, or formation of a lexicalized phrase. (Note: Because these are real-life examples, they will not always fall neatly into a single category; some words may have been formed by a combination of processes.)

leopard, clouded leopard, La Plata otter and giant otter. Times (London) 1/26/72, p16 **[1971]**

gigabit ('dʒɪgə,bɪt), *n.* a unit of information equivalent to one billion bits of binary digits. Compare KILOBIT, MEGABIT, TERABIT. *The four-minute-mile for electronics engineers has been the gigabit computer, a computer that can process a billion bits of information per second.* Science News 4/4/70, p345 **[1970,** from *giga-* one billion (from Greek *gígas* giant) + *bit*]

giggle-smoke, *n. U.S. Slang.* marijuana. . . . *the young soldier was saying that here in Vietnam cannabis, pot, the weed, giggle-smoke, grass, Mary Jane, call it what you will, is readily available and freely used.* Manchester Guardian Weekly 6/20/70, p6 **[1970]**

GIGO ('gaɪ,gou *or* 'gi:,gou), *n.* acronym for *garbage in, garbage out* (in reference to unreliable data fed into a computer that produces worthless output). *Most of us are familiar with GIGO—garbage in, garbage out—and we try in our systems to eliminate the vast printouts from the computer.* New Scientist and Science Journal 3/11/71, p575 *New technology and curriculum changes, he says, can be beneficial, but "it's a matter of GIGO—Garbage In, Garbage Out. You put garbage into a computer, you get garbage out." Simply investing money into new ideas isn't enough.* Science News 3/24/73, p186 **[1966]**

gimme cap ('gimi:), *U.S.* a visored cap with a clasp for adjusting it to any head size. . . . *Jay Dusard has photographed many modern cowboys with seeming realism . . . you will not see his cowboys fixing a baler or wearing the increasingly common "gimme" caps. They wear broadrimmed hats, chaps and kerchiefs. They ride horses, not pickups. They look just like cowboys should look.* Newsweek 12/12/83, p98 **[1978,** from *gimme* representing an informal pronunciation of *give me;* apparently so called from their being given out freely when requested ("gimme one") as a promotion item by various companies whose names often appear on the caps]

Ginnie Mae, *U.S.* **1** nickname for the Government National Mortgage Association. Compare FREDDIE MAC. *"Ginnie Mae" has been more active than ever before, particularly in the area of "pass-through" securities where "Ginnie" guarantees securities issued by lenders that represent loans in which the net principal and interest on the mortgage loan are passed through to investors each month.* Americana Annual 1975, p285 **2** a stock certificate issued by this agency. *Ginnie Maes—which normally come in minimum amounts of $25,000—provide both high interest yields and also return part of your investment to you each month. Any brokerage firm can provide you with complete details.* New York Post 12/1/78, p65 **[1975,** from pronunciation of the abbreviation *GNMA,* patterned after earlier (1953) *Fannie Mae,* nickname for the Federal National Mortgage Association (from its abbreviation, *FNMA*)]

girlcott, *v.t.* (said of women, in humorous analogy to *boycott*) to join in a boycott against someone or something prejudicial to women. *The Y.W.C.A., Feminists in the Arts, Radicalesbians, National Organization for Women—and anyone of taste—will find much to girlcott in Quiet Days in Clichy* [a motion picture]. Time 10/12/70, pJ9 **[1959]**

giveback, *n. U.S.* the surrendering of fringe benefits or other advantages gained previously by a labor union, usually in return for an increase in wages or other concessions by management. *New York City and its Transit Authority are both demanding givebacks to compensate for pay increases sought by their unions.* NY Times 3/26/78, p1 *Murdoch got most of the rest of the staff cut he was looking for by laying off eighteen people at the bottom of the seniority roll. That left an imposing list of givebacks still on Murdoch's "must" list.* New Yorker 1/22/79, p61 **[1978,** from the verb phrase *give back*]

given, *n.* something taken for granted; a fact. *Loneliness is a human given, and commitment and the public aspects of a relationship are probably things we'll always want.* New Yorker 11/28/70, p76 *The access of moneys to power is simply one of the givens in Washington.* Atlantic 3/71, p22 **[1965,** noun use of the adjective] ▶The noun has been formerly restricted in use to technical contexts in logic and mathematics.

give-up, *n. U.S. Stock Market.* a practice in which financial institutions, such as mutual funds, instruct brokers executing transactions for them to yield part of their commissions to other brokers, usually ones who have been performing services for the institution. *At issue was Fidelity's use of what are known as "give-ups." This is the cushion of the sales commissions on stock transactions that the broker actually handling the trade frequently gives to another broker on the instructions of his customer, generally a mutual fund.* NY Times 7/24/68, p53 **[1968]**

glam, *n. Informal.* short for *glamour. A champagne reception before the awards had the glitz and glam the Genies need, and the stars turned out in relative force—Jack Lemmon, Donald Sutherland, Helen Shaver, Margot Kidder, Lee Majors, Céline Lomez.* Maclean's 3/31/80, p49 **[1961]**

glasnost, *n.* an official policy of open and public discussion of problems and issues in the Soviet Union. *Furthermore, in this period of glasnost and uneasy détente, there are people in both governments who perceive the joint exploration of Mars as contributing to world peace.* New Yorker 6/8/87, p81 **[1985,** from Russian *glasnost'* a being public, public knowledge; also found in earlier references in English from 1972]

glasphalt, *n.* a material made from glass for paving roads. . . . *an experimental product called "glasphalt" . . . uses finely ground glass granules to replace the rock aggregates now used as a construction material for highways.* Time 3/16/70, p62 **[1970,** blend of *glass* and *asphalt*]

glass arm, an injured or sore arm resulting from tendons weakened or damaged by throwing or pitching balls. *Countless more suffered chronic maladies ranging from the annoying, like athlete's foot and jock itch, to the exotic and painful, like glass arm (loss of throwing ability from damaged tendons, common in baseball players), hollow foot (a strained instep found in ballet dancers) and web split (splitting of skin between the fingers).* Newsweek 4/2/73, p65 **[1966,** patterned after *glass jaw* (of a boxer)]

glass cord, cord made of fiberglass. *Another material that may make possible cheaper radials in glass cord. Glass cord can save tiremakers as much as $1 per tire, and some companies have already started to make glass-belted radials.* Encyclopedia Science Supplement (Grolier) 1972, p397 **[1968]**

glasshouse effect, British name for GREENHOUSE EFFECT. *According to Dr Sawyer the direct effect of carbon dioxide on mankind is negligible, with atmospheric content now being 319 parts per million to be compared with about 290 parts per million at the end of the nineteenth century. The indirect effect—the trapping of heat within the atmosphere, the so-called glasshouse effect—is however not so easily evaluated.* Nature 5/5/72, p5 **[1972]**

glassteel, *adj.* made of glass and steel. *The only trouble is that the Sondheim score does not have any integrity. It flirts with various styles, and is as neutral and eclectic as the glassteel skyscraper projections used as a backdrop.* Harper's 7/70, p108 **[1970]**

glass tissue, *British.* a fabric made of fiberglass. *Glass tissue, of which the initial annual production will be about 60 square metres, can be used as a base for roofing materials, wall covering, and other building purposes.* Times (London) 4/2/76, p20 **[1976]**

GLCM, abbreviation or acronym of *ground-launched cruise missile.* See CRUISE MISSILE. *The GLCM (or "glickum," in Pentagon jargon), to be deployed in Britain, West Germany and Italy, and later, perhaps, in Belgium and The Netherlands, is a dry-land version of the U.S. Navy's Tomahawk sea-launched cruise missile. It is designed to be a subsonic weapon with a range of about 1,500 miles and a lot of maneuverability. . . .* Time 12/24/79, p30 **[1979]**

gleamer, *n.* a cosmetic for making the skin of the face gleam. *Some* [candidates for Miss Teenage America Pageant in Texas] *wore pancake or foundation and blotches spread, islands of*

Figure 2.7 The *Third Barnhart Dictionary of New English,* **206.**

Exercise 26. Find ten invented words in the following poem by Quincy Troupe, and say how each word was formed. What is the effect of invented vocabulary in this poem?

take it to the hoop, magic johnson
by Quincy Troupe

take it to the hoop, "magic" johnson	*1*
take the ball dazzling down the open lane	*2*
herk & jerk & raise your six-foot, nine-inch frame	*3*
into air sweating screams of your neon name	*4*
"magic" johnson, nicknamed "Windex" way back in high school	*5*
'cause you wiped glass backboards so clean,	*6*
where you first juked & shook,	*7*
wiled your way to glory	*8*
a new-style fusion of Shake 'n Bake	*9*
energy, using everything possible,	*10*
you created your own space to fly through—	*11*
any moment now	*12*
we expect your wings to spread	*13*
feathers for that spooky take off of yours	*14*
then, shake & glide & ride up in space	*15*
till you hammer home a clothes-lining deuce off glass now,	*16*
come back down with a reverse hoodoo gem	*17*
off the spin & stick it in sweet, popping	*18*
nets clean from twenty feet, right side	*19*
so put the ball on the floor again, "magic"	*20*
slide the dribble behind your back,	*21*
ease it deftly between your bony stork legs, head bobbing everwhichaway	*22*
up & down, you see everything on the court	*23*
off the high yo-yo patter	*24*
stop & go dribble	*25*
you thread a needle-rope pass sweet home	*26*
to kareem cutting through the lane	*27*
his skyhook pops the cords	*28*
now, lead the fastbreak, hit worthy on the fly	*29*
now, blindside a pinpoint behind-the-back pass	*30*
for two more off the fake,	*31*
looking the other way,	*32*
you raise off balance into electric space	*33*
sweating chants of your name	*34*

turn, 180 degrees off the move, your legs scissoring space	*35*
like a swimmer's yo-yoing motion in deep water	*36*
stretching out now toward free flight	*37*
you double-pump through human trees	*38*
hang in place	*39*
slip the ball into your left hand	*40*
then deal it like a las vegas card dealer off squared glass	*41*
into nets, living up to your singular nickname	*42*
so "bad" you cartwheel the crowd	*43*
towards frenzy, wearing now your	*44*
electric smile, neon as your name	*45*
in victory, we suddenly sense your	*46*
glorious uplift your urgent need to be	*47*
champion	*48*
& so we cheer with you,	*49*
rejoice with you, for this	*50*
quicksilver, quicksilver,	*51*
quicksilver moment of fame,	*52*
so put the ball on the floor again, "magic"	*53*
juke & dazzle, Shake 'n Bake down the lane	*54*
take the sucker to the hoop, "magic" johnson	*55*
recreate reverse hoodoo gems off the spin	*56*
deal alley-oop dunkathon magician passes	*57*
now, double-pump, scissor, vamp through space	*58*
hang in place	*59*
& put it all up in the sucker's face, "magic" johnson,	*60*
& deal the roundball, like the juju man that you am	*61*
like the sho-nuff shaman that you am, "magic,"	*62*
like the sho-nuf spaceman you am	*63*

CHAPTER 3
GRAMMATICAL CATEGORIES, OR "PARTS OF SPEECH"

A part of speech . . . is not a kind of meaning; it is a kind of token that obeys certain formal rules, like a chess piece or a poker chip.

—Steven Pinker, 1994

3.1 Introduction

The way words combine to form new words, phrases, and sentences is determined by their membership in grammatical categories such as noun, verb, adjective, or adverb. Traditional grammarians identified eight grammatical categories, based on a classification that was developed, originally, by the ancient Greeks:

> *nouns*
> *pronouns*
> *verbs*
> *adjectives*
> *adverbs*
> *prepositions*
> *conjunctions*
> *interjections*

EXERCISE 1. Assign the following words to the categories in the list above: *her, thin, tall, and, honesty, ouch, under.*

Some of the traditional categories are very diverse. For example, the traditional category of adjectives includes words like *some* and *this* as well as those like *small* and *noisy*, and the traditional category of verbs includes words like *will* and *may* as well as those like *sing* and *sleep*. The category "adverb" is the most diverse, including words like *too, very, however* and *nevertheless,* as well as those like *sweetly* and *quietly*.

Modern grammarians find it useful to set up a longer list of categories, as shown in table 3.1, with a more precise definition of each category.

With this longer list, each category can be given a more uniform membership. For example, the words *some* and *this* are called "determiners" rather than "adjectives," and the words *very* and *too* are

Table 3.1 Modern Grammatical Categories

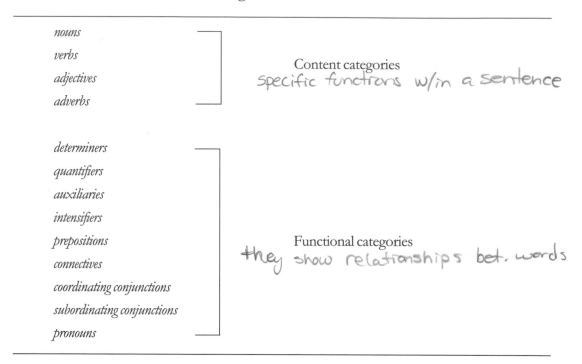

nouns
verbs
adjectives
adverbs

Content categories
specific functions w/in a sentence

determiners
quantifiers
auxiliaries
intensifiers
prepositions
connectives
coordinating conjunctions
subordinating conjunctions
pronouns

Functional categories
they show relationships bet. words

called "intensifiers" rather than "adverbs."

The grammatical categories can be divided into two broad groups, as shown above. The *content* categories (noun, verb, adjective, and adverb) provide most of the meaning of a sentence, while the *functional* (or *structural*) categories set up the syntactic structure. The functional categories are also sometimes called "closed" categories, because they seldom add new members; words are invented or borrowed into the "open" categories—noun, verb, adjective, and adverb. In this chapter, we will consider first the functional categories, one by one, and then the content categories. The content categories have the same names as their traditional counterparts but will be defined in a slightly different way. As you work through this chapter, you may find it useful to refer to the charts in figures 3.1a and 3.1b at the end of this chapter. Figure 3.1a shows the correspondence between the traditional and modern systems. Figure 3.1b provides a summary of the inflectional forms for each content category.

3.2 The Functional Categories

Determiners appear before a noun and indicate how the referent of the noun is to be chosen: *the* book, *a* house, *this* garbage, *my* dog, *every* assignment, and so on. The determiner helps the reader or listener to determine which book, house, garbage, or dog the speaker has in mind. **Definite determiners** such as *the, this, that, my, your,* and so on pick out entities whose identity is clear to both speaker and hearer. **Indefinite determiners** such as *a, every, some,* and *any* pick out referents whose identity has not yet been specified. A noun has at most one determiner: *the a book*; *this my house.* [The asterisk (*) indicates that a sentence or phrase is ungrammatical.]

Quantifiers are noun modifiers that indicate quantity: *one* world, *two* trees, *many* moons, *all people*, and so on. Quantifiers can co-occur with determiners: *these two trees, her many friends, all the members,* and so forth.

Auxiliaries appear before the verb in statements (*can* swim, *will* understand, *may* leave, and so on), but move to the left in questions. There are two classes of auxiliaries: the modal auxiliaries *can, could, may, might, will, would, shall, should,* and *must:*

Statement	Question
She *can* swim.	*Can* she swim?
They *will* understand.	*Will* they understand?
We *may* leave.	*May* we leave?

and the auxiliary verbs (*have$_{perf}$, be$_{progressive}$, be$_{passive}$,* and *do*):

	Statement	Question
have$_{perf}$	George *has left.*	*Has* George left?
be$_{prog}$	They *are* eating.	*Are* they eating?
be$_{pass}$	The desserts *are* made on the premises.	*Are* the desserts made on the premises?
do	You *do* understand.	*Do* you understand?

Both types of auxiliaries move to the left in questions, but auxiliary verbs have the additional property that they must agree with the subject: *she has spoken, they have spoken* vs. *she can swim, they can swim.* Please remember the auxiliaries. They are very important in the grammar of English, and you will be hearing a lot about them as you work through this text.

EXERCISE 2.

a. How can you tell whether a particular occurrence of *be* is the main verb *be* or one of the *be* auxiliaries (*She is here* vs. *She is studying*)?

b. How can you tell whether a particular auxiliary *be* is an instance of *be$_{prog}$* or *be$_{pass}$* (*He was leaving* vs. *He was left*)?

Intensifiers modify adjectives and adverbs. They indicate degree: *very tall, too tall, this tall, very slowly, too slowly, this slowly.* The intensifier *enough* is irregular in that it *follows* the adjective or adverb it modifies: *tall enough; slowly enough.*

Prepositions join with a noun phrase to form a prepositional phrase: *in the house, at the zoo,* *around* the block, *before* lunch, and so forth. Here is a list of common prepositions:

about	*above*	*across*	*after*	*against*
among	*around*	*ago*	*as*	*at*
before	*behind*	*below*	*beside*	*between*
but	*by*	*despite*	*down*	*during*
for	*from*	*in*	*inside*	*into*
off	*on*	*out*	*over*	*past*
since	*than*	*through*	*to*	*toward*
under	*until*	*up*	*with*	*without*

The preposition *ago* is irregular in that it *follows* its object: *three years ago.*

Connectives like *however* and *nevertheless* indicate a logical connection between two ideas. Words in this category are traditionally called *conjunctive adverbs.*

Coordinating Conjunctions such as *and, or, but,* and *yet* join two or more constituents of the same type, as in *Fish swim but birds fly* or *Jack and Jill went up the hill.* Coordinating conjunctions sometimes have two parts—e.g., *both Jack and Jill,* with one part at the beginning and one in the middle, as shown. Conjunctions of this type are called *correlative conjunctions.* Other correlative conjunctions are *either . . . or* and *neither . . . nor.*

Subordinating Conjunctions such as *that, because, if,* and *although* convert a sentence into a subordinate or "dependent" clause—that is, the sentence can no longer stand on its own but becomes part of a larger sentence:

> *Because the wind was behind us, we made better time.*
> *Although I told the truth, no one believed me.*
> *That he lost the election was hardly surprising.*
> *I didn't ask if he would be here.*

Pronouns substitute for noun phrases: *When the dog heard a noise, he* [=the dog] *began to bark. Personal pronouns* take various forms, depending on their person (first, second, or third), number (singular or plural), case (subject, object, or possessive) and gender (masculine, feminine, or neuter). Alternations of this sort are called inflection: English pronouns are said to be *inflected* for person, number, gender, and case. Table 3.2a illustrates the inflectional forms of pronouns in English.

Until the seventeenth century, English had an additional personal pronoun—the second person singular pronoun *thou* (subject), *thee* (object), and *thy/thine* (possessive). This was a "familar" pronoun, like the *tu* of French or Spanish or the *du* of German. As time went on, customs changed so that fewer and fewer people could be addressed with the familiar form; now, in modern English, it is used only in religious contexts, as a term of address for God. That leaves us with just one second person pronoun, *you,* which is used for both singular and plural (except in Southern American spoken English, where the second person plural pronoun is *y'all*).

A narrative is written in first, second, or third person. (But keep in mind that instances of first

Table 3.2a Pronouns in English

Number	Person		Subject or Nomina-tive Case	Object or Accusative Case	Possessive Case Determiner	Possessive Case Independ-ent Pronoun
Singular	First person		*I*	*me*	*my*	*mine*
	Second person		*you*	*you*	*your*	*yours*
	Third person	masculine	*he*	*him*	*his*	*his*
		feminine	*she*	*her*	*her*	*hers*
		neuter	*it*	*it*	*its*	—
		generic	*one/you*	*one/you*	*one's/your*	—
Plural	First person		*we*	*us*	*our*	*ours*
	Second person		*you*	*you*	*your*	*yours*
	Third person		*they*	*them*	*their*	*theirs*

and second person may be injected into what is, fundamentally, a third-person narrative.) In a first-person narrative, the story is told from one character's point of view, which may or may not be very reliable. A third-person narrative gives a more objective viewpoint. But even in a third-person narrative, the narrator may identify with one character more than others and, for example, show some of the thoughts that are passing through that character's mind, while the thoughts of other characters remain hidden.

EXERCISE 3.

Look through the passages in Appendix Section 1 and note the use of person in each narrative. (Some of the passages are mixed.) Make observations, if appropriate, about the effect of this choice. For example, the passage from Rachel Carson contains instances of second person. Why do you think Carson made this choice?

Reflexive pronouns are formed from the personal pronouns and, like them, are inflected for person and number, as shown in table 3.2b.

Table 3.2b Reflexive Pronouns in English

Reflexive pronouns		Singular	Plural
First person		*myself*	*ourselves*
Second person		*yourself*	*yourselves*
Third person	masculine	*himself*	*themselves*
	feminine	*herself*	
	neuter	*itself*	

EXERCISE 4.

Some speakers use the forms *hisself* and *theirselves* in place of the standard *himself* and *themselves*. What is the logic behind these nonstandard forms? (*Hint:* Try to state a "rule" for the formation of reflexive pronouns in Standard English and then in this non-Standard dialect, beginning with the first and second-person pronouns, and then moving to the third person.)

EXERCISE 5.

Pronouns generally have an *antecedent*—a preceding noun phrase that identifies the *referent* of the pronoun. Find the personal pronouns in the Lawrence, Thomas, and Morrison passages in the Appendix and identify the antecedent of each pronoun, if any. In which passage are the antecedents most difficult to determine?

Other Types of Pronouns. In addition to personal pronouns and reflexive pronouns, English also has reciprocal pronouns (*each other* and *one another*), *indefinite* pronouns (*one*[1], *everybody, everyone, somebody, someone, nobody, no one,* and so forth) and WH pronouns (*what, who, whose,* and so on.) Some determiners and quantifiers may also act as pronouns, including *this, that, some,* and *all.* For example, the determiner *this* functions as a pronoun in the sentence <u>*This* is my roommate,</u> and the quantifier *all* functions as a pronoun in the sentence <u>*All* of us are worried.</u>

Other Types of Proforms. In addition to the pro*nouns*, which substitute for nouns and noun

---

[1]This is the *one* of "*a green one*". It has the same spelling and pronunciation as the generic personal pronoun *one* (**One** *never knows who may show up for class*), but it has a different meaning and different grammatical behavior.

phrases, English also has other proforms, including *then* and *there*, which replace prepositional phrases:

> *If I see you on Sunday, we'll discuss it <u>then</u>* (i.e., *on Sunday*).
> *If I see you at the meeting, we'll discuss it <u>there</u>* (i.e., *at the meeting*).

and *do so,* which substitutes for a verb phrase:

> *I have never eaten snails and I hope never to <u>do so</u>* (i.e., *eat snails*).

Caution: Languages contain additional small sets of words that should, logically, be treated as separate categories. Some examples from English are the words *once* and *twice*, and the words *ever* and *never*. Because these classes are so small, they have not been given names. In practice, grammarians either call them adverbs (using the category "adverb" as a sort of default category) or assign them names, temporarily, for a particular discussion.

EXERCISE 6. Read through the transcription of the child "Eve" in Appendix Section 6.
a. At the age of twenty-seven months, Eve is using many function words, but also omitting some. What functional categories are included in her speech? Which are omitted? (Reminder: The functional categories are as follows: *determiners, quantifiers, auxiliaries, intensifiers, prepositions, connectives, coordinating conjunctions, subordinating conjunctions,* and *pronouns.*)
b. Which of the content categories (nouns, verbs, adjectives, and adverbs) does Eve use / not use? Obviously she would not be able to tell us the names of these categories, but does she know which category each word belongs to? How can you tell?

3.3 The Content (Open) Categories

The categories noun, verb, adjective, and adverb are called *content* categories because they carry the meaning (the semantic content) of the sentence. These categories are also called *open* categories, because they willingly accept new members; words that have been borrowed into English from other languages belong almost exclusively to the content categories.

EXERCISE 7. When space is at a premium, as in headlines and telegrams, we sometimes try to manage with content words alone (or *almost* alone), as in *Museum receives collection of books, Parking seen as last hurdle,* or *Arriving noon Sunday.* Sentences like these are called "telegraphic." (The term "telegraphic" is also used to describe the speech of two- and three-year-olds, as in the speech of the child "Eve," which you discussed in Exercise 6.) Add the missing function words in the telegraphic sentences above and identify the categories of the words you add.

Because function words play an important role in establishing the grammatical structure of the sentence, telegraphic sentences are often ambiguous. Explain the ambiguity in the following telegraphic sentences and eliminate the ambiguity, if possible, by inserting appropriate function words. (For example, try inserting *the* before a noun and an auxiliary such as *will* or *be* before a verb.)

Ship sails today.

Neighbors help burn victims.

Yellow perch decline to be studied.

Canada seals deal with creditors.

Spot searches dog bus riders.

Hershey bars protest.

(These examples are taken from various issues of the *Columbia Review of Journalism*, which regularly publishes erroneous or ambiguous headlines.)

You are probably familiar with the traditional definitions of the content categories:

Noun	The name of a person, place, or thing.
Verb	A word that expresses action or being.
Adjective	A word that modifies a noun.
Adverb	A word that modifies a verb, an adjective, or another adverb.

Modern grammarians find several problems in these definitions. First, they are inconsistent, in that two of them (noun and verb) are based on *meaning*, while the other two (adjective and adverb) are based on the function of the word in a sentence. To be consistent, we should define the categories *adjective* and *adverb* in semantic terms:

Adjective	A word that describes a person, place, or thing.
Adverb	A word that describes the manner, frequency, or degree of an action or condition.

Secondly, the application of the definitions is unclear in some cases. For example, the words *appetite* and *impossibility* are nouns, yet neither of them is the name of a person, place, or thing. Exceptions of this sort are usually dealt with by extending the definition of a noun to include qualities and ideas as well as persons, places, and things, but it is not clear, then, when the definition is complete. Similarly, the word *seem* is a verb even though it does not express action or being, and the word *action,* which does express action, is a noun rather than a verb.

The third and most serious problem with these definitions is that we can usually identify the syntactic category of a word in context even when we *do not know* its meaning, as in Lewis Carroll's (1897) poem "Jabberwocky," excerpted below from *Through the Looking Glass*:

44

'Twas brillig, and the slithy toves
Did gyre and gimble in the wabe;
All mimsy were the borogoves,
And the mome raths outgrabe.

Most people agree that *slithy, mimsy,* and *mome* are adjectives, that *toves, wabe, borogoves,* and *raths* are nouns, and that *gyre* and *gimble* are verbs. *Brillig* is either an adjective or a noun (on the pattern of *'Twas cloudy* or *'Twas evening*) and *outgrabe* is probably a verb. The fact that we can identify the categories of these words shows that, contrary to the traditional definitions, we do not rely entirely on meaning when we assign words to categories; our judgment is also based on formal characteristics such as the morphological composition of the word and its position in the sentence. For example, *slithy* can be identified as an adjective by its position between the determiner *the* and the noun *toves,* and this identification is further supported by the final *-y,* which appears to be the adjective forming suffix of *sand-y, slim-y,* and *water-y.*

EXERCISE 8. Give evidence for the syntactic category of each open-class word in the "Jabberwocky" stanza, as in the discussion of the word *slithy,* just above. *Caution:* Since you do not know the meanings of these words, you will have to rely on observations about the words' position or morphological composition.

The characteristic semantic, morphological, and syntactic properties of nouns, verbs, adjectives, and adverbs are set out in tables 3.3a through 3.3d. Note that members of these categories do not necessarily satisfy *all* these criteria; rather, a word is assigned to a category on the grounds that it satisfies some of the criteria for that category and none of the criteria for the other open-class categories.

Table 3.3a Noun

Meaning:	Names an entity such as a person, place, thing, or idea.
Affixation:	May end with a noun-forming suffix such as

-er/ -or	*owner, actor*
-ity	*brevity*
-ment	*government*
-ness	*happiness*
-th	*strength*
-(t)ion	*vision, rendition*
-ure	*creature*

Inflection: Takes one or more of the inflectional forms that are typical of nouns:

singular	*John*	*chair*	*appetite*
plural	—	*chairs*	*appetites*
singular possessive	*John's*	*chair's*	*appetite's*
plural possessive	—	*chairs'*	*appetites'*

Some nouns—including *man, child,* and *deer*—make their plural irregularly.

Syntactic position: Occupies positions such as the following:

a. May follow a determiner plus optional adjective within a noun phrase:

DET (ADJ) _____

b. (Together with a determiner) can function as the direct object of a verb like *see:*

see (DET) _____

c. (Together with a determiner) can function as the object of a preposition like *about:*

about (DET) _____

Nouns are divided into the subclasses *proper* vs. *common* and *count* vs. *noncount* or *mass.* Proper nouns name individual persons, places, or things and, in the singular, lack the determiner *the.* For example, *George Bush* is a proper name. Non-count nouns like *homework, happiness,* and *honesty* appear to be singular, in that they take a singular verb (*is* rather than *are*), but they do not accept the singular determiner *a(n)* and do not have a plural form.

Table 3.3b Verb

Meaning:	Indicates the occurrence of an action, event, process, or situation.
Affixation:	May carry a verb-forming affix such as

-ate	*designate*
-ify	*terrify*
-ize	*unionize*
-en	*darken*
en-	*enroll, ennoble*

Inflection: Takes the inflectional forms that are typical of verbs in English:

base form:	*go*	*put*	*play*
general present tense:	*go*	*put*	*play*
present tense third person singular:	*goes*	*puts*	*plays*
past tense:	*went*	*put*	*played*
present participle:	*going*	*putting*	*playing*
perfect participle:	*gone*	*put*	*played*
passive participle:	—	*put*	*played*

Verbs like *play,* which make their past tense, perfect participle, and passive participle with the suffix *-ed,* are called "regular" verbs. *Go* and *put* are "irregular" verbs.

Syntactic position: Occupies positions such as the following:

a. after *to* in an infinitive: *to jump, to seem*

b. after an auxiliary: *should go, may be, is going, has gone, was decided*

In Standard English, a verb is modified by an adverb rather than an adjective.

Drive carefully.   (**Drive careful.*)

(The asterisk, remember, indicates that the sentence is ungrammatical.)

Table 3.3c Adjective

Meaning:	Attributes a quality or condition to some entity.
Affixation:	May end with an adjective-forming suffix such as

-able	*readable*
-ed	*frightened*
-ful	*hopeful*
-(i)al	*controversial*
-ic(al)	*historic(al)*
-ing	*frightening*
-ish	*childish*
-ive	*defective*
-less	*hopeless*
-ous	*pompous*
-y	*sandy*

Inflection: Has positive, comparative and superlative forms:

positive:	*tall*	*intelligent*	*good*	*bad*
comparative:	*taller*	*more intelligent*	*better*	*worse*
superlative:	*tallest*	*most intelligent*	*best*	*worst*

Regular adjectives form their comparative with *-er* or *more* and their superlative with *-est* or *most*. Adjectives like *good* and *bad* are irregular (**gooder, *baddest*).

Syntactic position: Occupies syntactic positions such as the following:

a. Follows an intensifier such as *very* or *too* within an adjective phrase: *very tall, too rainy*.

b. Can be placed between the determiner and the noun of a noun phrase: *a tall tree, a rainy day*. Adjectives that occupy this position are called "attributive" or "pre-nominal" adjectives.

c. Can be placed after the linking verb *seem,* which, in American English, requires an adjective phrase as its complement: *The paper seemed satisfactory.* Adjectives that occupy this position are called "predicate adjectives."

Table 3.3d Adverb

Meaning:	Indicates the manner, frequency, or degree of an action or condition.
Affixation:	Is normally formed by adding the suffix *-ly* to an adjective:

slow	→	*slowly*
occasional	→	*occasionally*
terrible	→	*terribly*

Inflection: Has positive, comparative, and superlative forms, usually created by adding the intensifiers *more* and *most*:

positive	*slowly*
comparative	*more slowly*
superlative	*most slowly*

Syntactic position: Occupies positions such as the following:

   a. Follows an intensifier, as in *very <u>slowly</u>; too <u>slowly</u>*.

   b. Does not occupy the adjectival positions described earlier; for example, it cannot follow a linking verb like *seem*.

   c. Most adverbs can occur in the position *he did it* _____ or _____ *he did it*.

EXERCISE 9.

a. The following nouns lack one or more of the characteristic inflectional forms for nouns: *homework, trousers, pliers*. For each noun, determine which inflectional forms are present/absent.

b. Pick out the non-count nouns in the following list and give evidence for your answer: *milk, table, news, alphabet, cash, dollar, progress*. (Remember that non-count nouns do not have a plural form and do not accept the singular determiner *a(n)*.)

c. Some nouns may function either as count nouns or as mass nouns, depending on meaning. Give definitions for the following nouns as count nouns and as mass nouns: *beer, jelly, pie, agreement, activity*.

d. Determiners and quantifiers such as *a(n)*, *these* and *much* combine only with certain classes of nouns; for example, *a(n)* combines only with singular count nouns, *these* combines only with plural count nouns, and *much* combines only with mass nouns.

A list of determiners and quantifiers is given below. Decide which class of nouns each one combines with: singular count, plural count, mass, or some combination of these. (Hint:

Chair is a singular count noun, *chairs* is a plural count noun, and *money* is a mass noun.)

Articles: *the, a*

Demonstrative determiners: *this, that, these, those*

Possessive determiners: *his, her, their*

Indefinite determiners: *each, every, either, neither, another, several, a few, a little, no, more, less*

Quantifiers: *all, both, one, two, some, any, much, many*

e. The inflectional status of some nouns is in flux. Classify the following nouns as count singular, count plural, or mass, as you use them in speech: *data, criteria, alumni, slang*. After you have given your own answers, consult a dictionary and compare your answer with that of the dictionary.

EXERCISE 10. Convert the following words into nouns by adding suffixes. In some cases, there are two or more possible answers.

active	*stupid*	*please*
foolish	*invest*	*warm*
work	*follow*	*add*

EXERCISE 11. A verb can sometimes be converted to a noun without the addition of a suffix. This conversion, called "category shift" (see chapter 2), may be accompanied by a change in the position of stress; for example, the verb *record* has its stress on the second syllable, but the noun *record* is stressed on the *first* syllable. The following words can be either nouns or verbs. Decide, for each word, whether there is a change in the position of the stress when the word changes from a verb to a noun:

a. *record*	c. *remark*	e. *convict*	g. *surprise*
b. *journey*	d. *progress*	f. *reprint*	h. *protest*

EXERCISE 12. List the inflectional forms of the following verbs and identify each verb as regular or irregular. If you are like most people, the inflectional forms of some verbs in this list will be unclear: *think, enjoy, bring, swim, dive, lie down, wake up.*

EXERCISE 13. English verbs have a special form, called the *–s* form, which is used *in present tense only* when the subject of the verb is third person singular (*I think, you think, he/she/it thinks, we think, you (pl.) think, they think*). The use of an affix to make the verb agree with the subject is called "subject-verb agreement." English formerly had more subject-verb agreement than it does now. However, we have one verb, *be,* which still exhibits some of the agreement inflection that has been lost from other verbs. Write out the present and past tense forms of the verb *be* and specify when each form is used.

EXERCISE 14. Convert the following words into verbs by adding verb-forming affixes. In some cases, there is more than one possible answer.

light	*magnet*	*code*	*legal*
crystal	*sign*	*hyphen*	*weak*

EXERCISE 15.

a. Some adjectives, called *nongradable adjectives,* do not allow comparison or modification with intensifiers. This class includes adjectives such as *atomic, hydrochloric,* and *wooden* (with the meaning 'made of wood'). Give sentences to illustrate. (For example, **This bomb is very atomic.*)

b. The adjectives *unique, perfect, dead,* and *female* are identified in usage handbooks as nongradable adjectives, but in real life, they are often treated as gradable. What is your opinion of this usage? For example, would you ever say "very unique"? Note the opening lines of the Constitution:

> *We the people of the United States of America, in order to form a more perfect union . . .*

EXERCISE 16.

a. Give the comparative and superlative forms of the following adjectives: *young, good, bad, fast, happy, narrow, handsome, beautiful, flexible.* Which are irregular? For regular adjectives, what determines whether the adjective is inflected with *-er/-est* or with *more/most?*

b. Words ending in *-ed* or *-en* may be adjectives, or they may be verbs in the passive participle form. In the sentences below, say which words are adjectives and which are verbs. *Hint:* Consider whether the word can be modified with an intensifier like *very,* and whether the verb *be* could be replaced with *seem.*

    i.   The students will be *exhausted.*

    ii.   Their supplies will be *exhausted.*

    iii.   Their parents will be *worried.*

    iv.   Their money will be *stolen.*

c. (*Advanced*) Verbs in the present participle (*-ing*) form may, over time, be converted to the category noun or adjective. Determine the category of the *-ing* words in the following sentences and give evidence to support your answer. *Caution:* Some sentences may be ambiguous.

  i.   The movie was *boring.*
  ii.   The children had been *playing* in the alley.
  iii. We were startled by the sudden *opening* of the door.
  iv.   *Playing* tennis is good exercise.
  v.   *Swimming* is good exercise.
  vi.   The children *playing* in the yard belong to my next door neighbor.
  vii. Did you hear the *crying* of the loons?
  viii. We could hear a *crying* baby.
  ix.   We heard an *annoying* sound.

EXERCISE 17.

a. Some adjectives can be converted to adverbs without adding *-ly.* In the following sentences, determine whether the italicized word is an adjective or an adverb. (*Hint:* Try substituting a similar word which does distinguish between the adjective and the adverb form.)

  i.   You don't look *well.*   iii. This boat is *fast.*
  ii. She doesn't sing very *well.*   iv.   I spoke very *fast.*

b. Some dialects blur the distinction between adjectives and adverbs that are distinguished in Standard English. Would you use forms like the following?

  He sings good.

  Drive slow.

  Drive the car slow.

Speakers whose home dialects lack the distinction between the adjective form *good* and the adverb form *well* sometimes hypercorrect by creating sentences such as

  You look very well in that dress.

What is the problem with this sentence?

EXERCISE 18.

Name the syntactic category and inflectional form of the following words; for example, you should say that *toys* is a noun in the plural form and *tiny* is an adjective in the positive form.

toys	*tiny*	*children's*	*unremarkable*
calculating	*bookshops*	*listened*	*kitten's*
improbability	*happiest*	*disarms*	*untidiness*
fatherly	*repayment*	*realignments*	*realigned*

EXERCISE 19. Use affixation to fill in the blanks in the following word families. *Caution:* Some blanks cannot be filled.

Noun	Verb	Adjective	Adverb
		final	
	enjoy		
		eager	
fright			
	construct		
	think		
planet			
	compute		
		corrupt	
	reflect		
		perpetual	
		apparent	
	destroy		
sympathy			
colony			
		strong	
	describe		
mathematics			

EXERCISE 20. Writers sometimes rely particularly heavily on one or two parts of speech to do the descriptive work of a passage. For example, in the Hemingway passage in Appendix Section 1, the verbs provide very little information (*were, was, sat, come, stopped, went on,* and so forth); it is the nouns and adjectives that carry the description (*hills, valley, trees, station, rails, sun, shadow,* and *long, white, warm, open, hot*).

Look at the James Joyce passage and the passages from Rachel Carson and Lewis Thomas. What syntactic categories do the most descriptive work in these passages? Give examples to illustrate your answers.

EXERCISE 21. When a prefix or suffix is used to form a new word in English, it attaches to a complete word which belongs to a particular syntactic category. (Words like *stult-ify*, *re-sist*, or *log-ic*, in which affixes are attached to bound roots, were formed in Latin or Greek, not in English.) Consider the prefixes and suffixes below. From the examples given, determine a. what part of speech each affix combines with when it is used to form new words in English, b. what part of speech it forms, and c. the approximate meaning of the suffix. The first one is done for you, as an example:

    i.   *-able:* washable, doable, readable, understandable

           The suffix *-able* attaches to verbs and changes them to adjectives. The resultant word, *X-able,* means 'able to be X'd.'

    ii. *-ful:* helpful, thankful, hopeful, sorrowful, harmful, peaceful *to be full of*

    iii. *-ly$_1$-:* motherly, sisterly, friendly, homely, orderly *manner of*

    iv. *-ly$_2$-:* quickly, happily, conscientiously, notoriously, unpleasantly

    v.   *-ity:* sanity, rigidity, hostility, intensity, responsibility

    vi. *-ize:* unionize, crystallize, magnetize, hospitalize

    vii. *-ion:* invention, injection, narration, expression, pollution

    viii. *-en:* cheapen, worsen, shorten, weaken, redden, harden

    ix. *dis-:* dishonest, dissatisfied, disloyal, disinterested, disinherit, disintegrate, disinfect

    x.   *en-:* encamp, encapsule, entangle, encrust, endanger, empanel, embody

    xi. *in-:* inadequate, immeasurable, improper, insufferable, incorrigible, irreverent

    xii. *re:* rethink, redo, rework, reconsider, replay, rewrap

Traditional Category	Modern Category	Examples
NOUN	noun (N)	proper nouns: *Chicago, Bill Clinton, the Mississippi River*
		common nouns: *tree, honesty, life, river, president*
		count nouns: *dish, tree, president, assignment, law*
		noncount (mass) nouns: *soup, water, honesty, pie (the substance), life (the state)*
PRONOUN	pronoun (PRO)	personal pronouns: *I, me, you, they, one*
		reflexive pronouns: *myself, yourselves*
		reciprocal pronouns: *each other, one another*
		pronouns formed from determiners and quantifiers: *this, some, another, one, several*
		indefinite pronouns: *everybody, no one, one, some one*
		"WH" pronouns: *who, whose, what, which*
VERB	verb (V)	*sing, go, think, undergo, seem*
	auxiliary (AUX)	modal auxiliaries: *shall, should, can, could, may, might, must, will, would*
		auxiliary verbs: *have$_{perf}$, be$_{prog}$, be$_{pass}$, do*
ADVERB	adverb (ADV)	*slowly, happily, well, entirely*
	intensifier (INT)	*very, so, as, too, enough, this, that*
	connective (CONN)	*however, nevertheless, therefore, furthermore, thus, consequently*
ADJECTIVE	adjective (ADJ)	gradable: *polite, handsome, intelligent, unworthy, safe*
		nongradable: *entire, atomic, hydrochloric, wooden (—made of wood)*
	determiner (D)	possessive: *his, her, your, my*
		demonstrative: *this, that, these, those*
		articles: *a, the*
		definite: *the, this, that*
		indefinite: *a, any, some, either, a few*
	quantifier (Q)	numerals: *one, two, first, second*
		other quantifiers: *both, all, many, few*
PREPOSITION		
	preposition (P)	*in, at, under, beyond, around, near*
CONJUNCTION		
	coordinating conjunction (CONJ)	simple: *and, or, but, yet*
		correlative: *either . . . or; both . . . and, not only . . . but*
	subordinating conjunction (C)	*that, than, if, although, because, when, after*

Figure 3.1a Syntactic categories: A summary.

NOUNS

singular	plural	singular possessive	plural possessive
boy	*boys*	*boy's*	*boys'*
child	*children*	*child's*	*children's*
sheep	*sheep*	*sheep's*	*sheep's*
happiness	—	—	—
news	—	—	—
—	*trousers*	—	*trousers'*
Mount Washington	—	*Mount Washington's*	—
Susan	—	*Susan's*	—

VERBS

base	present tense		past tense	present participle	perfect participle	passive participle
	general	3rd pers. sg.				
go	*go*	*goes*	*went*	*going*	*gone*	—
think	*think*	*thinks*	*thought*	*thinking*	*thought*	*thought*
see	*see*	*sees*	*saw*	*seeing*	*seen*	*seen*
put	*put*	*puts*	*put*	*putting*	*put*	*put*
seem	*seem*	*seems*	*seemed*	*seeming*	*seemed*	—
have	*have*	*has*	*had*	*having*	*had*	*had*
be	*are (am)*	*is*	*were (was)*	*being*	*been*	—

ADJECTIVES AND ADVERBS

Positive	Comparative	Superlative
tall	*taller*	*tallest*
narrow	*narrower*	*narrowest*
pretty	*prettier*	*prettiest*
wonderful	*more wonderful*	*most wonderful*
bad	*worse*	*worst*
tired	*(?) tireder/ more tired*	*(?) tiredest/ most tired*
unique	*(?) more unique*	*(?) most unique*
dead	*deader*	*deadest*
slowly	*more slowly*	*most slowly*

Figure 3.1b Summary of inflection.

English has less inflection than many other languages. For example, there are fewer simple verb tenses in English than in French, Spanish, or Italian, and very little agreement of subject and verb. (Think of the long lists of verb inflections you have to memorize in these European languages.) In nouns, English lacks the gender classes of the European and African languages, and our adjectives do not "agree" with the noun they modify. Those who have studied German, Russian, or Latin will be aware of the complex *case* systems in these languages, whereby every noun is marked for its functional position (subject, object of verb, object of preposition, and so forth). English also had case inflection in Old English times, but we have now lost it in our nouns; in modern English, only personal pronouns are inflected for case.

CHAPTER 4
PRONUNCIATION AND SPELLING

School superintendent stands on principal in Michigan

—newspaper headline,
quoted in the *Columbia Journalism Review*

4.1 Pronunciation

Dictionaries provide representations of both forms of a word—its written form and its pronunciation. European dictionaries, including those published in Britain, represent pronunciation by means of the International Phonetic Alphabet, or IPA. This alphabet provides a symbol for every consonant and vowel sound that is known to occur in a human language. IPA symbols for the sounds of English are listed in table 4.1a.

The IPA can be difficult for English speakers for two reasons. First, it uses special symbols for certain sounds, such as [ð] for the initial sound of *this*, [ʃ] for the initial sound of *ship*, and so forth. Secondly, the symbols for the vowel sounds are based on the orthography of European languages rather than that of English; for example, the vowel of *see* is represented as [i] and the vowel of *say* as [e]. (This will make sense to you if you have studied French, Spanish, or Italian.) American dictionaries avoid these difficulties by using a system of symbols that corresponds more closely to the spelling system of English. The symbols from *The American Heritage Dictionary* are shown in figure 4.1b. Be sure to notice the [ə] (called "schwa") and its partner [ər]. The [ə] represents the most common vowel sound in English, that of unstressed (or "unaccented") vowels such as the *a* of *ahead*; [ər] represents the vowel sound of *bird*.

EXERCISE 1. Compare the symbols in figure 4.1b with those used in another dictionary.

EXERCISE 2. There may be more symbols in figure 4.1b than are needed for your speech. For example, it is possible that you do not distinguish between the sounds [w] 'witch' and [hw] 'which,' and if you are an American you probably do not make a three-way distinction among the vowel sounds [ä] 'father', [ŏ] 'pop', and [ô] 'law.'
a. How many distinctions do you make among these vowel sounds?
b. If you make a two-way distinction, which two symbols represent the same sound?

Table 4.1a International Phonetic Alphabet Symbols

Vowels	IPA Symbol	Example	IPA Symbol	Example
	[i]	*bead*	[o]	*code*
	[ɪ]	*bid*	[ɔ]	*caught*
	[e]	*fade*	[aɪ]	*lied*
	[ɛ]	*fed*	[aʊ]	*loud*
	[æ]	*fad*	[ɔɪ]	*boy*
	[ʌ]	*suds*	[ɪr] or [ɪə]	*here*
	[ə]	*sofa*	[ɛr] or [ɛː]	*wear*
	[a]	*father*	[ur] or [uə]	*tour*
	[u]	*cooed*	[ɔr] or [ɔː]	*more*
	[ʊ]	*could*	[ar] or [aː]	*car*

Consonants	IPA Symbol	Examples	IPA Symbol	Examples
	[p]	*pot, top*	[ʃ]	*ship, machine, wish*
	[b]	*big, bib*	[ʒ]	*measure, beige*
	[t]	*tip, pat*	[h]	*help*
	[d]	*dim, mad*	[tʃ]	*choose, match*
	[k]	*cat, tack*	[dʒ]	*judge, cage*
	[g]	*gun, tag*	[m]	*man, dim*
	[f]	*fill, phone, rough, off*	[n]	*nap, hen*
	[v]	*vine, love*	[ŋ]	*sing, think*
	[θ]	*think, bath*	[l]	*live, fill*
	[ð]	*this, loathe*	[r]	*ring, wrong*
	[s]	*sink, bus, kiss*	[w]	*wish*
	[z]	*zoo, lose*	[ʍ]	*which*
			[j]	*yellow*

PRONUNCIATION KEY

The system of indicating pronunciations in the Dictionary is explained in the section headed "Pronunciation" in the "Guide to the Dictionary." The column below headed AHD represents the pronunciation key used in the Dictionary. The right-hand column, labeled IPA, contains symbols from the International Phonetic Alphabet, widely used by scholars. The two systems do not precisely correspond, because they were differently conceived for somewhat different purposes.

spellings	AHD	IPA
pat	ă	æ
pay	ā	e
care	âr	ɛr, er
father	ä	ɑ:, ɑ
bib	b	b
church	ch	tʃ
deed, **milled**	d	d
pet	ĕ	ɛ
bee	ē	i
fife, **phase**, **rough**	f	f
gag	g	g
hat	h	h
which	hw	hw (also ʍ)
pit	ĭ	ɪ
pie, **by**	ī	aɪ
pier	îr	ɪr, ir
judge	j	dʒ
kick, **cat**, **pique**	k	k
lid, **needle**	l (nēd′l)	l, l̩ [ˈnidl̩]
mum	m	m
no, **sudden**	n (sŭd′n)	n, n̩ [ˈsʌdn̩]
thing	ng	ŋ
pot, **horrid**	ŏ	ɑ
toe, **hoarse**	ō	o
caught, **paw**, **for**	ô	ɔ
noise	oi	ɔɪ
took	o͝o	ʊ
boot	o͞o	u
out	ou	aʊ
pop	p	p
roar	r	r
sauce	s	s
ship, **dish**	sh	ʃ
tight, **stopped**	t	t
thin	th	θ
this	*th*	ð
cut	ŭ	ʌ
urge, **term**, **firm**, **word**, **heard**	ûr	ɝ, ɜr
valve	v	v
with	w	w
yes	y	j
zebra, **xylem**	z	z
vision, **pleasure**, **garage**	zh	ʒ
about, **item**, **edible**, **gallop**, **circus**	ə	ə
butter	ər	ɚ

FOREIGN

	AHD	IPA
French **feu**, *German* **schön**	œ	œ
French **tu**, *German* **über**	ü	y
German **ich**, *Scottish* **loch**	KH	x
French **bon**	N	õ, æ̃, ã, œ̃

STRESS

Primary stress	′	**bi•ol′o•gy** (bī-ŏl′ə-jē)
Secondary stress	′	**bi′o•log′i•cal** (bī′ə-lŏj′ĭ-kəl)

Figure 4.1b Amercan Heritage Dictionary Pronunciation Key. Copyright © 2000 by Houghton Mifflin. Reproduced by permission from *The American Heritage Dictionary of the English Language, Fourth Edition.*

EXERCISE 3. Identify the following words, written in dictionary symbols:

[brēth] *breath*	[ĭg.zăkt´]	[nô]	[rē´bat´]
berry [bĕr´ē]	[fə.tēg´]	[lā´sē]	[rōch]
choir [kwīr]	[flī]	[lŭv]	[säm´bə]
[kyōō]	[flŭngk]	[myōo´zĭk]	[sĭks]
[sĭ.mĕnt´] *cement* [frē´kwənt]	[prē´tĕkst´]	[wûrm]
concern [kən.sûrn´]	[jĕn´tl]	[pool]	[rĭst]
dissolve [dĭ.zŏlv´]	[gônt]	[pŏŏl]	[mē´nē]
easy [ē´zē]	[gōt]	[kwôrt]	[mŭ´nē]

EXERCISE 4. Transcribe the following words into pronunciation symbols. An answer key is provided on in figure 4.1c for the author's pronunciation. Your pronunciation may be different for some words.

ghost	*who*	*balanced*	*faith*	*ink*
tough	*gym*	*winked*	*finger*	*tango*
Thomas	*vision*	*taxis*	*xerox*	*hangs*
bath	*sword*	*taxes*	*long*	*skunk*
bathe	*fishing*	*high*	*longer*	*these*
scent	*elves*	*though*	*razor*	*shoes*
face	*composure*	*choke*	*racer*	*buy*
hose	*composer*	*batch*	*when*	*bury*
sure	*this*	*singer*	*thistle*	*watches*
garage	*the*	*thing*	*circle*	*while*

EXERCISE 5. The following words have two or more standard pronunciations. Give a representation for each pronunciation that you are aware of:

aunt	*vase*	*creek*	*roof*	*pecan*	*route*
harass	*abdomen*	*Uranus*	*dour*	*apricot*	

Students are sometimes told that the only correct pronunciation is the one that the dictionary lists first. In fact, *all* the pronunciations that are listed in dictionaries are standard pronunciations. Pronunciations that are considered nonstandard (such as [nōō´kyələr] for *nuclear*) are not listed at all.

[gōst]	[ho͞o]	[bă´lənst]	[fāth]	[ĭngk]
[tŭf]	[jĭm]	[wĭngkt]	[fĭng´gər]	[tăng´go]
[tŏm´əs]	[vĭ´zhən]	[tăk´sēz]	[zĭr´ŏks´]	[hăngz]
[băth]	[sôrd]	[tăk´sĭz]	[lông]	[skŭngk]
[bā*th*]	[fĭsh´ĭng]	[hī]	[lông´gər]	[*th*ēz]
[sĕnt]	[ĕlvz]	[*th*ō]	[rā´zər]	[sho͞oz]
[făs]	[kəm.pō´zhər]	[chōk]	[rā´sər]	[bī]
[hōz]	[kəm.pō´zər]	[băch]	[hwĕn]	[bĕr´ē]
[sho͝or]	[*th*is]	[sĭng´ər]	[thĭs´əl]	[wŏch´ĭz]
[gə.räzh´] or [gə.räj´]	[*th*ə]	[thĭng]	[sûr´kəl]	[hwīl]

Figure 4.1c Answers to Exercise 4.

EXERCISE 6.

a. Because we learn many words (especially Latinate words) from written texts rather than from speech, we sometimes find to our embarrassment that we have been pronouncing a word in a way that differs from its standard pronunciation. Here are some words that can be misleading; look them up in your dictionary to see whether you have been using the standard pronunciation:

something dominant *hegemony*   *desultory*   *gibbet*   *azure*   *plethora*   *mauve*

b. Are there other words whose pronunciation you have been confused about because you learned them from reading, without hearing them pronounced? *I word*

pinochle

4.2 Sound and Spelling: What a Child Has to Learn in Order to Read and Write

The spelling system of English is irregular, but not as irregular as is sometimes claimed.

4.2a Consonants. Most consonant sounds have a fairly consistent spelling; for example, the sound [b] is normally spelled as <b> or <bb>, the sound [g] as <g> or <gg>, the sound [h] as <h>, and so forth. (Notice the notation—square brackets for *sounds,* angle brackets for *letters.*)

EXERCISE 7. Identify the most common spellings for the following consonant sounds and provide an example of each. Note that some consonant sounds have different spellings for word-initial and word-final position, and that some sounds do not occur at all in initial (or final) position:

Sound	Word-initial spelling	Word-final spelling
[p]		
[d]		
[j]		
[k]		
[kw]		
[ks]		
[g]		
[f]		
[v]		
[s]		
[z]		
[l]		
[r]		
[m]		
[h]		

4.2b Digraphs. Because our alphabet was borrowed from the Romans, it provides letters to represent the sounds of *Latin*, not English. Where English and Latin had corresponding consonant sounds, the Roman letters were simply carried over into English, but English consonants that had no Latin correspondent had to be represented in another way. The solution was to spell some consonant sounds as *digraphs* (a sequence of two letters used to represent a single sound), as shown in table 4.2b. Each of these letter sequences represents a single consonant sound.

Table 4.2b Digraphs in English

Digraph	Pronunciation	Example
th	[th]	*th*ing, ba*th*
th	[*th*]	*th*is, ba*th*e
sh	[sh]	*sh*ow
ch	[ch]	*ch*ew
wh	[hw] or [w]	*wh*en
ng	[ng]	ri*ng*

4.2c The Consonants <c> and <g>. There are two consonants—<c> and <g>—whose behavior is very complex, as the result of a Late Latin rule that "softened" <c> and <g> before the vowels <i> and <e>. When English borrowed words from French and Latin, that rule was carried over into English. Thus we have *gap* [găp], *got* [gŏt], and *gun* [gŭn] with hard <g>, but *gem* [jĕm] and *gin* [jĭn] with soft <g>; *cat* [kăt], *cot* [kŏt], and *cut* [kŭt], with hard <c>, but *city* [sĭt´ē] and *cell* [sĕl] with soft <c>.

EXERCISE 8.

  a. Give additional examples to show that <c> is hard (i.e., pronounced as [k]) before <a>, <o>, and <u> and soft (i.e., pronounced as [s]) before <e> and <i>.

  b. Before <i> and <e>, the sound [k] is spelled with the letter <k> rather than <c>. Give examples.

  c. Give additional examples to show that <g> is hard (i.e., pronounced as [g]) before the vowels <a>, <o>, and <u>.

  d. Before <e> and <i>, <g> is sometimes hard (*get, gear, geek, gefilte fish, gift, gig, gill, gild, gilt, give,* and *gimlet.*) and sometimes soft (*gel, gelatin, general, genetic, gender, gem, German, giant, gibberish, gigolo,* and *gin*). What is the difference between these two sets of words? (*Hint:* It has to do with their historical origin.)

  e. The sound [g] is spelled as *gu* in the words *guess, guest, guise, guilt,* and *guide.* Why is this spelling necessary?

  f. The sound [j] is normally spelled <j> before <a>, <u>, and <o>. Give examples. What is strange about the word *George*?

  g. What is the effect of the "silent" <e> at the end of the following words: *force, notice, peace, advantage, enlarge, merge, bulge*?

  h. What happens when a suffix is added to a word that ends in <ce> or <ge>? (Try *-able, -ing, -ous,* and *-ment*).

  i. Explain why <k> is inserted in the following words: *picnic* + *-ing* → *picnicking; mimic* + *- ed* → *mimicked.*

4.3 The Spelling of Vowel Sounds: Long vs. Short Vowels

The spelling of vowel sounds in English is very complex. The basic problem is that our alphabet, which was borrowed from the Romans, provides only five vowel letters (<a>, <e>, <i>, <o>, and <u>), but English has thirteen vowel sounds—sixteen if we count the diphthongs [oi] as in *noise,* [ou] as in *cow,* and [yoo] as in *cute.*

Our spelling system for vowels is based on the division of vowel sounds into "long" and "short":

a. Long Vowel Sounds, including Diphthongs

[ā] *pay*	[ē] *bee*	[ī] *pie*	[ō] *toe*	[ô] *taught*
[o͞o] *boot*	[yo͞o] *cute*	[oi] *noise*	[ou] *cow*	[ä] *father*

b. Short Vowel Sounds

[ă] *pat*	[ĕ] *pet*	[ĭ] *pit*	[ŏ] *pot*	[ŭ] *cut*	[o͝o] *took*

4.3a The Spelling of Short Vowel Sounds. A single vowel letter followed by two consonants or by a single consonant at the end of a word is pronounced as a short vowel:

*b*a*g, b*asset, m*et, m*essage, h*ip, l*isten, c*od, c*ollege, r*um, r*ustle*

EXERCISE 9.

a. Explain why the vowel sound is short in each of the words above.

b. When the plural suffix *-s* is added to a word like *potato, hero,* or *go,* an *e* must be added as well: *potato**es,** hero**es,** go**es.** Why? (*Hint:* What would happen if the <s> were added alone, without the <e>?)[1]

4.3b The Spelling of Long Vowel Sounds. English has two distinct systems for spelling long vowels:

a. Long vowel sounds are often represented by a digraph (a sequence of two vowel letters), as in the examples below (note that at the end of a syllable <w> and <y> act as vowels).
   [ā] *paid, say, vein, hey*

EXERCISE 10. Find as many different spellings as you can, using digraphs, for the following long vowel sounds: [ē], [ī], [ō], [ô], [o͞o], and [yo͞o].

---

b. Alternatively, a long vowel sound may be represented by a single vowel letter followed by CV (a single consonant plus a vowel).[2] Often, as in the examples below, the vowel that makes the boldfaced vowel long is the silent <e>.

[1]But note *ratios, radios,* and *rodeos,* which are exceptions.

[2]This rule holds true only at the righthand edge of the stem; inside the stem of a word, a single vowel followed by CV may be either long or short:

Long vowel	Short vowel
*m**a**de*	*m**a**d*
*m**e**te*	*m**e**t*
*f**i**ne*	*f**i**n*
*h**o**pe*	*h**o**p*
*t**u**be*	*t**u**b*

In all, there are four uses of silent <e> in English:

    i. To spell the consonant sound [v] at the end of a word: *give, love, have.*

    ii. To make a <c> or <g> "soft" at the end of a word: *silence, peace, courage, large.*

    iii. To make the preceding vowel long: *made, mete, fine, hope,* and *tube.*

    iv. For no purpose at all: *some, none, there.*

EXERCISE 11. *explain*

a. Account for the silent <e> in each of the following words: *ride, sieve, once, ledge, name, cede, dove, bone, rube, these, whole, fumes, one.*

b. Uses (ii) and (iii) above sometimes collide. What is the motivation for the *dg* spelling in the words below? (*Hint:* What would happen if the [j] sound were spelled simply as <ge>)? *badge, ridge, edge, lodge, judge*

4.4 Adding Suffixes: What Happens to Silent <e>?

When a suffix is added to a word that ends with silent <e>, the <e> is dropped if it is no longer needed. For example, if the silent <e> is serving to make a vowel long, then it is dropped before a suffix that begins with a vowel, because the vowel of the suffix will take over that function: *elope* + *-ing* → *eloping* (**elopeing*). If, on the other hand, the suffix begins with a consonant, the silent <e> is still needed to make the vowel long, and it must be retained in the spelling: *elope* + *-ment* → *elopement* (**elopment*).

2 (cont'd)	Long vowel sound	Short vowel sound
	*v**a**lence*	*b**a**lance*
	*pl**a**cate*	*pl**a**card*
	*ven**e**tian*	*fr**e**netic*
	*m**e**ter*	*m**e**taphysics*
	*m**i**ser*	*comm**i**serate*
	*Fr**i**day*	*fr**i**gate*
	*s**o**lar*	*s**o**lid*
	omen	*ominous*
	*p**u**nitive*	*p**u**nish*

66

EXERCISE 12.

(a.) Add suffixes as indicated and explain why the silent *e* is dropped or retained:

hope + *-ful*	*confine* + *-ed*	*note* + *-able*	*rope* + *-like*
hopp -ing	confine -ment	not -ation	rop -er
hop -ed		hot -ing	ropp -ing
			rop -y

b. Explain the difference between *notable* (*note* + *-able*) and *noticeable* (*notice* + *-able*). Why is the silent <e> dropped in *notable*, but not in *noticeable*?

When a word with a *short* vowel adds a suffix beginning with a vowel, the final consonant must be doubled, to keep the vowel short. For example, *bag* + *-ed* → *bagged* (**baged*); *sin* + *-er* → *sinner* (**siner*); *fit* + *-ing* → *fitting* (**fiting*).

EXERCISE 13.

Add suffixes as indicated and explain why the final consonant is doubled. What would happen if the consonant were *not* doubled?

hop +p *-ing*	*sin* +n *-ing*	*knot* +t *-ed*	*pop* +p *-er*
hopp -ed	sinn -ed	knott -ing	pupp -ing
hopp -er	sinn -er	knott -y	popp -able

There is one exception to the consonant-doubling rule above. In polysyllabic words, the final consonant is *not* doubled if the final syllable is unstressed. The reason is that unstressed syllables in English are pronounced with a "reduced" vowel sound ([ĭ], [ə] or [ər]); thus an unstessed vowel *cannot* be long, and no signal is needed in the spelling: *pro·fit* + *-ed* → *profited* (cf. *re·mit´* + *-ed* → *remitted* and *ben´e·fit´* + *-ed* → *benefitted*, which have a stress on their final syllable and so must double the final consonant when adding a suffix that begins with a vowel).

EXERCISE 14.

Add suffixes as indicated, and explain why the final consonant is or is not doubled:

travel	+	*-ing*	*rebel*	+	*-ing*	*abet*	+	*-ed*
	+	*-er*		+	*-ious*		+	*-or*
begin	+	*-ing*	*beckon*	+	*-ing*	*picket*	+	*-ed*
	+	*-er*					+	*-er*

4.5 The Letter <y>

The letter <y> is used in three ways:

a. As a consonant: <y> at the beginning of a word or syllable represents the consonant sound [y]:*yes, yippee, yellow, young, be·yond.*

b. As part of a digraph. Some long vowel sounds are spelled with <y>, as we saw above: *day, key, buy, boy.*

EXERCISE 15. Give the dictionary symbol for the vowel sound that is represented by each of the digraphs above.

---

c. As a vowel. At the end of a word after a consonant, <y> represents the sound [ē] or [ī]: *worry, baby, happy, friendly, sky, identify.*

EXERCISE 16. What vowel sound is represented by the <y> in each of the words above?

If a suffix is added to a word that ends with vocalic <y>, then the <y> changes to <i>: *baby* + *s* → *babies*; *hurry* + *-ed* → *hurried*. This spelling rule preserves the generalization that vocalic <y> normally appears only at the end of a word.

EXERCISE 17.

a. Add suffixes, as indicated, and explain what happens to the <y> and why. You will find one exception to the <y> → <i> rule. What is it, and why does it occur?

pity	+	*ed*	*happy* + *er*	*identify*	+ *able*
		ful	*ness*		*er*
		ing			*ing*

b. *pity* + *-s* → *pities:* The <y> changes to <i>, and the <s> is the third person singular present tense suffix, but why do we also have to add <e>?

4.6 Irregularities in English Spelling

Though the English spelling contains many systematic features, as we have seen, there are some genuine irregularities. These have two main sources. First, the pronunciation of English has changed since our spelling system was established, and this has left us with odd spellings for such common words as *would, could,* and *should; knee, know, gnat,* and *gnaw;* and *might, light, right,* and *enough.* When representations were first created for these words, the <l> of *would* and *should* was pronounced,[3] as were the <k> and <g> of *knee, know, gnat,* and *gnaw.*

The <gh> of *might, light, right,* and *enough* originally represented a consonant sound that was present in Old English. (It is the final sound of the name *Bach,* when pronounced in German.) Over the course of our history, this sound came to be pronounced as [f] in some words (*tough, rough, enough,* and so forth) and was dropped from others (*light, right, night, though, thought,* and so on). There is no longer a [gh] sound in English, but the letters remain in the spelling of some words.

A more important source of spelling irregularities is borrowing. Words such as *sauté, hibachi,* and *garage,* which were borrowed into English from other languages, often retain some spelling features of the parent language.

EXERCISE 18. Use the examples below to identify spellings that were borrowed into Modern English from other languages. Your answer should take the form: "The [f] sound is normally spelled <f> in English, but in words borrowed from Greek, it is represented as <ph>." Or "<ch> in English represents the sound [ch], but in words borrowed into Modern English from French, <ch> represents the sound [sh]."

French:	*chic, beige, quiche, mauve, bureau, hour, savoir-faire*
Greek:	*pneumonia, psychology, rhythm, telegraph, euphony*
Italian:	*spaghetti, gnocchi, pizza, bologna*
Spanish:	*hombre, adobe, marijuana, tortilla, tequila*
German:	*sauerkraut, waltz*

4.7 The Morphological Basis of English Spelling

Even where it is regular, the spelling system of English is not directly phonetic; our system is more concerned with providing a consistent spelling for each morpheme than with representing the exact pronunciation of a word. Thus, although prefixes, roots, and suffixes often change their pronunciation from one word to another, their spelling usually remains constant. Consider, for example, the past tense suffix *–ed.* This morpheme has three distinct pronunciations—[id] (in words like *waited*), [d] (in words like *jogged*), and [t] (in words like *jumped*)—but it is spelled consistently as <ed>. Similarly, the plural suffix *-s* is given the same spelling (<s>), whether it is pronounced as [s] (*cats*) or [z] (*dogs*).

---

[3] The <l> of *could* was added later, by analogy with *would* and *should.*

EXERCISE 19. The pronunciation of the plural and past tense suffixes is determined by the sound (not letter) that directly precedes the suffix. Use the examples below to work out the rules for the pronunciation of the suffix *–ed*. First, determine whether the suffix is pronounced as [t], [d], or [ĭd] in each example. Then, list the set of sounds that causes each pronunciation. (Your answer should take the following form: "When the past tense suffix is preceded by the sounds … , it is pronounced [t].")

waited	*rubbed*	*ringed*	*raised*	*helped*
tilted	*waltzed*	*passed*	*pawed*	*bathed*
filled	*sighed*	*baked*	*hatched*	*frothed*
waded	*planned*	*cared*	*judged*	*sloshed*
thanked	*chimed*	*laughed*	*booed*	*plowed*

Roots and stems also maintain a consistent spelling from word to word.[4] This is particularly noticeable in the spelling of vowel sounds. Because of a pronunciation rule called *Vowel Reduction*, unstressed vowels in English are normally pronounced as [ĭ] or [ə]. For example, in the word *chrysanthemum*, only the second syllable is stressed. Thus, it receives a full vowel sound [ă], but the other three vowels, being unstressed, are pronounced as [ĭ] or [ə]: [krĭ.săn´thə.məm].

EXERCISE 20. Give pronunciations for the following words, using dictionary symbols. Mark the stressed vowels, and notice that all *un*stressed vowels are pronounced as [ĭ] or [ə]:

magnet	*definite*	*accuse*	*disposition*	*absent*
tutor	*final*	*decorate*	*definite*	*indicate*
grammar	*composition*	*existence*	*influence*	*symbol*

The vowel sound [ə] can be spelled with *any* vowel letter:

rel<u>a</u>tive	[rĕl´ə·tĭv]	([ə] spelled <a>)
arithm<u>e</u>tic	[ə·rĭth´mə ·tĭk]	([ə] spelled <e>)
ind<u>i</u>cation	[ĭn´də·kā´shən]	([ə] spelled <i>)
dem<u>o</u>crat	[dĕm´ə·krăt]	([ə] spelled <o>)
inj<u>u</u>re	[ĭn´jər]	([ə] spelled <u>)

---

[4] English being English, there are, of course, a few exceptions to this rule, and words spelled with <ou> = [ou] are among them. Thus we have *pronounce ~ pronunciation* and *denounce ~ denunciation* not **pronounciation* and **denounciation*.

Thus, a writer cannot depend on auditory cues in determining the spelling of this sound. Sometimes, however, it is possible to find a related word in which the vowel can be heard in its full form; for example, the <a> of *relative* can be heard in the word *related*, the <e> of arithmetic can be heard in the word *arithmetical*, the <i> of *indication* can be heard in the word *indicative*, the <o> of *democrat* can be heard in the word *democracy*, and the <u> of *injure* can be heard in the word *injurious*.

Word families can also help with the spelling of silent consonants. For example, the silent <g> of *malign* shows up in the pronunciation of the related word *malignant* and the silent <n> of *condemn* shows up in the related word *condemnation*.

EXERCISE 21.

a. Find related words that justify the spelling of the underlined [ə] sound in the following words:

magnet	*definite*	*accuse*	*disposition*	*absent*
professor	*final*	*decorate*	*definite*	*indicate*
grammar	*composition*	*existence*	*influence*	*symbol*
college	*family*	*degradation*	*numerous*	*academy*

b. Find the silent consonant in each word below; then, find a related word in which that consonant is no longer silent:

bomb	*autumn*	*solemn*	*sign*
iamb	*column*	*hymn*	*resign*

c. If, like the author of this text, you are sometimes tempted to spell *rhythm* as **rhythmn*, how can you remember not to do this?

4.8 Morphological Spelling: Further Consequences

Except for the changes described in sections 4.4 and 4.5, each morpheme in a complex word retains its own spelling.

EXERCISE 22. Write out the spelling of each of the following complex words:

un + easy	*book + ish*	*mis + inform*
un + necessary	*book + keeping*	*mis + spell*
dis + obey	*in + expensive*	*over + eat*
dis + satisfied	*in + numerable*	*over + rule*
under + take	*final + ly*	*magical + ly*
under + rate	*sole + ly*	*accidental + ly*

Prefixes borrowed from Latin are a special case, in that the final consonant of the prefix often assimilates to (i.e., changes to agree with) the initial consonant of the stem; for example, when the prefix *ad-* is added to the stem *fect*, the <d> of the prefix changes to <f>: *affect*. Examples are given in table 4.8, with the assimilated forms marked with an asterisk.

Except for this assimilation rule—and the rules we observed earlier regarding the addition of suffixes—the spelling of a complex word is normally the sum of its parts—its prefixes, root(s),

Table 4.8 Spelling of Latin Prefixes

ad- 'toward'	*con-* 'together'	*in-* 'not'	*sub-* 'under'
ad-apt	*co-alesce	in-appropriate	sub-alpine
*ab-breviate	*com-bat	*im-balanced	
*ac-cept	con-cur	in-conceivable	*suc-ceed
ad-dict	con-duct	in-direct	sub-due
ad-ept	co-efficient	in-ept	
*af-fect	con-fection	in-formal	*suf-fer
*ag-gregate	con-gress	in-glorious	*sug-gest
ad-here	*co-here	in-hospitable	sub-human
ad-it	*co-incide	in-imitable	
ad-junct	con-jecture	in-justice	sub-ject
*al-lege	*col-lect	*il-legible	sub-lime
ad-mit	*com-mit	*im-measurable	sub-merge
an-nex	con-nect	in-nocuous	sub-normal
ad-opt	*co-opt	in-oper-able	sub-orn
*ap-point	*com-pose	*im-possible	*sup-port
*ac-quiesce	con-quer	in-quietude	
*ar-rive	*cor-rect	*ir-reverent	sub-rogate
*as-sist	con-sensus	in-satiable	sub-sist
*a-scribe	con-scription	in-scribe	sub-scribe
*at-test	con-tact	in-tolerable	sub-tend
ad-umbrate	con-urbation	in-utile	sub-urbia
ad-vance	con-vert	in-voluntary	sub-vert

and suffixes. Thus the single best strategy for improving spelling at the intermediate and advanced levels is to become more aware of the internal structure—the morphological composition—of words.

4.9 Double Consonants: A Summary

One very common question about English spelling is when to double a consonant. As we have seen, there are four main sources of double consonants in English:

1. As you discovered in Exercise 7, certain consonant sounds such as [l] and [s] are normally spelled with a double letter when they appear at the end of a word after a single vowel. For example, we find *hill* not **hil* and *mess* not **mes.*[5]

2. A consonant may be doubled with the addition of a suffix, to keep the vowel sound short: *hop + -ing* → *hopping.*

3. When two morphemes are combined, each of which contains an instance of the consonant in question, both consonants are retained in the spelling: *book + keeping* → *bookkeeping; un- + necessary* → *unnecessary.*

4. The Latin prefixes *ad-, con-,* and *in-* often assimilate to the initial consonant of the stem, creating a double: *in + logical* → *illogical.*

Of all these double consonants, only those of type 3 are pronounced with the sound of a double consonant.

EXERCISE 23.

a. Account for the double consonant in each of the following words:

admitted	*hugged*	*connected*	*irresponsible*	*illegal*
unnatural	*interrupt*	*kiss*	*immodest*	*jabbed*
approve	*buzz*	*roommate*	*really*	*running*

b. *(Advanced)* Account for the spelling of *accommodate.*

EXERCISE 24. (*Summary Exercise*)

a. Figure 4.9 displays spellings of English words by first-grade children. Each horizontal row represents spellings by a particular child; each vertical row represents spellings for a particular word. Make whatever observations you can about the spelling strategies of

---

[5]But note exceptions such as *until, wonderful,* and *bus.*

these children. What does each child understand or not understand about the spelling system of English? What would be your immediate goals for each child if you were the teacher?

b. Collect ten to twenty spelling errors made by you or other adult spellers. Try to identify the cause of each error. In other words, why was the speller confused about the spelling of that word? Have you learned anything in this chapter that would help the speller to avoid that error in the future?

Correct Spelling	camp	zero	hill	tack	five	pickle	muffin	wife	job	quick
Student 1	kip	siro	hl	tak	fifv	pikl	mifn	wif	gob	kwik
Student 2	kmb	zoz	ely	tgk	vin	plp	mad	woe	gbo	vew
Student 3	kap	zao	hla	tak	fiv	pegl	mife	wif	job	kwe
Student 4	kip	sit	hill	tag	foif	pigll	maf	wuf	job	qic
Student 5	cap	sro	hill	tac	fiv	pagl	mvn	wru	job	job
Student 6	kamp	zero	hlri	tac	fiv	pikl	mifn	wif	job	kwak
Student 7	camp	zero	hill	tack	five	pickel	muffin	wife	jobe	quic
Student 8	camp	zero	hill	tack	five	pickle	muffin	wife	job	quick
Student 9	kp	sro	ul	tk	ff	pl	mfa	waf	gb	kwk
Student 10	cep	zeo	hel	tac	fiv	peg	muf	wif	gob	wec

Figure 4.9 Spelling of first-grade children.

CHAPTER 5
THE DICTIONARY

The first English dictionaries, published in the seventeenth century, were lists of "hard words":

Robert Cawdry, *Table Alphabeticall of Hard Words*, 1604
John Bollokar, *An English Expositor*, 1616
Henry Cockeram, *The English Dictionarie*, 1623

Not until John Kersey's dictionary in the early eighteenth century was there a dictionary that included ordinary words such as *tree* and *have*. Kersey's dictionary was followed in 1734 by Bailey's *An Universal Etymological English Dictionary*, which contained about 40,000 entries and exhibited many of the features of a modern dictionary: etymologies (often incorrect), marks showing the position of accent, and the division of words into syllables.

Samuel Johnson's famous *Dictionary of the English Language* was published in 1755. Although some of Johnson's definitions were unorthodox, they were, for the most part, clearer and more complete than Bailey's, and they were accompanied by illustrative quotations from reputable authors. Johnson also began the tradition of making judgements on the proper use of words.

The first comprehensive American dictionary, *An American Dictionary of the English Language*, was published in 1828 by Noah Webster. Webster pointed out differences between British and American usage, often drawing his illustrative quotations from American authors. He also introduced spelling reforms that were intended to simplify the system: *honor* (for *honour*), *center* (for *centre*), *tire* (for *tyre*), and *draft* (for *draught*). It is because of Noah Webster that the American spelling of words like these differs from that of the British.

The Oxford English Dictionary (OED) was put together between 1858 and 1928. A new edition is currently being developed. The OED contains 414,000 entries in thirteen volumes, and it records the history and development of English words since the time of King Alfred (899 A.D.). Dated quotations are provided to illustrate the use of each word at various times in our history.

The G. & C. Merriam Company's *Third New International Dictionary*, published in 1959, is the descendant of Noah Webster's dictionary of 1828. It contains some 450,000 entries, based on ten million "citations" collected between 1934 and 1959. When this dictionary was first published, there was heated controversy over its policy of simply recording current usage without making judgements about whether the usage is good or bad; for example, it listed the word *irregardless*, which is considered by many to be incorrect. It also substituted the usage labels *substandard* 'not used by cultivated speakers of the language' and *nonstandard* 'not recognized in standard usage, but used by some speakers of cultivated English' for the more judgemental earlier terms such as *vulgar*, *illiterate*, and *erroneous*.

In response to the controversy over *Webster's Third*, recently-published dictionaries have included more information about usage. For example, *The American Heritage College Dictionary* employs the usage labels *informal* ('wish list'), *slang* ('cool'), *nonstandard* ('anyways'), *offensive* (racial, ethnic, and gender slurs), *vulgar,* and *obscene.* Special problems, discussed in a "Usage Problem" section, provide advice to the reader based on the judgements of a Usage Panel that includes such members as Julian Bond, Alistair Cooke, John Kenneth Galbraith, Charles Kuralt, Nina Totenberg, and Eudora Welty. We are told, for example, that eighty-nine percent of the Usage Panel rejects the use of the word *disinterested* to mean 'not interested' (rather than 'unbiased').

5.1 Dictionary Entries

Dictionaries list words (including compound words such as *ice cream*), prefixes and suffixes, abbreviations, and lexicalized (i.e., idiomatic) phrases such as *trial and error.* Some lexicalized phrases are given separate entries, but others are listed under one word of the phrase.[1] Many dictionaries also list proper names, including names of famous people and geographical place names.

Exercise 1.

a. Find in your dictionary an example of each of these items: a compound word, a prefix or suffix, an abbreviation, a proper name, and a lexicalized phrase.

b. Explain the ambiguity in the sentences below. Which *down hill* and which *red tape* are lexicalized phrases? (That is, which meanings of these expressions are listed in the dictionary?)

    i. From a selectman at town meeting: "*A lot of our roads have been going down hill lately.*"

    ii. From *The Daily Messenger*, quoted in *The Columbia Journalism Review*, September 1997: "*Red tape holds up outlet bridge.*"

Look closely at some of the individual entries in your dictionary. Each entry begins with the spelling and syllabification of the word, followed by its pronunciation and then its definitions, which are the heart of the entry. The etymology (the origin) of the word may appear near the beginning of the entry or at the end. The definitions are numbered, with closely related definitions under a single number; for example, for the word "ground," *The Concise Oxford Dictionary* provides two definitions under the number 1:

    "*1a. the surface of the earth.*
    1b. a part of this surface, qualified in some way (low ground)."

---

[1] It can be hard to predict which one; for example, in one dictionary, the phrases *take advantage of* and *take charge* are both listed under *take*; in another, these phrases are listed under *advantage* and *charge,* and in a third *take advantage of* is listed under *advantage,* while *take charge of* is listed under *take.*

Other, more distinct meanings are listed under separate numbers:

> *"2. Soil; earth.*
> *3. a limited or defined area (the ground beyond the farm).*
> *4. (often pl.) a foundation, motive, or reason (excused on the grounds of ill health)."*

Lexicalized phrases may be listed at the end of the entry; for example, in *Webster's New World College Dictionary* the phrases *get hold of (one)self, hold a candle to, hold one's own, hold out on (someone), hold (someone's) feet to the fire, hold the fort, hold the line, hold water, no holds barred,* and *on hold* are listed at the end of the entry for *hold.*

Dictionary definitions are organized by syntactic category (V, N, Adj, and so forth). In the *Merriam Webster* dictionaries, as we noted above, each part of speech is given a separate listing. American dictionaries use the traditional category labels; for example, the word *those* is identified as an adjective or definite article rather than as a determiner, the word *very* is identified as an adverb rather than as an intensifier, and no distinction is made between coordinating conjunctions like *and* and subordinating conjunctions like *that* and *if.* The *American Heritage* and *Merriam Webster* dictionaries use the following category labels:

adjective	*(adj.)*
adverb	*(adv.)*
conjunction	*(conj.)*
definite article	*(def. art.)*
indefinite article	*(indef. art.)*
interjection	*(interj.)*
noun	*(n.)*
preposition	*(prep.)*
pronoun	*(pron.)*
verb	*(v.).*

The *Concise Oxford Dictionary* adds the labels *auxiliary (aux.)* and *determiner (det.).*

Verbs are further classified as *transitive (tr.)* or *intransitive (intr.)*, depending on whether the verb does or does not take a direct object. (*Close the door* is transitive, whereas *Stop!* is intransitive.) Inflectional forms (past tense, perfect participle, present participle, and the third person singular present tense) are listed for verbs; the plural form is given for irregular nouns such as *foot~feet,* but not for "regular" nouns such as *tree.* The *Oxford Learners' Dictionary,* which is intended for students of English as a foreign language, gives more detailed information about the syntactic properties of words.

Dictionaries also list *phrasal verbs* (sometimes called "two-word verbs") such as *give away, give back, give in, take off, throw up,* and *set out.* These are usually listed under the entry for the head word; for example, *give in, give off, give up,* and *give out* are listed under the entry for *give.* However, nouns formed from phrasal verbs by category shift are listed separately: *a giveaway, a giveback.*

Words formed by *affixation* are listed at the end of the entry for the base word if the meaning is predictable; for example, *adaptability* and *adaptableness* are listed at the end of the entry for *adaptable*. However, if the meaning is idiosyncratic, a separate entry is provided; thus, *adaptable* itself is listed as a separate word rather than under the entry for *adapt*, because its meaning, when applied to a person, is 'able to adapt', rather than the expected meaning 'able to *be adapted*' (cf. *washable* 'able to be washed,' *lockable* 'able to be locked,' *doable* 'able to be done,' and so on). A useful feature of American dictionaries is the list of synonyms at the end of some entries; for example, at the end of the listing for *fat*, *The American Heritage College Dictionary* provides the synonyms *obese, corpulent, fleshy, portly, stout, pudgy, rotund, plump,* and *chubby*, with a helpful discussion of the differences in meaning. Finally, dictionaries also give information about usage, if only a labeling of some uses of a word as *informal, slang, nonstandard, offensive, vulgar,* or *obscene*. (Recall that this was the source of much of the controversy surrounding the publication of *Webster's Third International*.) Some examples from *The American Heritage College Dictionary* are given below; see if you agree with their usage labels:

informal	*egghead, slob, fix up* 'provide with a date', *give (someone) the slip, mug* 'face'
slang	*nerd, wimp, cat* 'person,' *kiddo, bitch* 'complain'
nonstandard	*ain't, anyways, irregardless*
vulgar slang	*prick* 'penis' / 'contemptible man,' *bastard* 'mean, disagreeable person,' *suck*
obscene	*shit, fuck*
offensive	*Jap, kike, broad* 'woman,' *bitch* 'a spiteful or overbearing woman,' *queen* 'homosexual man'

EXERCISE 2.

a. Check the words above with one or two other dictionaries. Usage labels are one of the places where dictionaries often disagree. Which dictionary seems to be the most conservative?

b. If you were writing a dictionary, what usage labels, if any, would you apply to the following words? *Clueless, veggies, cough up* 'give up unwillingly', *whitey,* and *screw up*?[2] Look to see what your dictionary says about these lexical items.

5.2 Word Meaning: Referential Meaning vs. Affective and Social Meaning.

Referential meaning is the part of the word's meaning that indicates the object(s), event(s), or quality(ies) that the word indicates or refers to. *Affective* meaning is the information the word provides about the speaker's attitude. The *social meaning* or *register* of the word is the social context in which the word is appropriately used. For example, the words *dine* and *eat* have similar referential meanings but different registers; I was startled when a Burger King employee asked whether I

---

[2]Based on an exercise from Frommer, Paul R. and Edward Finegan, 1994, p. 297.

78

would be *dining* in the restaurant.

As for differences in *affective meaning,* if I say that an unmarried man and woman are *living together,* then I am describing the situation in neutral terms, but if I say they are *shacking up,* then I indicate not only what they are doing (the referential meaning), but also something about my attitude—that I disapprove of their behavior (the affective meaning). Another word with the same referential meaning, *cohabiting,* is affectively neutral but has a special social meaning, or register, in that it is usually employed in scholarly contexts such as a sociology report. These three expressions have identical referential meanings, but very different affective and social meanings.

EXERCISE 3. Discuss referential meaning, affective meaning, and register in the following words.

    a. *fat, obese, corpulent, portly, stout, pudgy, plump, chubby*

    b. *talk, converse, gossip, gab, prattle, yak, gab*

    c. *man, guy, dude, jock, gentleman, hunk, boy*

    d. *stupid person, idiot, nerd, ass, jerk, turkey, wimp, punk, airhead, bastard* [3]

Example: *Referential meaning:* All the words of set 1 refer to the state of being overweight, but *obese* and *corpulent* are stronger than the others: they mean 'extremely overweight.' *Stout* means 'heavily built,' rather than 'fat.' *Portly* means 'stout in a dignified way,' and it applies only to adults, usually male adults. *Obese* means 'unhealthily fat.'

Affective meaning: The words *fat, obese,* and *corpulent* usually indicate a negative attitude on the part of the speaker. The word *portly* has positive connotations, as does *stout,* to a lesser degree. The words *pudgy, plump,* and *chubby* indicate that the speaker considers the fatness to be cute or charming.

Register: The words *obese, corpulent,* and *portly* are formal in register. *Obese* is more likely to be used in a medical context than in ordinary conversation.

Most of the time when we consult a dictionary, it is the *referential* meaning of the word that we are after. Unfortunately, the meanings of words are not easy to pin down, even for lexicographers. To see how difficult this can be, try Exercise 4, based on an experiment by the sociolinguist William Labov (1978), in which he asked his subjects to think about the meanings of the words *cup, bowl, glass,* and *bottle*:

EXERCISE 4.

a. Look closely at the drawings of containers in figure 5.2a and decide which containers could be called *cups,* which could be called *glasses,* and which could be called *bowls.* Then

---

[3]Based on an exercise from Finegan, Edward (1999, 218).

use this classification to determine what properties are essential or desirable in a *cup, bowl,* or *glass*. In doing the exercise, you should consider not only the shape of the container, but also what it is composed of and what it might contain. Here are some results you may find:

  i. It is easy to list *desirable* properties of cups, bowls, and glasses, but harder to find properties that are *essential;* the absence of some properties can be forgiven if enough other relevant properties are present.

  ii. Different speakers have slightly different definitions for these terms.

  iii. Our definition of a particular term depends partly on what other terms we use. For example, speakers who customarily use the word *tumbler* for a drinking glass that is not made of glass may be reluctant to apply the term *glass* to such a container. Similarly, speakers who use the term *mug* for a cup with straight-up-and-down sides may hesitate to call such a container a *cup*.

b. When you have finished the *cup/bowl/glass* exercise, try the exercise in figure 5.2b; here you are to decide whether a given container is or is not a bottle. After you have made your classification, try to determine what properties a container must have to be a bottle.

c. Here are some other sets of terms you might try to define:

  i. *chair, bench, stool, sofa;*
  ii. *fry, bake, boil, broil.*

Given the difficulty we find in determining the exact referential meanings of words, you will not be surprised to learn that even dictionary definitions are flawed. For example, *The American Heritage College Dictionary* gives, as one meaning of the verb *paint*, the definition 'coat with paint,' but the linguist Jerry Fodor has pointed out that if we spill a can of paint, thereby coating a large section of the floor, we would not then say that we had *painted* the floor. In response to a suggestion that what is missing from the definition is the notion of *deliberateness,* Fodor pointed out that if I deliberately stick my brush into the paint can and coat its bristles with paint, I cannot say that I have *painted* my paintbrush bristles. Apparently, something must also be said about the *purpose* of the paint-coating—it must be done for the purpose of decoration or protection. Look to see what your dictionary says about the meaning of the word *paint*.

To give another example, consider the word *water*. *The American Heritage College Dictionary* defines water as 'a clear, colorless, odorless, and tasteless liquid, H_2O.' In fact, however, the meaning of this word can be shown to vary according to the purpose for which the liquid is used. If we are concerned with *drinking*, then lack of color and odor are, indeed, important; even a small number of tea molecules introduced by dipping a teabag for 30 seconds or so is sufficient to change *water* into *tea*. However, chlorine or other chemicals that are added for the purpose of killing germs do not have the same effect—chlorinated water is still water. If the water is *not* for drinking, but is flowing in a river, then it may contain almost anything; certainly it does not have to be 'clear, odorless, and tasteless,' nor does it have to consist entirely of 'H_2O.'

Figure 1
Containers used in the cup/bowl/glass experiments

Figure 5.2a Containers used in the cup/bowl/glass experiments (from Labov, 1978, 222).

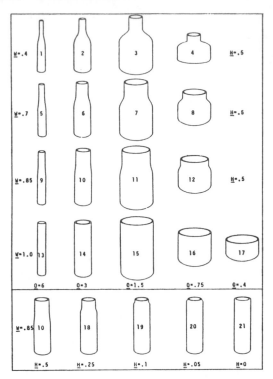

Figure 5.2b Series of bottle-like containers from Harmon S. Boortien, *Vagueness of Container Nouns and Cognate Verbs.* Unpublished University of Texas dissertation, 1975. Reprinted in Labov (1978, 230).

5.3 Homonyms and Polysemous Words

What looks like a single word from the point of view of spelling and pronunciation may sometimes be given multiple dictionary entries. For example, *The Concise Oxford Dictionary* list three words *bank*:

> *bank*[1]: 'the sloping edge of land by a river'
> *bank*[2]: 'a financial establishment'
> *bank*[3]: 'a set of similar object, espl of keys, lights, or switches'

Sets of words like this, with identical spelling and pronunciation, are called *homonyms*.[4] The motivation for representing the three *banks* as distinct words is partly semantic (the meanings seem not to be related to one another) and partly etymological: *bank*[1] is a borrowing from Old Norse, *bank*[2]

---

[4] Students sometimes ask about the terms *homophone* and *homograph*. Homophones are words like *their* and *there*, which have identical pronunciations; homographs are words like *read* (present tense) and *read* (past tense), which have identical spellings; *homonyms* have identical spellings *and* identical pronunciations.

was borrowed during Middle English times from the Old French word *banque* or the Old Italian word *banca*, and *bank*[3] was borrowed into Middle English from the Old French word *banc*.

The *Merriam Webster* dictionaries provide a separate entry for each part of speech; thus *Webster's* lists *five* words *bank,* with the verb 'to raise a pile or mound' listed separately from the noun 'a pile or mound,' and the verb 'to carry out the business of banking' listed separately from the noun meaning 'an establishment where money is kept.' Look to see how many *bank*s your own dictionary lists.

Dictionaries make a distinction between homonyms, which have separate entries, and *polysemous words* like *platform* and *eye*, which have more than one meaning under a single entry. The meanings of the word *platform* include 'a horizontal surface raised above the level of the adjacent area,' and 'a formal declaration of the principles on which a group makes its appeal to the public'; the meanings for the word *eye* include 'an organ of vision,' ' the faculty of vision, ' and 'a detective.'

EXERCISE 5.

a. The distinction between homonyms and polysemous words is not easy to make. Try your hand on the words below: Are these separate words (homonyms) or different meanings of a single polysemous word? After making your best guess, check with a dictionary. On what basis does the dictionary make this decision?

sound 'a sensation perceived by the sense of hearing'

sound 'healthy'   *sound* 'a long body of water'

shark 'a species of fish'   *shark* 'a person who preys greedily on others'

fire 'to set on fire'   *fire* 'to inflame with passion'

fire 'to hurl or throw'   *fire* 'to dismiss from a job'

bill 'a statement of money owed'   *bill* 'parts of a bird's jaw'

bill 'a written or printed public notice'

b. Ambiguity in the meaning of words is sometimes the basis of jokes. Explain the jokes below, and determine whether the semantic ambiguity is a matter of homonymy or polysemy:

   i. Q: *Why don't you get hot at a baseball game?*
      A: *Because there are so many fans there.*

   —From a children's joke book

   ii. Headline from the *San Francisco Business Times,* quoted in *The New Republic,* 1 April 1996: *Del Monte Foods to can 150 employees.*

c. Most words are polysemous—that is, they have more than one meaning, sometimes a very large number of meanings. Thus the words *cup, bowl,* and *glass* each have several other meanings in addition to the "container" meanings that you defined above. List as many definitions as you can think of for each of these words. Then consult your dictionary to find any additional meanings you may have missed.

5.4 How Words Acquire New Meanings

There are four common methods by which new meanings are added to a word:

a. Generalization. A word with a specific meaning begins to be applied more generally, as when a copy machine is called a "xerox machine" or the word *kleenex* comes to mean "tissue."

b. Narrowing. A word with a general meaning is applied more specifically, as when the verb *drink* is used to mean "drink alcohol" or the word *smoke* to mean "smoke cigarettes." (*She neither drinks nor smokes.*)

c. Metaphor. A word is applied to something that it *resembles* in some way, as when the words *bright, brilliant,* and *dim* are used to refer to intelligence (or its opposite), based on the underlying simile: "Intelligence is like light."

d. Metonymy. A word is applied to an event or object with which it is associated, as when the word *hand* is used to mean "assistance." (*Would you give me a hand?*) Similarly, the word *wheels* can be used to refer to a car, and the word *pad* can be used to mean "apartment."

These methods may be combined with **category shift** (the use of the word as a different part of speech).

EXERCISE 6. *The Oxford English Dictionary* (OED) gives very detailed information about the history of words in English, with examples from original texts. Look up one word that interests you in the OED. State (in one sentence) how the word came into English, and then write a one-page essay describing, as simply as you can, the development of the word after it entered the English language. You should pay particular attention to the development of extended meanings for the word, but you might also mention changes in spelling or the incorporation of the word into compounds and/or lexicalized phrases. If you can, identify extensions of meaning as instances of generalization, narrowing, metaphor, or metonymy. *Caution:* The OED provides very detailed, technical information about the history of words. Your assignment is to condense that information into a brief, readable account that an ordinary reader will be able to follow.

5.5 Ordering of Definitions

Dictionaries follow three systems for the ordering of definitions in polysemous words: The *Merriam Webster* dictionaries list the historically oldest definition first. Other dictionaries start with the most *common* use of the word or with a *central* meaning from which other meanings seem to be derived. Look to see what system your dictionary follows. (You'll find it in the explanatory material at the beginning of your dictionary.)

EXERCISE 7. Definitions for the words *drip, skirt,* and *tough* are set out below, with the order scrambled. How would you order the definitions if you were compiling a dictionary? This question has two parts:

a. Which part of speech would you list first?

b. How would you order the definitions within each category? What principle(s) are you following in ordering your definitions?

skirt (skûrt)

n. _____. The lower outer section of a rocket vehicle.

n. _____. An outer edge; a border.

n _____. A garment hanging from the waist and worn by women and girls.

n. _____. **skirts.** The edge, as of a town; the outskirts.

n. _____. *Offensive slang.* A girl or woman.

n. _____. The part of a garment, such as a dress, that hangs freely from the waist down.

tr. v. _____. To pass along or around the border or edge of.

tr. v. _____. To lie on or along the border of.

tr. v. _____. To evade, as by circumlocution: *skirted the issue.*

drip (drĭp)

n. _____. The process of falling in drops.

n. _____. *Slang.* A tiresome or annoying person.

n. _____. The sound made by liquid falling in drops.

tr. v. _____. To let fall in or as if in drops.

intr. v. _____. To shed drops.

intr. v. _____. To fall in drops.

tough (tŭf)

v. __10__. *Idiom.* **tough it out.** *Slang.* To get through despite hardship; endure.

adj. __4__. Hard to cut or chew.

adj. __5__. Able to withstand great strain without tearing or breaking; strong and resilient.

adj. __1__. Demanding or troubling; difficult: *tough questions.*

adj. __6__. Severe; harsh: *a tough winter.*

adj. __7__. Physically hardy; rugged.

adj. __8__. Aggressive; pugnacious.

adj. __9__. *Slang.* Unfortunate; too bad.

adj. __2__. Strong-minded; resolute.

n. __3__. A violent or rowdy person; a hoodlum or thug.

Figure 5.5 Definitions of the word "face." Based on a proposal by Richard R. Lodwig and Eugene F. Barrett, *Words, Words, Words: Vocabularies and Dictionaries* (Montclair, NJ: Boynton/Cook, 1981, 98).

In attempting to show the relationship among the various meanings of a polysemous word, dictionary writers are hampered by the linear character of the printed page and by their decision to organize the definitions by syntactic category, with nominal (noun) definitions in one section and verbal definitions in another. Thus, for example, one of the *noun* meanings for *skirt* 'an outer edge or border'—is closely related to the verbal meaning 'to lie on or along the border of,' but under the organization that dictionaries use, these two definitions must be presented in different sections of the lexical entry. Perhaps now that dictionaries are being put on computers, dictionary writers might experiment with more revealing graphic representations such as the one represented in figure 5.5 for the noun *face*.

EXERCISE 8. Redo the definitions for *skirt, drip,* and *tough* using a graphic notation similar to that shown in figure 5.5.

5.6 Basic Semantic Concepts

People learn new words with astonishing speed; the linguist Steven Pinker (1994) has estimated that children learn a new word every two hours, up until the time they start school. How do we do this? One hypothesis suggests that word meanings are composed at least partly of basic (perhaps innate) concepts such as *flat, rigid, round, heavy, bright, dark, hard, soft, loud, quiet, happy, sad, move, grasp,* and *ingest*. The idea is that when we look for the meanings of words, we already know, in part, what to look for.

In carefully composed writing such as poetry or advertising slogans, a particular semantic concept may be repeated over and over to create an image.

EXERCISE 9. Read the following poem, "Safe in their Alabaster Chambers," by Emily Dickinson.

a. One basic semantic notion is repeated over and over in the second stanza; try to find it.

b. The repetition of this semantic concept is reinforced by repetition of certain consonant sounds. Try to find those, also.

> *Safe in their Alabaster Chambers—*
> *Untouched by Morning—*
> *And untouched by Noon—*
> *Lie the meek members of the Resurrection—*
> *Rafter of Satin—and Roof of Stone!*
> *Grand go the Years—in the Crescent—above them—*
> *Worlds scoop their Arcs—*
> *And Firmaments—row—*
> *Diadems—drop—and Doges—surrender—*

Soundless as dots—on a Disc of Snow—

—Emily Dickinson (version of 1861)

When children learn new words, they often fail at first to understand the entire meaning. Underextensions are common, as when one twenty-month-old child refused to accept that a blank page could be *white*, since she had previously associated that word only with snow. Overextensions are also frequent, as when a child applies the word *doggie* to every four-legged animal, or the word *moon* to various shiny crescent-shaped objects such as a lemon slice or a crescent-shaped piece of paper.[5] Children may also fail to understand idiomatic expressions, as when a two-year-old of the author's acquaintance ran to her mother one evening, crying "Dad said a bad word!" "What did he say?" the mother asked. "Time for bed," answered the child, thereby revealing her less-than-complete understanding of the lexicalized phrase *bad word*.

Words whose meaning is relative to the context are particularly difficult. Young children sometimes use the word *daddy* to refer to any adult male, not understanding that a man is a *daddy* only in relation to his own children. Similarly, a three-year-old may not understand that a glass may be *little* for the child, but *big* for the dolls who are to "drink" out of it. Primary-school children have been found to have difficulty with the words *before* and *after,* and even university students sometimes confuse words like *precede* and *follow* when asked, for example, whether a given consonant agrees in voicing with the consonant that *precedes* it or the consonant that *follows* it.

EXERCISE 10.

a. In the selection from the speech of a young child in Appendix Section 6, Eve asserts that her ice cubes are "in the refrigerator, cooking." Which word does Eve not completely understand? Does she understand *anything* about the meaning of this word?

b. When a two-year-old, pretending to read a newspaper, was asked what she was doing, she replied, "Watching the newspaper." What does this child not understand about the meaning of the word *watching*?

Adults also learn new vocabulary and, just as we saw with children, they sometimes fail to comprehend the complete meaning of a new word, though they may have a partial understanding. One of the most common writing errors is the use of a word that is almost but not quite appropriate, as in the examples below, which were collected from college students' papers:

a. *American Sign Language is an **ample** form of communication.*

---

[5]Examples from Aitchison (1994, 173-5).

b. *When criticized about the grammatical error, Winston* **countered right back** *with the slogan, "What do you want, good grammar or good taste?"*

c. *The English language has* **transformed** *considerably over the past five centuries.*

d. *I'm* **apt** *to agree with Chomsky's contention that language is innate.*

e. **Abolishing** *the importance of correct spelling would . . .*

f. *If we spent more time* **revising** *our mistakes . . .*

g. *The* **fact** *that one doesn't think in sentences is true.*

h. *The demand for jobs has* **prolifically** *declined.*

i. *My knowledge of grammar is a little* **sparse.**

j. *Unless precautions are* **formulated,** *dozens of animal species will die out. More thought and research needs to be* **enacted**.

k. *Baseball has always been* **commonplace** *to me every year as summer rolls around.*

l. (In a note from a local elementary school) *Children may not play in the gym in sock feet. Socks* **enhance** *slipping.*

EXERCISE 11. If you agree that the boldfaced words in the examples above are misused, try to say exactly what is wrong (and right) about the use of the word in that context.

Having noted how difficult it is to define the meaning of a word (see section 5.2), I was curious to see whether my students' errors could have been avoided by consulting a dictionary. Based on definitions from the *Merriam Webster's* and *American Heritage* dictionaries set out in table 5.6, I decided that the dictionary is not always helpful to the student who wants to avoid such errors. Clearly, when we learn a word by hearing or reading it in context, we learn more about its meaning than can be found by consulting a dictionary. Dictionary writers do their best to represent the word meanings that *people* know, but they do not completely succeed.

5.7 Specialized Dictionaries

In addition to the general dictionaries that we have been discussing so far, there are also many specialized dictionaries, which are included in the following list. For the convenience of readers who want to look at these dictionaries, the Library of Congress call number is provided for each item.

a. Dialect Dictionaries

Blevins, W. *Dictionary of the American West*: Facts on File, 1993. PE 2970.W4 B5 1993

Cassidy, F.G., ed. *Dictionary of American Regional English* 2 vols.: Belknap Press, 1985. PE 2843.D52 1985

A Dictionary of Canadianisms on Historical Principles: W.J. Gage, 1967. PE 3243.D5

Holloway, J.E., and W.K Vass. *The African Heritage of American English*: Indiana University Press, 1993. PE 3102.N4 H65 1993

Hughes, J.M., et al., eds. *The Australian Concise Oxford Dictionary*: Oxford University Press, 1992. PE

Table 5.6 Dictionary Definitions vs. Students' Usage of Words

Dictionary definition	Student's use of word
ample 'generously sufficient to satisfy a requirement or need.'	*American Sign Language is an* **ample** *form of communication.*
counter, intr. 'to adduce an answer'	*When criticized about the grammatical error, Winston* **countered right back** *with the slogan,"What do you want, good grammar or good taste?"*
transform, intr. 'to become transformed; change.'	*The English language has* **transformed** *considerably over the past five centuries.*
apt 'ordinarily disposed; inclined.'	*I'm* **apt** *to agree with Chomsky's contention that language is innate.*
abolish 'do away with.'	**Abolishing** *the importance of correct spelling would . . .*

3601.Z5 A863 1992

Major, C. *Juba to Jive*: Viking, 1994. PE 3727.N4 M34 1994

Ramson, W.S. *The Australian National Dictionary*: Oxford University Press, 1988. PE 3601.Z5 A97 1988

Smitherman, G. *Black Talk*: Houghton Mifflin, 1994. PE 3102.N4 S65 1994

b. Dictionaries of Foreign Words and Phrases in English

Bell, A.J. *A Dictionary of Foreign Words and Phrases in Current English*: E.P. Dutton, 1966. PE 1670.B55 1966a

Guinagh, K. *Dictionary of Foreign Phrases and Abbreviations*: H.W. Wilson, 1972. PE 1670.G8 1972

Newmark, M. *Dictionary of Foreign Words and Phrases*: Philosophical Library, 1950. PE 1582.A3 N4

c. Dictionaries of New Words

Barnhart, R. and Sol Steinmetz, with Clarence Barnhart. *The Third Barnhart Dictionary of New English*: H.W. Wilson, 1990. PE 1630.B3

The Oxford Dictionary of New Words: Oxford University Press, 1991. PE 1630.094 1991

d. Dictionaries of Slang

Ayto, J. and J. Simpson. *The Oxford Dictionary of Modern Slang*: Oxford University Press, 1992. PE 3721.94 1992

Lightner, J. E., ed., *Random House Historical Dictionary of American Slang* 2 vols.: Random House, 1994. PE 2846.H57 1994

Partridge, E. *A Dictionary of Slang,* 8th ed.: Macmillan, 1984. PE 3721.P3 1984

e. Etymological Dictionaries

Klein, E. *A Comprehensive Etymological Dictionary of the English Language* 2 vols.: Elsevier, 1966. PE 1580.K4

Morris, W. and M. Morris. *Dictionary of Word and Phrase Origins* 2 vols.: Harper & Row, 1962. PE 1580.M6

Onions, C.T., ed. *The Oxford Dictionary of English Etymology*: Clarendon Press, 1966. PE 1580.05

Partridge, E. *Origins: A Short Etymological Dictionary of Modern English*: Macmillan, 1958. PE 1580.P3

Shipley, J.T. *Dictionary of Word Origins*: Philosophical Library, 1945. PE 1580.S45

Shipley, J.T. *The Origins of English Words*: Johns Hopkins, 1984. PE 1571.S46 1984

f. Pronouncing Dictionaries

Bollard, J.K., ed. *Pronouncing Dictionary of Proper Names*: Omnigraphics, 1993. PE 1137.982 1993

Jones, D. *Everyman's English Pronouncing Dictionary,* 14th ed.: E. P. Dutton, 1977. PE 1137.G53 1977

Kenyon, J.S., and T.A. Knott, *A Pronouncing Dictionary of American English*: G. & C. Merriam, 1944. PE 1137.K37

Pointon, G.E., ed. *BBC Pronouncing Dictionary*. Oxford University Press, 1990. PE 1660.B3 1990

g. Rhyming Dictionaries

Lees, G. *The Modern Rhyming Dictionary*: Cherry Lane Books, 1981. PE 1519.L37

Stillman, F. *The Poet's Manual and Rhyming Dictionary*: Thos. Y. Crowell, 1965. PE 1505.S8

Young, S. *The New Comprehensive American Rhyming Dictionary*: Wm. Morrow, 1991. PE 1519.Y68 1991

h. Other Specialized Dictionaries

Barlough, J.E. *The Archaicon: A Collection of Unusual, Archaic English*: Scarecrow Press, 1974. PE 1667.BC

Cowie, A.P., et al. *Oxford Dictionary of Current Idiomatic English* 2 vols.: Oxford University Press, 1983. PE 1460.87

Cowie, A.P. and Mackin, R. *Oxford Dictionary of Phrasal Verbs*: Oxford University Press, 1993. PE 1319.C69 1993

Maggio, R. *The Dictionary of Bias-Free Usage*: Oryx Press, 1991. PE 1460.M26 1991

McCutcheon, M. *Descriptionary: A Thematic Dictionary*: Facts on File, 1992. PE 1591.M415 1992

Smith, R.W.L. *Dictionary of English Word-Roots*: Littlefield, Adams, and Co., 1967. PE 1580.S65

Taylor, M. *The Language of World War II*: H.W. Wilson, 1948. PE 3727.S7 T3 1948

EXERCISE 12. Find three dictionaries from the list above and write down one interesting fact you learn from each one.

EXERCISE 13. As a summary exercise for chapter 5, create a dictionary of slang. Begin by collecting slang words that are used in a group to which you belong, such as a fraternity or sorority, athletic team, or simply a group of friends. When you have collected twenty words or more, compile your words into a dictionary. Be as professional as possible: include a pronunciation, inflectional forms, parts-of-speech labels, and an etymology. (If you can't figure out the etymology, do what the dictionary writers do—put [origin unknown] or [?].) Write definitions, and if the word has more than one definition, organize them carefully. Include usage labels where relevant. If appropriate, provide a list of synonyms at the end of the entry, with a discussion of differences in meaning and usage.

EXERCISE 14. As a summary exercise for chapters 2–5, discuss the vocabulary of one or more of the literary passages in Appendix Section 1. Some questions you might consider are listed below. *Caution:* Write your answer as a coherent essay, with references to the selection you are discussing; don't just go through the questions and answer *yes* or *no*. Also, choose questions that are relevant to the passage you are discussing; not all questions are relevant to every passage. Finally, confine this discussion to the question of *vocabulary*; you will have opportunities to discuss sentence structure in future exercises.

a. Consider the *register* of the words: Are they formal, informal, or neutral; conversational or literary? Are they characteristic of a particular mode of discourse, such as poetry or legal language? Is there a relationship between the register of the words and their historical origin?

b. Consider the author's dependence on certain syntactic categories. Some writers depend primarily on adjectives for description, while others use nouns and verbs with strong meanings.

c. Is the passage written in first, second, or third person, and is this significant?

d. Now consider the meanings of the words: Are the nouns concrete or abstract? Do the adjectives describe qualities that could be measured objectively, or are they entirely subjective (a judgement by the narrator)? Do the nouns, verbs, and adjectives rely primarily on a particular sense such as sight or hearing? Do the verbs express actions or states? Is there any figurative language?

e. Are there repetitions of sounds, and are they connected to meaning?

CHAPTER 6
THE STRUCTURE OF STATEMENTS

6.1 What is a Sentence?

This is an important theoretical question, because the sentence is the basic unit of written discourse (though not necessarily of spoken discourse, as we will see), but it is also an important practical question: Teachers spend countless hours trying to help children understand what units should be punctuated as sentences. Notice, for example, that the first-grade author of "Mafin" (Appendix Section 2) has misjudged the punctuation of the sentence

> *When my mom washsi mafin. he scashed my mom and it hse [hurts] a lot.*

The second-grade author of "Your Own Monster" has written two sentences together as one:

> *I like him he's just kind of hard to take care of.*

In the examples in the Appendix, the children seem to be identifying sentences correctly by third or fourth grade, but don't be fooled. These compositions have been edited with the help of the teacher. In their study of freshman writing errors, Connors and Lunsford (1988) found that even college students sometimes have difficulty identifying sentences; improper identification of sentences was the fourth most frequent error in freshman writing. (See table 6.1.)

Teachers traditionally give two sorts of definitions for the sentence:[1]

> 1. *A sentence is a group of words that expresses a complete thought.*
> 2. *A sentence is a group of words that contains a subject and a predicate.*

Note that these definitions address two different issues. The following sentence from "My Nightmare" (Appendix Section 2) is grammatically well-formed, but contains too many unrelated thoughts for one sentence; in other words, it violates the first definition given above:

> *They put me in a space jail, but I had a good idea and all I had to do is get that space gun.*

---

[1] Notice that we are actually talking not about sentences in general, but about *statements*: Questions like "What are you doing?" and imperatives like "Please shut the door" will have to be approached in a slightly different way; we'll return to that issue in chapter 10.

Table 6.1 Categories of Grammatical Errors in Freshman Compositions, in the Order of Their Frequency (Connors and Lunsford (1988))[2]

Spelling

Punctuation, especially commas and apostrophes

Use of inflectional forms such as past tense and subject-verb agreement

Formation of complete sentences (vs. fragments, run-ons, and comma splices)[3]

Word choice

NP reference, especially pronouns

Consistency of verb tense

This is a different problem from the writing of fragments or run-ons, which violate the second definition:

> *When my mom washsi Mafin.* (an incomplete sentence or "fragment")
>
> or   *I like him he's just kind of hard to take care of.* (two sentences written together as one—a "run-on")

The first problem—too many thoughts in one sentence—lies outside the purview of a textbook on English grammar. How many thoughts should be included in one sentence is a matter of judgement and taste, not grammatical structure. But the second problem—whether a given sequence of words has the necessary structure to be punctuated as a sentence—is a proper subject of discussion for this text. This issue is addressed by the second definition above: *A sentence is a group of words that contains a subject and a predicate.* In this chapter, we will explore this definition and introduce some revisions to make it more consistent with current linguistic theory.

EXERCISE 1. Find other examples of fragments and run-ons in the samples of children's writing in Appendix Section 2.

---

[2]Connors and Lunsford provide a more specific list of writing errors; for our purposes here, I have collapsed errors of the same general type into a single category. For example, the fourth category is a combination of three types of errors having to do with the formation of sentences: fragments, run-ons, and comma splices.

[3]A comma splice is two sentences separated by a comma rather than a conjunction or semi-colon:

> *I like him, he's just kind of hard to take care of.*

6.2 The Structure of a Sentence

Traditionally, as we have said, a statement is divided into two parts, a subject and a predicate:

Subject	**Predicate**
Gaul	*is divided into three parts.*
People who live in glass houses	*shouldn't throw stones.*
My mom	*gets mad at Muffin.*

In this section, I will give evidence to show that a statement actually has *three* parts rather than two. We will begin our examination of the sentence with a set of very simple statements such as the following:

> *An intelligent dog would bark.*
> *The old girl should find a good bike.*
> *A conscientious teacher will sit on this soft bench.*

These sentences could serve as models for other sentences, as in tables 6.2a, 6.2b, and 6.2c on the following page; if we don't worry about whether the statement makes sense, we can create a large number of well-formed statements from each table by choosing one word—any word—from each column. Additional statements like those of tables 6.2a, 6.2b, and 6.2c can be constructed by following the formulas below:

Table 6.2a: S(entence) = D + Adj + N + AUX + V
Table 6.2b: S = D + Adj + N + AUX + V + D + Adj + N
Table 6.2c: S = D + Adj + N + AUX + V + P + D + Adj + N

EXERCISE 2.

a. Give the full names of the categories in these formulas.

b. Generate five sentences from each formula.

6.3 Words Are Grouped into Phrases

Although the three formulas at the end of the previous section will generate a very large number of sentences (2,346,875 of them, using just the words that are listed in the tables), they hardly scratch the surface of the sentence-making capacity of human English speakers. Formulas of this type, which assume that sentences are made up of individual words strung together one by one, will not get us very far in understanding how sentences are constructed. In fact, words do not enter sentences one by one, but as groups of words called *phrases*. In this section, we will revise our sentence formulas to reflect this insight.

Table 6.2a Sentence Pattern 1

D	Adj	N	AUX	V
A(n)	*intelligent*	*dog*	*would*	*bark*
Any	*healthy*	*teacher*	*can*	*swim*
The	*lucky*	*girl*	*could*	*laugh*
Your	*pesky*	*computer*	*should*	*run*
This	*old*	*man*	*will*	*talk*

Table 6.2b Sentence Pattern 2

D	Adj	N	AUX	V	D	Adj	N
The	*old*	*girl*	*should*	*find*	*a(n)*	*good*	*bike*
Any	*conscientious*	*teacher*	*would*	*remove*	*this*	*old*	*hat*
A(n)	*good*	*computer*	*can*	*ruin*	*your*	*dependable*	*car*
Your	*pesky*	*cat*	*would*	*disturb*	*any*	*tired*	*man*
This	*lucky*	*man*	*will*	*steal*	*the*	*helpful*	*cat*

Table 6.2c Sentence Pattern 3

D	Adj	N	AUX	V	P	D	Adj	N
A(n)	*conscientious*	*teacher*	*will*	*sit*	*on*	*this*	*soft*	*bench*
Any	*old*	*girl*	*can*	*recline*	*in*	*a(n)*	*old*	*chair*
The	*good*	*computer*	*could*	*play*	*by*	*your*	*dependable*	*car*
Your	*pesky*	*cat*	*would*	*run*	*near*	*any*	*large*	*tree*
This	*lucky*	*man*	*should*	*hide*	*under*	*the*	*helpful*	*hat*

6.3.1 The Noun Phrase (NP). The sequence "D Adj N" occurs in all three tables above, and twice in table 6.2b. If we pull out this sequence and identify it as a *noun phrase* (NP), then the formulas of tables 6.2a–6.2c will be greatly simplified, as shown below:

> **Table 6.2a:** S = NP AUX V   (*An intelligent dog would talk.*)
> **Table 6.2b:** S = NP AUX V NP   (*A conscientious teacher would remove this old hat.*)
> **Table 6.2c:** S = NP AUX V P NP   (*The lucky dog will hide under a helpful tree.*)
>   where NP = D Adj N

Linguists use *constituency tests* such as the following to determine whether a given string of words constitutes a phrase.[4]

1. The Pro-form Test
If a string of words can be replaced with a pro-form, then it is a phrase.
> **A conscientious teacher** *would remove* **this old hat.** → **She** *would remove* **it.**

The pro-form test shows that the NPs *a conscientious teacher* and *this old hat* are both phrases.

2. The Movement Test
If a string of words can be moved, as a unit, to another position in the sentence, then it is a phrase.
> **This old hat,** *any conscientious teacher would remove.*

The movement test shows that the NP *this old hat* is a phrase.

3. The Short-Answer Test
If a string of words can serve as the short answer to a question, then it is a phrase.
> **Q:** *What would a conscientious teacher remove?*   **A:** *This old hat.*
> **Q:** *Who would remove this old hat?*   **A:** *A conscientious teacher.*

The short-answer test shows that the NPs *this old hat* and *a conscientious teacher* are both phrases.

4. The Cleft Test
If a string of words can be placed in focus position in a *cleft,* as in the example below, then it is a phrase:
> Original sentence: *A conscientious teacher would remove this old hat.*

> **Cleft 1:** *It's* | *this old hat* | *that a conscientious teacher would remove.*

> **Cleft 2:** *It's* | *a conscientious teacher* | *that would remove this old hat.*

---

[4]Notice that these tests depend on the assumption that speakers of English already know, intuitively, how words are grouped into phrases. Otherwise, we couldn't make use of the constituency tests; we wouldn't be able to judge whether the string of words we are testing passes the tests or not.

The cleft test shows that the NPs *this old hat* and *a conscientious teacher* are both phrases.

6.3.2 The Prepositional Phrase (PP). A preposition together with the NP that follows it (the *complement* of the preposition) also creates a phrase: *in the house, about social security, by the author, under the sink, near Chicago, around the block,* and so on are all prepositional phrases (PPs).

---

* If v can move PP is adverbial phrase

EXERCISE 3. Consider the following sentences from table 6.2c:
  a. *A conscientious teacher should recline in this old chair.*
  b. *The lucky man will hide under a helpful hat.* PP adverbial
First identify the PP in each sentence. Then use the pro-form test, the movement test, the short answer test, and the cleft test to show that the sequence of words you have identified is a phrase. *Hint:* The pro-form for a PP is *then* or *there*.

Now that we have identified the phrasal categories NP and PP, the formula of table 6.2c can be simplified as follows:

S = NP AUX V PP, where NP = D ADJ N and PP = P NP
(*The lucky man will hide under a helpful hat.*)

6.3.3 The Verb Phrase (VP). There is an additional constituent that can be identified in the sentences of Tables 6.2a–6.2c: the sequence of words consisting of the verb plus the phrase that follows it (the complement of the verb). This string of words is called the *verb phrase* (VP):[5]

*An intelligent dog can **talk**.*   *She will **steal your car**.*   Direct object   *He should **sit in that chair**.*

EXERCISE 4. In each of the boldfaced VPs above, identify the verb and the complement of the verb. What category does the complement belong to?

Our constituency tests show that the VP is a phrase:

[5]Unfortunately, the term *verb phrase* is used in traditional grammar with another meaning, to designate the string of words consisting of the auxiliary verb plus the main verb: *should have gone; will notice; was decapitated.* In this text, we will use the term *verb string* rather than *verb phrase* for sequences of this sort. In the sense in which we are using the term *phrase*, the verb string is not a phrase at all.

1. The Pro-form Test

Given an appropriate context such as the parenthesized material in the examples below, a VP can be replaced by the pro-form *do so*:

> *(Most animals cannot talk, but) an intelligent dog can* **do so.**
>> *Talk* has been replaced, in the second clause, by the proform *do so*.
>
> *(I said she would steal your car, and) she will* **do so.**
>> *Steal your car* has been replaced, in the second clause, by the proform *do so*.
>
> *(I told him to sit in that chair, and) he should* **do so.**
>> *Sit in that chair* has been replaced, in the second clause, by the proform *do so*.

2. The Movement Test

Given an appropriate context such as the parenthesized material in the examples below, the VP can be moved to the beginning of its clause:

> *(I said this dog could talk, and)* **talk** *he can.*
>> *Talk* has moved to the front of its clause.
>
> *(I said she would steal your car, and)* **steal your car** *she will.*
>> *Steal your car* has moved to the front of its clause.
>
> *(I said he should sit in that chair, and)* **sit in that chair** *he should.*
>> *Sit in that chair* has moved to the front of its clause.

3. The Short-Answer Test

A VP can serve as the short answer to a question:

> **Q:** *What can an intelligent dog do?*   **A:** *Talk.*
> **Q:** *What will she do?*   **A:** *Steal your car.*
> **Q:** *What should he do?*   **A:** *Sit in that chair.*

4. The Cleft Test

VPs will not participate in clefts of the sort we saw above. [Remember that the asterisk (*) indicates that the sentence is not well-formed.]

> **It's* | *steal your car* | *that she will.*

> **It's* | *talk* | *that an intelligent dog can.*

But there is another type of cleft, called a *WH-cleft*, that *does* allow a VP in focus position:

> *What an intelligent dog can do is* | *talk* |

> *What she will do is* | *steal your car* |

The evidence from the constituency tests—the Pro-form Test, the Movement Test, the Short-

Answer Test, and the Cleft Test (WH-Cleft)—shows that the sequence consisting of the verb plus its complement(s) is a phrase. A phrase of this type is called a *verb phrase* (VP).

With the recognition of the phrases NP and VP, the formulas of tables 6.2a–6.2c now reduce to a single formula, shown in the righthand column of table 6.3.

Table 6.3 Sentence Formulas: Two Versions

	Original formula	Revised formula
Table 6.2a	S = D + Adj + N + AUX + V	S = NP AUX VP
Table 6.2b	S = D + Adj + N + AUX + V + D + Adj + N	S = NP AUX VP
Table 6.2c	S = D + Adj + N + AUX + V + P + D + Adj + N	S = NP AUX VP

where	NP =	D Adj N,
	VP =	V *or* V NP *or* V PP
	PP =	P NP

In other words, the sentences of tables 6.2a–6.2c all consist of a NP, an AUX, and a VP, in that order, where the VP, in turn, is made up of a verb alone, a verb plus a NP, or a verb plus a PP, depending on the requirements of the particular verb.

Formulas like those above, which specify what elements can be combined to form a statement or phrase, are called *phrase structure rules*. Note that there are three positions in the sentence where a NP can occur. The NP at the beginning of the sentence (**NP** AUX VP) is called the *subject* of the sentence. A NP that follows the verb within the VP (V **NP**) is called *the object of the verb.* A NP that follows the preposition within a PP (P **NP**) is called *the object of the preposition.*[6]

6.4 Tree Diagrams

The structure of a statement can be represented schematically by means of a tree diagram, as

---

[6]The reader may be wondering about the difference between a complement and an object. *Complement* is a general term for the phrase that belongs after a particular verb or preposition. For example, in the VPs *close the door* and *look at the camera,* the NP *the door* is the complement of the verb *close* and the PP *at the camera* is the complement of the verb *look.* A complement which is a NP is also called an *object.* Thus, for example, the NP *the door* is both the complement and the object of the verb *close* and the NP *the camera* is both the complement and the object of the preposition *at.* But the PP *at the camera* cannot be called the object of the verb *look*—it is not an object because it is not an NP.

shown in figure 6.4, where S = statement, NP = noun phrase, and VP = verb phrase:[7]

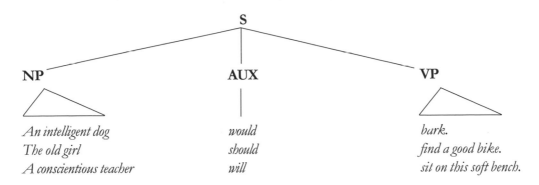

Figure 6.4 A tree diagram

The triangles under the labels **NP** and **VP** indicate that we could say more about the internal structure of these phrases, but we have chosen not to do so because it is irrelevant to our present purposes. This use of triangles is called the *triangle notation*.

EXERCISE 5. Draw tree diagrams of the following sentences, following the model in figure 6.4. (That is, you should assume that S = NP + AUX + VP and use the triangle notation for NP and VP.)

  a. *This old man can swim.*
  b. *A conscientious cat would find an old bike.*
  c. *The lucky girl should sit near the old tree.*
  d. *Choosy mothers will choose Jiff.*
  e. *The cow would jump over the moon.*
  f. *Nobody could do the exercise.*

Caution: Draw your tree diagrams *very neatly* and exactly as shown above. For example, do not draw the tree upside down or put the labels inside the triangles rather than on top. A notation like this is useful only if it is applied in a uniform way, so that we become accustomed to it and recognize it immediately, rather than having to puzzle out the notation each time.

---

[7]In sentences like *Beth gets a haircut* and *The dog ate my homework,* the tense marker [present tense] or [past tense] serves as the AUX. Sentences of this type will be discussed in section 6.6.

A note about diagrams: The practice of diagramming sentences has gained a bad reputation as a result of the traditional practice of asking students to do Kellogg-Reed diagrams such as the following:

Students and their teachers have pointed out that the notational conventions for these diagrams are arbitrary and difficult to learn, and that learning to diagram sentences does not help students become better writers. Let me say at the outset that I am under no illusion that diagramming sentences will greatly improve your writing. However, if we are going to talk about the *structure* of sentences, then we need a way to illustrate that structure—a way to draw a picture of a sentence. Diagrams are very useful for that purpose. Tree diagrams are more logical and easier to learn than the traditional Kellogg-Reed diagrams, and their usefulness is enhanced by the triangle notation, which allows us to omit irrelevant details.

6.5 Sentence families

In the previous sections, we saw that a statement has three parts rather than two, with the auxiliary element (AUX) as a separate, independent constituent: NP, AUX, VP. This section will give further evidence for the status of AUX as an independent element, separate from the verb. The argument will be based on observation of other sentence types such as emphatics, negatives, and *yes/no* questions. Let us begin by noting that for each affirmative statement we can construct a family of corresponding sentences, as follows:

Affirmative Statement:	*This old man can swim.*
Emphatic Statement:	*This old man **can** swim.*
Negative Statement:	*This old man cannot swim.*
	(or, with contraction, *This old man can't swim.*)
***Yes/no* question:**	*Can this old man swim?*

EXERCISE 6. Give the emphatic, negative, and *yes/no* question that corresponds to each of the statements in Exercise 5. Then state a rule for forming each type of sentence.

If you did Exercise 6, you will have seen that our three-part analysis of the sentence allows a simple statement of the relationship among the various members of a sentence "family":

1. Emphatic statement: Emphasize AUX.

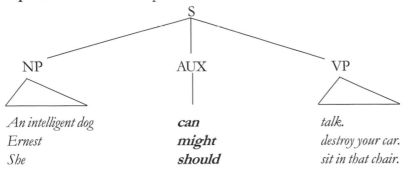

An intelligent dog	***can***	talk.
Ernest	***might***	destroy your car.
She	***should***	sit in that chair.

2. Negative statement: Place the negative particle *not* immediately after AUX.

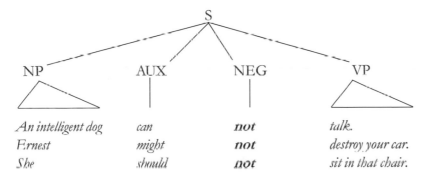

An intelligent dog	can	***not***	talk.
Ernest	might	**not**	destroy your car.
She	should	***not***	sit in that chair.

3. *Yes/no* question: Move AUX to the left of the subject NP.

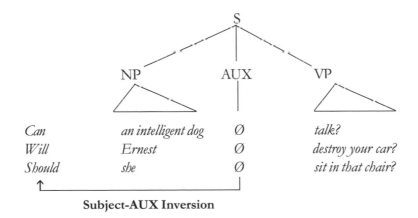

Can	an intelligent dog	Ø	talk?
Will	Ernest	Ø	destroy your car?
Should	she	Ø	sit in that chair?

Subject-AUX Inversion

Note that the original position of the AUX is marked in the diagram with a null sign—Ø. The idea is that, in sentences of this type, the auxiliary in some sense occupies *two* positions: its basic position between the subject NP and the VP, and the position before the subject of the sentence. The rule that moves the AUX to the position preceding the subject is called *Subject-AUX Inversion*.

Rules of this type, which move constituents from one position to another, are called *transformations*.

In addition to its usefulness in elucidating the relationship among the members of a sentence family (statement, emphatic statement, negative statement, question), our three-part analysis of the sentence also allows a simple description of the distribution of sentential adverbs like *probably*, *surely*, and *sometimes:* Adverbs of this type can be placed at the boundary of any of the major constituents of the sentence (that is, in any of the positions labeled *ADV* in the tree diagram in figure 6.5).

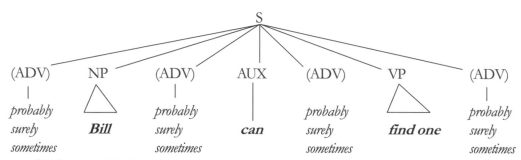

Figure 6.5 Sentential adverbs

Notice how difficult it would be to understand the position of these adverbs if we were assuming the traditional view that the sentence has only two parts—subject and predicate, and that the auxiliary is part of the verb *(can find, will destroy, should sit)*. We would have to say that an adverb can be placed right in the middle of the verb (*. . . can probably find . . .*).

6.6 Sentences with No Visible AUX

We are now ready to deal with sentences like *Beth got a haircut* and *The dog ate my homework,* which have no visible AUX. To understand the structure of these sentences, consider what happens when they are converted into emphatics, questions, or negatives.

Emphatic statement

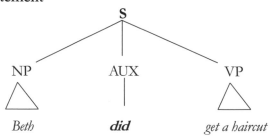

Question

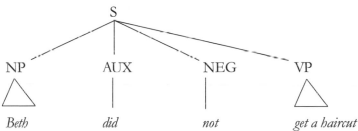

Subject-AUX Inversion

Negative statement

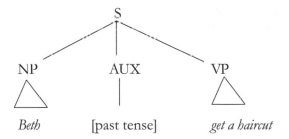

These examples show that when the statement *Beth got a haircut* is converted into one of its related forms, it *does* have an auxiliary, the "dummy" auxiliary *did*. This auxiliary is present in all forms of the sentence except the affirmative statement, and it, rather than the main verb, carries the tense marker—in this case [past tense]. This suggests that the tense marker belongs, inherently, to the AUX position. In other words, the sentence *Beth got a haircut* has the underlying structure:

The affirmative statement is created from this underlying structure by means of a transformation called *Tense Hopping*, which attaches the tense marker to the main verb:

Affirmative statement

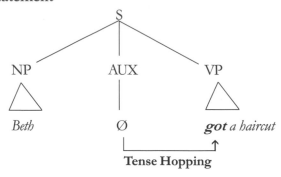

In the emphatic form of this statement, which requires emphasis on AUX, the past-tense marker is pronounced as *did*, by a transformation called *Do*-Insertion or *Do*-Support:

Emphatic statement

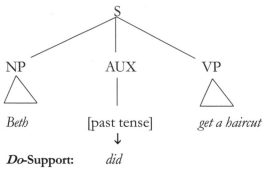

In questions, the past tense marker is again pronounced as *did*, and, like any other AUX, it moves to the front of the sentence by Subject-AUX Inversion:

Yes/no **question**

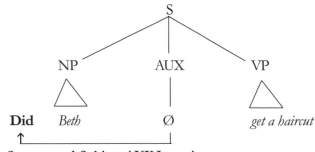

In the negative form, *Beth did not get a haircut*, the past-tense marker is again pronounced as *did,* by *Do*-Support:

Negative statement

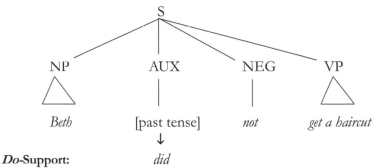

Do-Support:

And a further transformation called *Contraction* converts the sentence (optionally) to

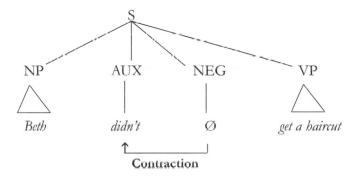

Note that, just as in the example above with Subject-AUX Inversion, the underlying position of the *not* is marked with Ø in the tree diagram.

In conclusion, sentences like *Beth got a haircut* do have an AUX—the tense marker *[past tense]*, which takes either of two forms: it attaches to the verb by Tense Hopping, or it is pronounced as *did* by the transformation of *Do*-Support. English has three tense markers, shown below, each of which can be pronounced either as part of the verb or separately, as a form of *do*:

Tense Marker	**With *Do*-Support**
[past tense]	*did*
[general present tense]	*do*
[3rd singular present tense]	*does*

EXERCISE 7.

a. Give tree diagrams for the sentences *The dog ate my homework, Did the dog eat my homework? The dog didn't eat my homework,* and *The dog **did** eat my homework,* showing the effects of Tense Hopping, *Do*-Support, Contraction, and Subject-AUX Inversion, as in the models above.

b. Give tree diagrams for the sentences *Beth gets a haircut, Beth **does** get a haircut, Does Beth get a haircut?* and *Beth doesn't get a haircut,* showing the effects of Tense Hopping, *Do*-Support, Contraction, and Subject-AUX Inversion, as in the models above. What is the AUX in these sentences? (Your answer should be [past tense], [general present tense], or [3rd singular present tense]).

c. Give tree diagrams for the sentences *Some people like squash, Some people **do** like squash, Do some people like squash?* and *Some people don't like squash,* showing the effects of Tense Hopping, *Do*-Support, Contraction, and Subject-AUX Inversion, as in the models above. What is the AUX in these sentences?

6.7 Conclusion

In this chapter, we have established that a sentence has three parts: NP, AUX, and VP. Some sentences also contain the negative particle *not,* or a sentential adverb such as *probably* or *certainly.* In the examples we have seen, AUX consists of a modal (*can, could, will, would, shall, should, may, might,* or *must*) or a tense marker ([past tense], [general present tense], or [3rd singular present tense]).

We have also identified four transformations, which adjust the word order in certain types of sentences:

Subject-AUX Inversion (SAI):	To form a question, move AUX to the left of the subject NP.
Tense Hopping:	If AUX = [general present tense], [3 singular present tense] or [past tense], then attach it to the following verb.
***Do*-Support:**	In questions, negatives, and emphatics, pronounce the tense marker as *did* ([past tense]), *do* ([general present tense]), or *does* ([3rd singular present tense])
Negative Contraction:	(Optional) Contract the negative particle *not* onto the AUX.

6.8 Applications for Students and Teachers of English

In his book *Grammar and the Teaching of Writing,* Rei Noguchi (1991) suggests the rule of Subject-AUX Inversion as a test for the completeness of a statement: If the statement is complete, then it can be converted to a *yes/no* question, by Subject-AUX Inversion:

Statement to be tested:	*A trained chimpanzee can change the oil in a car.*
***Yes/no*question:**	***Can** a trained chimpanzee Ø change the oil in a car?*

SAI

Since the statement above has a corresponding *yes/no* question, it must be complete. In contrast, the statement below is *not* a complete sentence, and it has no corresponding *yes/no* question:

> *Which is more than I can say for some people!*
> ('There is no corresponding *yes/no* question, so it must be a fragment.)

Notice the principle that underlies the Noguchi test: A well-formed statement contains a subject (usually a NP), AUX, and VP. By applying the rule of Subject-AUX Inversion, we locate two of the major parts of the statement—subject and AUX— and establish that both are present. If a string of words contains a subject, AUX, and VP and does not begin with a subordinating conjunction such as *although* or *because*, then the transformation of Subject-AUX Inversion will convert it into a *yes/no* question, showing that it is a complete sentence.[8]

EXERCISE 8. Use the Noguchi test to determine which of the "statements" below are complete and which are only fragments. Identify the subject, AUX, and VP of each complete statement. (Examples based on Noguchi 1991, p. 88)

a. *Sam ended up cleaning his room.*

b. *Which he doesn't like.*

c. *The soldiers were marching straight ahead.*

d. *Into an ambush.*

e. *Arthur will miss a surprise quiz.*

f. *If he skips class.*

g. *It should soon become obvious.*

h. *That we aren't going to Chicago.*

---

[8]The Noguchi test is actually a test for an *independent clause* rather than for a sentence. Compound sentences like the following contain two independent clauses connected by a coordinating conjunction (*and, but, or,* or *yet*):

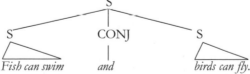

In a sentence of this type, each independent clause can undergo Subject-AUX Inversion:

> *Can fish Ø swim and can birds Ø fly?*

but it is impossible to apply Subject-AUX Inversion just once to the entire sentence:

> **Can fish Ø swim and birds can fly?*

Fragments are common in conversation, but in formal writing we are usually expected to use complete sentences. However, writers sometimes employ fragments deliberately to create a special effect. For example, there are several fragments in the following advertisement for Papermate pens:

> *Air-cushioned grip. Smooth Lubriglide*^{TM} *ink system. Bold, vivid lines. Does all this make Dynagrip the perfect pen? In a word, yes.*

In fact, in this advertisement there is only one sentence that is *not* a fragment—the *yes/no* question, *Does all this make Dynagrip the perfect pen?*

EXERCISE 9.

a. Find the fragments in the following narrative from an article by Paul Brown entitled "The Night I Befriended the Fog," which appeared in *Points East Magazine* (2001). Would you consider these fragments to be errors, or are they an effective use of the fragment? You should also be able to find a comma splice (independent clauses joined together with nothing but a comma).

I stepped up onto the lazarette and let down the boarding ladder at the transom. I was	1
slightly apprehensive about this impulse. Was I being foolish? Had I had too much to drink?	2
No matter. When my toes touched the water, it was as any Mainer would expect; not your	3
average bath water, but not shockingly cold. Actually, rather refreshing.	4
I lowered myself into the water, holding onto a rung of the ladder, then I kicked my	5
legs and stroked gently with my free arm. Millions of luminescent globules swirled about me.	6
Then, holding with both hands to the bottom rung, I kicked my feet forward and watched	7
the cascade of glitter trailing from each individual toe.	8
It was, as they say, almost a religious experience. Does an angel reclining on a soft, fluffy	9
cloud, plunking on his harp, enjoy the same sensuous feeling? I'm not ready to find out, but	10
I can tell you that this earthly experience was one not to be forgotten.	11
Presently, I hauled myself out of the radiant brine, clambering slippery-wet and pant-	12
ing slightly from my exertion into the cockpit. One more deep inhalation and a silent thanks	13
for a few moments to remember.	14

—Paul Brown, "The Night I Befriended the Fog"

b. We said that fragments are common in conversation. Look over the sample of conversational English that you inserted in Appendix Section 4. To what extent do the participants in your conversation employ fragments rather than complete sentences?

c. "Realistic" representations of conversation in literature also use fragments. Turn to the dialogue passage from Ernest Hemingway's "Hills Like White Elephants" in Appendix Section 5. Find as many fragments as you can (I found eight), and use Subject-AUX Inversion to *show* that they are fragments.

Caution: In doing this exercise, please confine your attention to statements only. Imperatives such as *Cut it out!* will not pass the Subject-AUX Inversion test even though they are complete. You should also ignore truncated statements such as *You wouldn't have.* This sentence has a subject NP, AUX, and part of a VP, and it passes the Subject-AUX Inversion test; however, part of the VP is omitted because it can be understood from the context.

CHAPTER 7
THE STRUCTURE OF PHRASES

7.0 Types of Phrases

In this chapter we will delve more deeply into the grammar of English by working out the internal structure of phrases: PP (prepositional phrase), VP (verb phrase), AdjP (adjective phrase), AdvP (adverb phrase), and NP (noun phrase). The main idea to be developed in this chapter is that all phrases have essentially the same structure—a *head* word (the N of a noun phrase, the P of a prepositional phrase, the V of a verb phrase, and so forth) plus the dependents of the head word—its *complements,* its *modifiers,* and its *subject* or *specifier.* (These terms will be defined in the course of the chapter).

7.1 The Prepositional Phrase (PP)

A prepositional phrase consists of a preposition (the head word of the phrase) together with its complement. A *complement* is a phrase that, in English, comes after the head word and completes its meaning.[1]

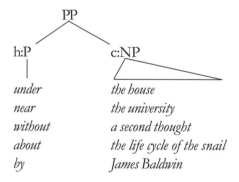

The uppercase labels (PP, P, NP) indicate the *category* of each constituent (prepositional phrase, preposition, noun phrase); the lowercase labels (h, c) indicate the *function* of the constituent (head or complement). The internal structure of the c:NP has been left unspecified, using the triangle notation.

Prepositions typically take NPs as complements, as in the examples above, but it is possible for a preposition to make up a PP all by itself, as in the sentence *She ran **by**.* Some prepositions take a PP complement, as in the following examples.

---

[1]Notice the spelling of the word *complement*. Its middle syllable is spelling with <e>, not <i>, because it is related to the word *complete*. English also has a word *compliment*, spelled with <i>, which is what you receive when people say they like your smile.

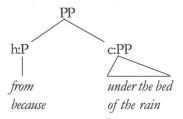

In addition to the head word and its complement, a PP may also contain a *modifier*—an optional descriptive element that is not necessary for the well-formedness of the phrase:

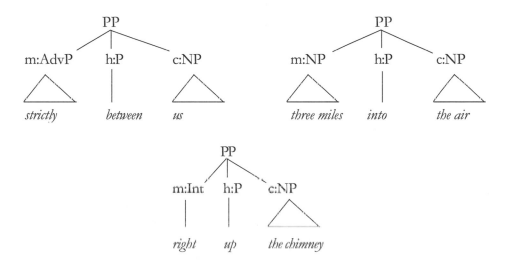

Exercise 1. Draw tree diagrams for the following PPs, showing the category and function of each constituent: *out the window, about the American Revolution, right around the block, completely off the mark.*

For the student who wants a challenge: *a year after the accident.*

7.2 The Verb Phrase (VP)

A verb phrase, like a prepositional phrase, consists of a head word (in this case, a verb) together with its complements and modifiers:

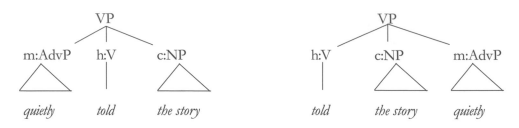

The modifier of the verb can go either at the beginning or the end of the VP; however, the complement always follows right after the head.

Verbs can be classified into seven categories, shown in table 7.2a on the following page, depending on what sorts of complements they require.[2]

Exercise 2. For each VP in table 7.2a, draw a tree diagram showing the category and function of each constituent.

↳ each part of speech of a phrase.

Let's go through these patterns one by one.

[2]Those of you who have studied traditional grammar will notice that these VP patterns correspond to the traditional seven basic sentence patterns, listed below (from Greenbaum 1989).

SV	**Subject**	**Intransitive verb**	
	Someone	*is talking.*	
SVO	**Subject**	**Transitive verb**	**Direct object**
	We	*have finished*	*our work.*
SVP	**Subject**	**Intransitive verb**	**Prepositional complement**
	My parents	*are living*	*in Chicago.*
SVOO	**Subject**	**Transitive verb**	**Indirect object** / **Direct object**
	She	*has given*	*me* / *the letter.*
SVOP	**Subject**	**Transitive verb**	**Direct object** / **Prepositional complement**
	You	*can put*	*your coat* / *in my bedroom.*
SVC	**Subject**	**Linking verb**	**Subject complement**
	I	*feel*	*tired.*
SVOC	**Subject**	**Transitive verb**	**Direct object** / **Object complement**
	You	*have made*	*me* / *very happy.*

114

Table 7.2a Verb Phrase Patterns

Name of category	Formula	Example
Intransitive	V	*Sing.*
Transitive	V NP	*Eat your vegetables.*
Prepositional	V PP	*Insist on precision.*
Ditransitive	V NP NP	*Give the man the money.*
Transitive Prepositional	V NP PP	*Put your socks in the drawer.*
Linking	V $\left\{ \begin{array}{l} \text{AdjP} \\ \text{NP}_{\text{pred}} \end{array} \right\}$	*Be quiet.* *Be a good sport.*
Complex transitive	V NP $\left\{ \begin{array}{l} \text{AdjP} \\ \text{NP}_{\text{pred}} \end{array} \right\}$	*Make us rich.* *Call me Ishmael.*

1. Intransitive Verbs: Verbs in this category do not need a complement:

$$\begin{array}{c} \text{VP} \\ | \\ \text{h:V} \\ | \\ \textit{talk} \\ \textit{run} \\ \textit{swim} \\ \textit{grow} \\ \text{etc.} \end{array}$$

2. Transitive Verbs: Verbs in this category take a NP complement, traditionally called the *direct object* of the verb:[3]

---

[3]From this point on, I will omit the label *h* for the head word and mark only the functions complement *c*, modifier *m*, and subject or specifier *s*; in this abbreviated notation, the unmarked element in each phrase is the head of the phrase.

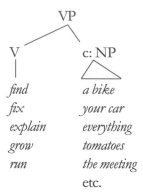

Many verbs accept more than one pattern; for example, the verb *run* is listed above for both the transitive and intransitive patterns, and it also appears in the prepositional pattern below. Sometimes there is a difference in meaning from one pattern to another; for example, the intransitive *run* of *She runs* has a different meaning from the transitive *run* of *She runs the office.*

3. Prepositional Verbs: Verbs in this category take a PP complement, traditionally called the *prepositional complement*.

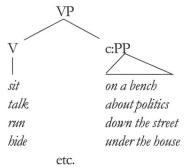

Some prepositional verbs require a particular preposition, as shown below:

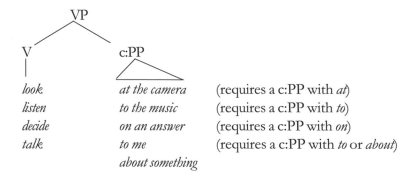

With verbs of this type, the preposition is often rather meaningless. Why do we look *at* something but listen *to* it? And what is the meaning of the preposition *on* in the VP *decide on an answer*? As we learn the prepositional verbs, we simply memorize which preposition goes with each verb.

4. Ditransitive Verbs: Verbs in this category take *two* NP complements. The first c:NP is traditionally called the *indirect object* of the verb; the second is called the *direct object* (cf. the transitive pattern just above):

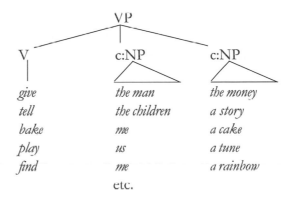

5. Transitive Prepositional Verbs: Verbs in this category also take two complements: first a NP (called the *direct object*) and then a PP (called the *prepositional complement*):

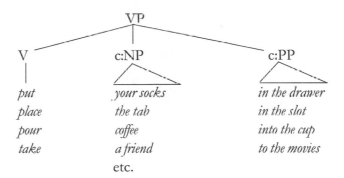

Like the intransitive prepositional verbs we looked at earlier, transitive prepositional verbs sometimes require a particular preposition:

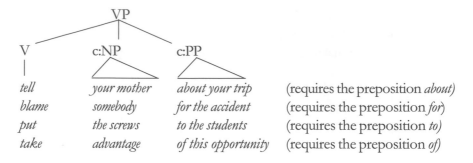

tell	*your mother*	*about your trip*	(requires the preposition *about*)
blame	*somebody*	*for the accident*	(requires the preposition *for*)
put	*the screws*	*to the students*	(requires the preposition *to*)
take	*advantage*	*of this opportunity*	(requires the preposition *of*)

6. Linking Verbs: Verbs in this category take *predicate complements* which describe a NP that appeared earlier in the sentence—in this case, the subject NP *the instructor,* who is said to be *angry, upset, irritated,* and so forth. For most linking verbs, the predicate complement is an AdjP, as in the examples below:

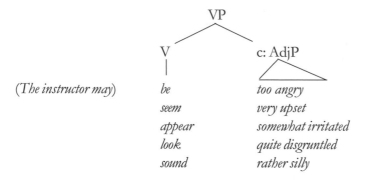

However, some linking verbs take NPs as predicate complements:

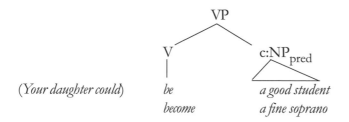

A predicate NP (NP_{pred}) acts like an adjective phrase in that, rather than introducing one of the participants in the event or situation, as NPs normally do, it attaches an attribute to a previous NP—in this case, the subject NP *your daughter,* who is said to be (potentially) *a good student* or *a fine soprano.* Because of its adjective-like meaning, the c:NP in this pattern is called a *predicate complement* rather than a *direct object* (cf. the transitive pattern above).

7. Complex Transitive Verbs: Verbs in this category take a direct object plus a predicate complement:

With AdjP as predicate complement:

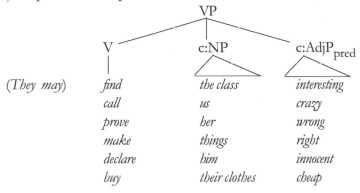

With NP~pred~ as predicate complement:

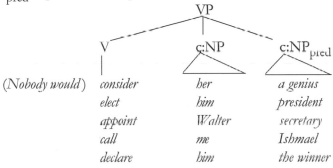

The predicate complement in this pattern describes the direct object of the verb—that is, it is the direct object of the verb that is said to be *interesting, crazy, a genius, president,* and so forth.

EXERCISE 3.

a. Find the VP in each sentence and identify the pattern.

    i. *The baby was crying.*

    ii. *The doctor cancelled all his appointments.*

    iii. *Your father may not like the house.*

    iv. *The clinic gives elderly people free vaccinations.*

    v. *No one could see.*

    vi. *We will explain the procedure to everybody.*

    vii. *The students might take advantage of a substitute teacher.*

    viii. *Bill can look after his own interests.*

    ix. *This is disgusting!*

    x. *Nobody would call her stupid.*

b. Explain the ambiguity of the sentence *You could take her flowers.* (You should be able to draw two distinct tree diagrams for the VP of this sentence, one corresponding to each meaning.)

c. Explain the ambiguity of the sentence *Call me a taxi*. (Smart answer: *Okay, you're a taxi.*) Again, you should be able to draw two distinct tree diagrams for the VP, one corresponding to each meaning.

d. Write *brief* sentences with the verbs in table 7.2b, in whatever patterns they will accept. This is a difficult exercise, so here are some cautions: (i) Don't force it; no verb will fit in every pattern. (ii) Stick with simple statements in active voice; passive verbs and some types of questions distort the complement structure. (iii) Be careful to include only *complements* (phrases that are required by the verb in one of its meanings), not modifiers like *slowly* or *on Sunday*. Modifiers are not chosen by a particular verb, but can be added, optionally, to almost any VP. (We will have more to say about the distinction between complements and modifiers in section 7.7.)

Table 7.2b Complementation Patterns for Verbs

	Intransitive V	Transitive V NP	Prepositional V PP	Ditransitive V NP NP	Transitive Prepositional V NP PP	Linking V $\left\{\begin{array}{l}\text{AdjP}\\\text{NP}_{pred}\end{array}\right.$	Complex Transitive V NP $\left\{\begin{array}{l}\text{AdjP}\\\text{NP}_{pred}\end{array}\right.$
ask							
buy							
call							
elect							
find							
give							
grow							
make							
run							
smile							
wish							

7.2.2 Applications for Students and Teachers of English

How important are the seven basic VP patterns? It depends on what use you are making of your knowledge of grammar. Native speakers of English intuitively choose the correct pattern for each verb; we do not often make mistakes. Furthermore, with the possible exception of the ditransitive pattern (*Give the man the money*) and the complex transitive pattern (*Make someone happy*), children who learn English as a native language use all the VP patterns correctly by the time they enter school. These patterns are sometimes listed in school grammars as a way of helping students identify well-formed sentences, as opposed to fragments and run-ons. In the opinion of this author, however, they are too complicated to be useful for this purpose. To help students identify sentences, I would prefer to teach the NP-AUX-VP pattern that we developed in chapter 6.

The situation is different for students and teachers of English as a second language (ESL). ESL students do always not know what complements are permitted for a given verb, and a familiarity with the list of patterns can be very helpful. Dictionaries for ESL students, such as the *Longman Dictionary of American English* and the *Oxford Learner's Dictionary*, provide detailed information about what patterns each verb permits.

EXERCISE 4.

a. What VP patterns can you find in the speech of a young child aged eighteen months and twenty-four months (Appendix Section 6), and in the writing of first- and second-graders (Appendix Section 2)?

b. Consider the sentences below based on an exercise from O'Grady, Archibald, Aronoff, and Rees-Miller (2001). First, decide which sentences are ungrammatical, and say why. Then explain why an ESL student might be confused:

    i. *We will drink to your victory.*
    ii. *We will toast to your victory.*
    iii. *He gave the church $500.*
    iv. *He donated the church $500.*
    v. *They told us the answer.*
    vi. *They said us the answer.*
    vii. *She should suggest this plan to the clients.*
    viii. *She should ask this question to the clients.*
    ix. *They finally got to their destination.*
    x. *They finally reached to their destination.*

7.3 The Adjective Phrase

An adjective phrase (AdjP) consists of an adjective with its complements and modifiers, if any:

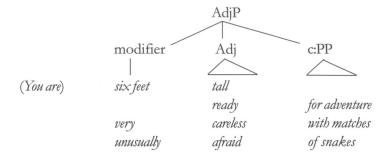

(*You are*)   modifier   Adj   c:PP

six feet   tall

ready   for adventure

very   careless   with matches

unusually   afraid   of snakes

The complement of an adjective is usually a PP.

EXERCISE 5.

a. Fill in complements for these adjectives:

> *tired*
> *interested*
> *guilty*
> *surprised*
> *nervous*
> *loyal*

b. The choice of preposition for the complement of an adjective can sometimes be a usage issue. Some authorities object to the following choices in formal writing:

> *angry at (a person)*   *different than*   *bored of* (cf. *tired of*)

Do you agree that these are errors? If so, what would you say instead?

There are a handful of adjectives—including *fond, averse, tantamount* and *subject*—that *require* complements, as well as many adjectives that do not accept complements: *tall, beautiful, black, white, dull, square, unexpected, sandy, old, possible, excellent*, and so forth.

The *modifier* of an adjective may be an intensifier (Int), a NP, or an AdvP:

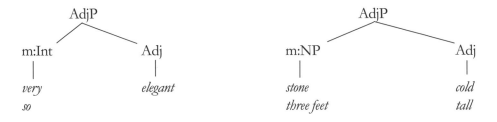

m:Int   Adj   m:NP   Adj

very   elegant   stone   cold

so   three feet   tall

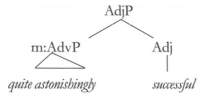

7.4 The Adverb Phrase

An adverb phrases (AdvP) has the same structure as an adjective phrase, except that adverbs do not take complements:

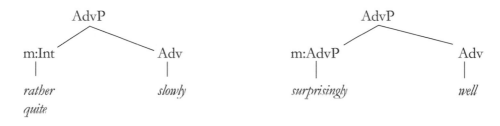

Exercise 6. Draw tree diagrams for the following AdjPs and AdvPs, showing the category and function of each constituent: *very excited about the game, three feet deep, incredibly naive, very foolishly.*

7.5 Summary of PP, VP, AdjP, and AdvP

As we have seen, PP, VP, AdjP, and AdvP all have the same basic structure—a head word (P, V, Adj, or Adv) with its complement(s) and modifier(s), if any:

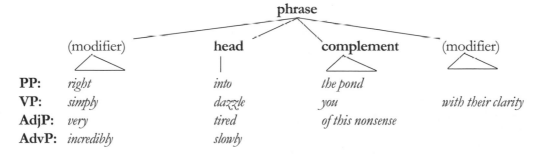

The head word is always present, and determines the category of the phrase. The choice of complement, if any, depends on the head word. For example, the preposition *into* and the verb *dazzle* both require NP complements (into **the pond,** *dazzle* **you**), and the adjective *tired* wants a PP with *of* (*tired* **of this nonsense**). The adverb *slowly* does not take a complement at all. In English, complements always follow the head word. Modifiers are added, optionally, at the beginning or end of the phrase.

7.6 Noun Phrases (NP)

Noun phrases contain an additional element—the *specifier*—which was not present in the phrases we have looked at so far:

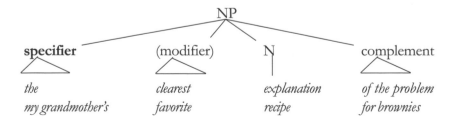

The specifier is a determiner (D) or possessive NP (NP_{poss}) that helps to identify *which* explanation, recipe, crackers, etc. the speaker has in mind:

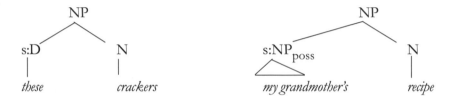

Modifiers may be AdjPs, NPs, VPs, PPs, or QPs (*quantifier phrases*):

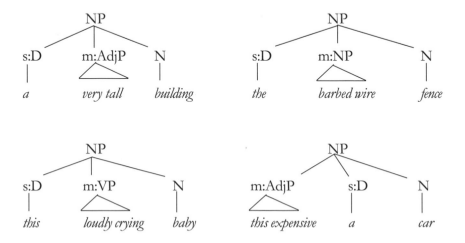

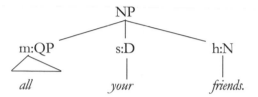

If the modifier is long, it goes after the head noun rather than before it:

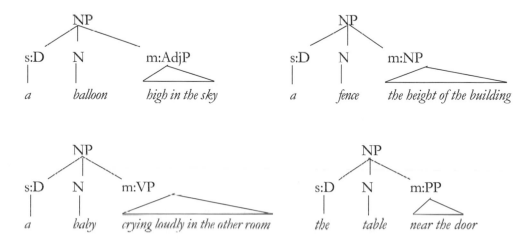

Nouns that are related to complement-taking verbs and adjectives may also take complements; for example,

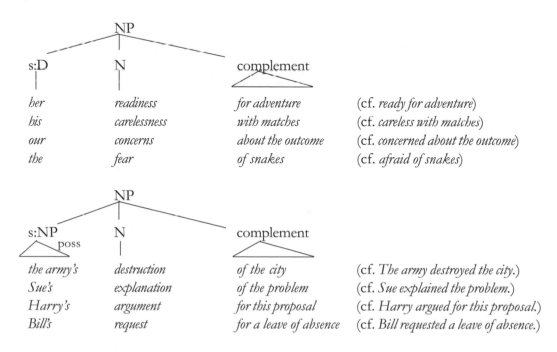

her	readiness	for adventure	(cf. *ready for adventure*)
his	carelessness	with matches	(cf. *careless with matches*)
our	concerns	about the outcome	(cf. *concerned about the outcome*)
the	fear	of snakes	(cf. *afraid of snakes*)

the army's	destruction	of the city	(cf. *The army destroyed the city.*)
Sue's	explanation	of the problem	(cf. *Sue explained the problem.*)
Harry's	argument	for this proposal	(cf. *Harry argued for this proposal.*)
Bill's	request	for a leave of absence	(cf. *Bill requested a leave of absence.*)

EXERCISE 7.

a. First identify the complement of the adjective or verb below. Then fill in the corresponding NP, and notice that the noun can have the same complement:

Complement-taking adjective	Corresponding NP
<u>extravagant</u> with money	
<u>thoughtful</u> towards others	
<u>honest</u> about her opinions	
<u>loyal</u> to her friends	
<u>polite</u> to her teachers	
<u>interested</u> in biology	

Complement-taking verb	Corresponding NP
The school board <u>dismissed</u> the teacher.	
We <u>anticipated</u> the results.	
Some people <u>prefer</u> chocolate.	
John <u>returned</u> to Chicago.	
John <u>fled</u> to Chicago.	
The parents <u>quarreled</u> with the principal.	

b. Draw tree diagrams of the following NPs, showing the category and function of each constituent: *my earliest memories, the daring rescue of the fishermen, the trees in the park, your father's Oldsmobile, people.*

7.7 The Sentence (S)

A sentence is also a type of phrase, with the AUX as its head word. As in the other phrases we have looked at, the head word (AUX) has a complement (the VP), and may have modifiers, as well. However, like the NP, a sentence also contains an additional element—the subject (s):

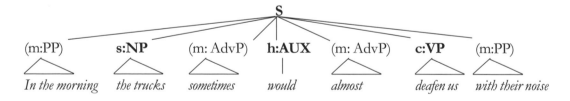

There is a close correspondence between the subject of a sentence and the specifier of a NP:

Sentence	Corresponding NP
The teacher will explain the instructions.	**the teacher's** explanation of the instructions
She understands the issues.	**her** understanding of the issues
We insisted on immediate results.	**our** insistence on immediate results

Because of this correspondence (namely, that the subject of a sentence is like the specifier of a NP), linguists usually collapse these two functions into a single function which we will call *s*. NP and S can then be said to consist of a head word (N or AUX) with its subject or specifier (*s*), its complement (*c*), and its modifiers (*m*).

7.8 Phrases are Nested Inside Phrases

In the end, phrases have a nested structure, with phrases inside phrases inside phrases, as shown below:

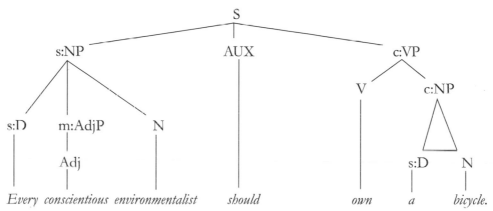

In this diagram, subjects/specifiers are identified as *s*, complements as *c*, and modifiers as *m*. The head of each phrase is left unmarked.

EXERCISE 8.

a. In the diagram above, identify the category and function of each constituent. For example, *every conscientious environmentalist* is an NP that functions as the subject of the sentence and *should* is an AUX that functions as the head of the sentence.

    i. *own a bicycle*
    ii. *a bicycle*
    iii. *every*
    iv. *conscientious*
    v. *bicycle*

b. Draw complete tree diagrams, including the functional labels *s, c,* and *m* for the following sentences:

    i. *The baby was crying.*
    ii. *The doctor canceled his appointments.*
    iii. *Your father may not like the house.*
    iv. *The clinic gives elderly people free vaccinations.*
    v. *We will explain the procedure to everybody.*

Caution: In this exercise you are asked to draw complete tree diagrams so that you can see whether you understand how to do it. Once you are sure you understand, however, there are very few circumstances in which you will need to draw a complete tree diagram of a sentence. Normally, we show the part of the structure in which we are interested and then abbreviate the rest, using the triangle notation. There is no virtue in showing more structure than is necessary.

7.9 Determining the Structure of a Sentence

As we begin dealing with more complicated sentences, you may sometimes be unsure where a particular constituent fits into the syntactic structure. For example, consider the two sentences below:

> a. *They bought a house with three bedrooms.*
> b. *They bought a house with their savings.*

The PP in the first sentence—*with three bedrooms*—is a modifier of the noun *house*, and it therefore hangs from the NP in the tree structure:

a.

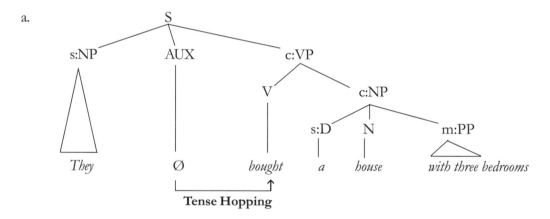

However, the PP in the second sentence—*with their savings*—is a modifier of the verb *bought*, and it therefore hangs from the VP:

b.

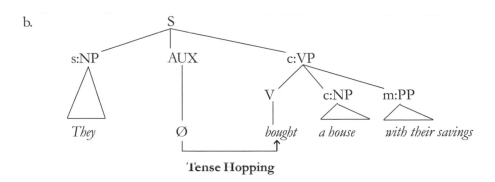

Tense Hopping

To determine where a PP should be placed in the tree, we rely partly on the meaning of the sentence, as we did above. However, there is also another way to determine where a particular PP belongs, and that is to make use of the constituency tests that were described in chapter 6: the cleft test, the pro-form test, and the short-answer test. The string *a house with three bedrooms* in sentence (a) above is a constituent—a NP—and it therefore passes the constituency tests:

The cleft test: *It was* | *a house with three bedrooms* | *that they bought.*

WH-cleft: *What they bought* *was* | *a house with three bedrooms.*

The pro-form test: *They bought* **one.** (where **one** = *a house with three bedrooms*)
The short-answer test: Q: *What did they buy?* A: **A house with three bedrooms.**

The constituency tests show that *a house with three bedrooms* is a phrase, thereby confirming our hypothesis that the PP *with three bedrooms* is a constituent of the NP.

In contrast, the string *a house with their savings* in sentence (b) above is *not* a constituent, and so it does not pass the tests:[4]

The cleft test: **It was* | *a house with their savings* | *that they bought.*

WH-cleft: **What they bought* *was* | *a house with their savings.*

The pro-form test: **They bought* **one.** (where **one** = *a house with their savings*)
The short-answer test: Q: *What did they buy?* A: * **A house with their savings.**

The constituency tests show that *a house with their savings* is not a constituent, thereby confirming our hypothesis that the PP *with their savings* is not part of the NP.

---

[4]The asterisk, you will recall, indicates that the sentence is ungrammatical.

EXERCISE 9.

a. Draw tree diagrams showing the position of the PP in each of the following sentences. Then support your answer, using the cleft test, the pro-form test, and the short- answer test:

    (i) *I put your socks in the drawer.*

    (ii) *I like the sparkle in his eye.*

b. (Advanced) The following VP is ambiguous: It has a sensible meaning and a silly meaning. Draw two different tree diagrams to show the ambiguity. Which tree corresponds to which meaning?

    Try on that dress in the window.

7.10 Phrasal Verbs: An Exercise in Constituent Structure

English, like other Germanic languages, has a large class of *phrasal* or *two-word* verbs which consist of a verb plus a *particle* (an intransitive preposition). Examples are *break up, put on, take off, take over,* and so forth. Verbs of this type are often ignored in traditional grammars, perhaps because they tend to be conversational in register; however, they are very important in the grammar of English.

EXERCISE 10.

a. List five additional phrasal verbs.

b. Most phrasal verbs are polysemous (that is, they have more than one meaning). Find as many meanings as you can for the phrasal verbs *break up, put on, take off,* and *take over.*

Phrasal verbs take the same complementation patterns as simple verbs:

Intransitive:	*The plane took off.*
	I think I'm going to throw up.
Transitive:	*Please take off your shoes.* or *Please take your shoes off.*
	He brought in the pie. or *He brought the pie in.*
Prepositional:	*I won't put up with this nonsense.*
	Look out for the cars!
Ditransitive:	*Pick me up some milk,* please.
	Would you throw me down a towel?
Transitive prepositional:	*We handed over our notes to the authorities.*
	Please turn in your paper to the instructor.

or	We *handed our notes over to the authorities*.
	Please *turn your paper in to the instructor*.
Linking:	Everybody *called in sick*.
	Your brother *came in drunk*.
Complex transitive:	You shouldn't *put your shoes on wet*.
	I wouldn't *turn a child away hungry*.

Exercise 11. *Advanced*: Draw tree diagrams of the underlined VPs above. [Treat the phrasal verb as a verb (V) with two parts—V and P, as in diagram (b) below.]

There is a surface similarity between a simple verb in the prepositional pattern and a phrasal verbs in the transitive pattern, as shown below:

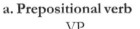

a. Prepositional verb   **b. Transitive phrasal verb**

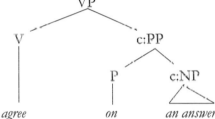
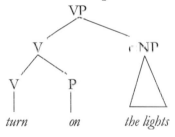

To distinguish these constructions, we can make use of the following properties: First, if the preposition is part of a phrasal verb, then it can move to the right of its direct object by a transformation called *Particle Movement*.

The Particle-Movement Test:

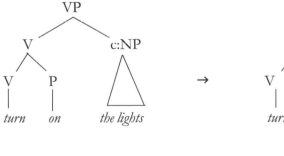
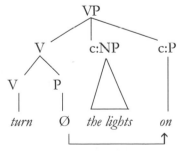

Particle Movement

Table 7.10 Complementation Patterns for Phrasal Verbs

	Intransitive V	Transitive V NP	Prepositional V PP	Ditransitive V NP NP	Transitive Preposi-tional V NP PP	Linking $V \begin{cases} AdjP \\ NP_{pred} \end{cases}$	Complex Transitive $VNP \begin{cases} AdjP \\ NP_{pred} \end{cases}$
come out							
take off							
fill in							
try out							
put away							

In contrast, a preposition that is part of a PP cannot be moved; its position is fixed:

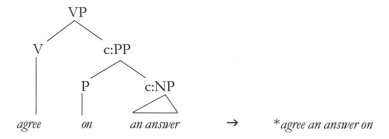

Secondly, these constructions can also be distinguished by the constituency tests of chapter 6; for example, they can be distinguished by the Short-Answer Test:

    The Short-Answer Test: *What did they agree on?*   <u>*An answer*</u> or <u>*On an answer*</u>

In this construction, the NP *an answer* and the PP *on an answer* are both constituents [see diagram (a) above]; therefore, either phrase can serve as a short answer.

    Compare the transitive phrasal pattern:

    The Short-Answer Test: *What did they turn on?*   <u>*The light*</u> but not <u>**On the light*</u>.

In this construction the P NP sequence (*on the light*) is not a constituent [see diagram (b) above]; consequently, it cannot serve as a short answer.

EXERCISE 12.

a. [*Based on an exercise from Farmer and Demers (2001).*] Use the particle-movement test and the short-answer test to determine whether the VP in each of the following sentences follows the prepositional pattern [diagram (a) above] or the transitive phrasal pattern [diagram (b) above]. Draw a tree diagram for each VP.

    i. *The witch turned into a bat.*

    ii. *The car turned into the road.*

    iii. *I put on my jacket.*

    iv. *Little Miss Muffet sat on a tuffet.*

    v. *We threw out the trash.*

    vi. *We climbed out the window.*

    vii. *The applicants must fill in all the blanks.*

b. Find VP patterns in the following poem by Robert Frost. (Your choices are intransitive, transitive, prepositional, ditransitive, transitive prepositional, linking, and complex tran sitive.) *Hint:* These are imperative sentences which consist of nothing but a VP; you can think of them simply as VPs, or, if you prefer, you can assume an understood subject and AUX: *you will.* There are four lines (4, 6, 7, and 8) that you may not know how to handle, but you should be able to do the rest. There is one instance of a phrasal (*two-word*) verb.

To the Thawing Wind

Come with rain, O loud Southwester!	1
Bring the singer, bring the nester;	2
Give the buried flower a dream;	3
Make the settled snowbank steam;	4
Find the brown beneath the white;	5
But whate'er you do tonight,	6
Bathe my window, make it flow,	7
Melt it as the ice will go;	8
Melt the glass and leave the sticks	9
Like a hermit's crucifix;	10
Burst into my narrow stall;	11
Swing the picture on the wall;	12
Run the rattling pages o'er;	13
Scatter poems on the floor;	14
Turn the poet out of door.	15

—Robert Frost

c. *Advanced:* Put the phrasal verbs in table 7.10 into VP patterns, as appropriate. Remember to stick with very simple, active-voice sentences.

7.11 Distinguishing Complements from Modifiers

You may have been wondering how to tell whether a particular phrase is a complement or a modifier. Modifiers of a verb can be distinguished from complements in the following ways:

1. A complement is necessary to complete the meaning of the verb. Modifiers are more loosely connected with the verb. For example, look at this sentence:

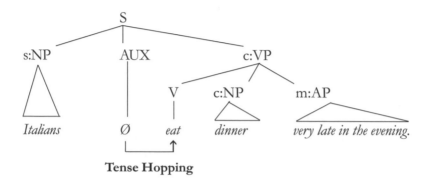

Tense Hopping

The c:NP *dinner* is closely associated with the verb *eat* and could not appear, for example, with the verb *wonder*. However, the m:AP *very late in the evening* is not dependent on the verb *eat*. One can do anything very late in the evening, not just eat.

2. The verb's complements normally come first, before its modifiers:

h	c	m	*h	m	c
raise	*your hands*	*slowly*	*raise*	*slowly*	*your hands*
lock	*the door*	*with the key*	*lock*	*with the key*	*the door*
decide	*on an answer*	*this week*	*decide*	*this week*	*on an answer*
look	*at the camera*	*for Daddy*	*look*	*for Daddy*	*at the camera*

3. The string of words consisting of the verb plus its complement(s) can be replaced by the pro-form *do so*. Modifiers *can* be included under the pro-form, but do not have to be. This difference can be used as a test to determine whether a particular phrase is a complement or a modifier. To apply the *do so* test, substitute *do so* for the verb plus one or more following constituents. Phrases that follow *do so* must be modifiers:

VP to be tested: *raise your hands slowly.*
Do so [slowly].   *Slowly* is a modifier; it can follow *do so.*
*Do so [my hands] [slowly].   *My hands* is a complement; it can't follow *do so.*

VP to be tested: *write often during the fall.*
Do so [often] [during the fall].   *Often* and *during the fall* are both modifiers.

VP to be tested: *run into the yard*
*Do so [into the yard].   *Into the yard* is a complement.

EXERCISE 13. Draw tree diagrams of the following VPs, identifying each underlined constituent as a complement or a modifier:

    a. (I will) *think of a number.*
    b. *throw the ball into the yard.*
    c. *leave on Sunday.*
    d. *open the door with the key.*
    e. *stay out of trouble.*
    f. *decide on an answer.*
    g. *decide on the boat.*
    h. *decide on an answer on the boat.*
    i. *plant spinach in the spring.*
    j. *this package with care.*
    k. *bake a cake for a friend.*
    l. *go to the movies with Susan.*

7.12 Conclusion

7.12.1 The Structure of Phrases. As we have seen, phrases are constructed according to a consistent pattern:

PP, VP, AP:[5]   head + complement   (plus modifiers)

NP, S: $\left\{ \begin{array}{l} \text{subject} \\ \text{specifier} \end{array} \right\}$ + head + complement   (plus modifiers)

The presence and nature of the complement(s) depends on the head word. (For example, the verb *enjoy* takes a NP complement, but the verb *elapse* does not.) Modifiers are optional and may be placed at various points within the phrase.

    All languages construct their phrases with the same ingredients, but the *order* of elements may differ somewhat from language to language. English is an *s h c* language, because our phrases follow the order *specifier head complement.* The great majority of human languages employ one of the following three word orders:[6]

---

[5]AdjP and AdvP are collapsed here into a single "super" category, AP.
[6]Klingon, a language spoken by nonhuman inhabitants of a far-distant planet, has the order *c h s,* but this order is almost never found in *human* languages.

s c h	This is the most common order, found in Japanese, Turkish, and Korean.
s h c	This is the second most common order, found in English, Swahili, and Chinese.
h s c	This is a less common order, found in Welsh and Arabic.

In many languages, word order is consistent for all phrases. For example, in English the complement always follows the head word, but in Japanese, where the complement *precedes* the head, *all* phrases are turned around backwards from our point of view: Instead of *shut that door,* Japanese speakers say *that door shut,* instead of *on that table, that table on,* instead of *You should go, You go should.* (Of course, they use Japanese words, rather than English!) In languages such as Latin, where word order is fairly free, it is hard to be sure about the basic order.

EXERCISE 14.

a. Give the phrase-structure rules (formulas) for constructing S, VP, and PP in Japanese.

b. What word order would we find in the Japanese sentence for *I am speaking to the teacher?* Draw a tree diagram for the English and Japanese versions of this sentence.

c. The Japanese version of this sentence is *Watashi-wa sensei ni hanashite imasu.* What is the meaning of each Japanese word? (Hint: Japanese has no word corresponding to English *the.*)

d. In poetry, words are sometimes placed outside their normal order, so that an English phrase may take on the order of Japanese. Find examples of nonstandard word order (for English) in the following poem by Christopher Marlowe (I count four), and say what constituents are out of order; for example you might say that the verb precedes the subject or that the direct object comes before the verb. What is the purpose of the nonstandard word order?

The Passionate Shepherd to His Love

Come live with me and be my love,		1
And we will all the pleasures prove	*(prove = try)*	2
That valleys, groves, hills, and fields,		3
Woods, or steepy mountain yields.		4
And we will sit upon the rocks,		5
Seeing the shepherds feed their flocks		6
By shallow rivers, to whose falls		7
Melodious birds sing madrigals.		8
And I will make thee beds of roses		9
And a thousand fragrant posies,		10
A cap of flowers and a kirtle	*(kirtle = gown)*	11
Embroidered all with leaves of myrtle;		12

A gown made of the finest wool	13
Which from our pretty lambs we pull;	14
Fair-lined slippers for the cold,	15
With buckles of the purest gold;	16
A belt of straw and ivy buds,	17
With coral clasps and amber studs,	18
And if these pleasures may thee move,	19
Come live with me and be my love.	20
The shepherds' swains shall dance and sing	21
For thy delight each May morning:	22
If these delights thy mind may move,	23
Then live with me and be my love.	24

—Christopher Marlowe

7.12.2 Category ≠ Function. Another important point to take from this chapter is the distinction between **category** and **function**. For example, the phrase *this old house* belongs to the **category** NP by virtue of its internal composition—it has a noun (*house*) as its head word. Like other NPs, it may serve any of the following **functions**:

Subject of sentence:[7]	*This old house must be theirs.*
Complement of V:	*They bought this old house in 1985.*
Complement of P:	*They moved into this old house in 1985.*

These examples show that a single category (NP) may serve any of several different functions. The converse is also true; a given function can be performed by any of several different categories. For example, while the subject of a sentence is usually a NP, other types of phrases can also act as subject:

NP as subject:	*This old house must be his.*
PP as subject:	*In front of the library would be a good place for the statue.*
AdjP as subject:	*Very rich is what I'd like to be.*
AdvP as subject:	*Very slowly is how I run.*
VP as subject:	*Sail across the Atlantic is what he'd like to do.*

---

[7]Strictly speaking, this is the subject of AUX (since the AUX is the head of the sentence); however, we will stick with the more standard terminology *subject of the sentence.*

The possible functions of each phrasal category are set out in table 7.12. VPs in subject or complement position are traditionally called *gerunds*; VPs in modifier positions are traditionally called *participles*.

EXERCISE 15. Identify the category and function of each identified constituent; for example, you would say that *the hills across the valley of the Ebro* in example (a) is a NP which functions as the subject of the sentence.

a. *The hills across the valley of the Ebro were very white.*
    i. *across the valley of the Ebro*
    ii. *very white*

b. *Accompanied by a plague of robins, Sula came back to Medallion.*
    i. *a plague of robins*
    ii. *accompanied by a plague of robins*
    iii. *came back*
    iv. *to Medallion*

c. *The sky was black for hours.*
    i. *the sky*
    ii. *black*
    iii. *for hours*

d. *The morning's post had given the final tap to the family fortune.*
    i. *the morning's post*
    ii. *the morning's*
    iii. *the final tap*
    iv. *final*
    v. *to the family fortune*
    vi. *family*

7.12.3 Phrasing. A final point to take from this chapter is the importance of phrases. We cannot understand a sentence until we know how the words are grouped into phrases. (Reading theorists call this *chunking* or *segmenting*.) When language is difficult as, for example, a foreign language or a Shakespeare play, it can be surprisingly helpful to hear the text read aloud, while reading along. That is because spoken language contains *intonation* (changes in pitch and rhythm) that help the listener to locate the boundaries of the major phrases.

Studies have shown that children who read poorly are sometimes helped by having the words grouped *for them* into meaningful phrases[8]:

---

[8]These examples and discussions are taken from Perrera (1984), pp. 303-305.

Table 7.12 Functions of Phrasal Categories

NP	subject of sentence	*The army may destroy the city.*
	specifier of N	*the army's destruction of the city*
	complement of AUX	—
	complement of V	*close the door*
	complement of P	*in the closet*
	complement of N	—
	complement of A	—
	sentential modifier[9]	*Every weekend he would practice his putting.*
	modifier of V	*Do it this way.*
	modifier of P	*three miles from the village*
	modifier of N	*the renovation of the building last year*
	modifier of A	*three miles high*
PP	subject of sentence	*Next to the library would be a good place for the statue.*
	specifier of N	—
	complement of AUX	—
	complement of V	*decide on an answer*
	complement of P	*from under the couch*
	complement of N	*an investigation of the incident*
	complement of A	*afraid of snakes*
	sentential modifier	*On Monday, she will fly to Chicago.*
	modifier of V	*sing the song with gusto*
	modifier of P	—
	modifier of N	*a cat with a long tail*
	modifier of A	*high in the air*
AP[10]	subject of sentence	*Very rich is what I'd like my husband to be.*
	specifier of N	—
	complement of AUX	—
	complement of V	*(They) seem very upset.*
	complement of P	—
	complement of N	—
	complement of A	—
	sentential modifier	*Occasionally, the sky would clear.*

[9]In strictly formal terms, this should be called *modifier of AUX* (because, in the grammatical system that has been developed in this chapter, every constituent of a phrase must be identified as a subject, complement, or modifier of the *head* of the phrase). However, the term *sentential modifier* is much more commonly used.

[10]AdjP and AdvP are collapsed here into a single "super" category, AP.

Table 7.12 Functions of Phrasal Categories *(continued)*

AP	modifier of V	*close the door <u>quietly</u>*
	modifier of P	*<u>completely</u> beside himself*
	modifier of N	*a <u>very fast</u> car*
	modifier of A	*<u>extremely</u> upset*
VP	subject of sentence	*<u>Walking rapidly</u> can be good exercise.*
	specifier of N	—
	complement of AUX	*You may <u>open the window</u>.*
	complement of V	*enjoy <u>playing tennis</u>*
	complement of P	*by <u>playing tennis</u>*
	complement of N	—
	complement of A	—
	sentential modifier	*<u>Holding the match to the wood</u>, he waited for the flame to take hold.*
	modifier of V	*(She would) sit <u>listening for the sound of the car</u>.*
	modifier of P	—
	modifier of N	*the man <u>standing in the corner</u>*
	modifier of A	—

The dog   bit the man   on the leg.

Readers that are intended for young children commonly avoid line breaks that disrupt the phrasing, especially if they occur at the beginning of the sentence where the structure is still highly unpredictable:

The
dog bit the man on the leg.

An arrangement like the following is easier to read, because the NP *the dog* is kept together on one line.

The dog
bit the man on the leg.

The breaking of a phrase is less disruptive if it occurs towards the end of the sentence, after the structure has already been worked out:

The dog bit the man on the
leg.

In poetry, the placement of line breaks can be an important element in how the poem works. Some poems have *end-stopped lines*, meaning that the ends of the lines coincide with the boundaries of major phrases, often marked by a comma, semicolon, or period. The following sonnet by William Shakespeare has end-stopped lines:

My Mistress' Eyes Are Nothing like the Sun

My Mistress' eyes are nothing like the Sun,	1
Coral is far more red, than her lips red,	2
If snow be white, why then her breasts are dun:	3
If hairs be wires, black wires grow on her head:	4
I have seen Roses damasked, red and white,	5
But no such Roses see I in her cheeks,	6
And in some perfumes is there more delight,	7
Than in the breath that from my Mistress reeks.	8
I love to hear her speak; yet well I know,	9
That Music hath a far more pleasing sound:	10
I grant I never saw a goddess go,	11
My Mistress when she walks treads on the ground.	12
And yet by heaven I think my love as rare,	13
As any she belied with false compare. (she – woman)	14

—William Shakespeare

In some poems there is a mismatch between ends of phrases and the ends of lines, so that the lines break in the middle of a phrase. The running over of a phrase from one line to another is called *enjambment*. You saw an instance of enjambment in lines 9 and 10 of the Robert Frost poem "To a Thawing Wind" (in Exercise 12), where line 10 completes the VP that is begun in the middle of line 9:

Melt the glass and leave the sticks	9
Like a hermit's crucifix;	10

This mismatch between line-end and phrase-end creates a momentary confusion in the mind of the reader: Is the VP *leave the sticks* or is it *leave the sticks like a hermit's crucifix*?—a small puzzle that adds to the interest of the poem.

Exercise 16. Consider the following poem by Gerard Manley Hopkins. How many sentences are there in this poem? [For the purposes of this question, count the semi-colon (;) and the colon (:) as marking the ends of sentences.] Where does each sentence begin and end? Locate the line ends that do not coincide with major phrase boundaries. What is the effect of breaking the lines at these points?

Spring and Fall
To a young child

Márgarét, are you grieving		1
Over Goldengrove unleaving?	*(unleaving = losing its leaves)*	2
Leáves, like the things of man, you		3
With your fresh thoughts care for, can you?		4
Áh! Ás the heart grows older		5
It will come to such sights colder		6
By and by, nor spare a sigh		7
Though worlds of wanwood leafmeal lie;		8
And yet you will weep and know why.		9
Now no matter, child, the name:		10
Sórrow's springs áre the same.		11
Nor mouth had, no nor mind, expressed	*(Nor = neither)*	12
What heart heard of, ghost guessed:	*(ghost = spirit)*	13
It is the blight man was born for,		14
It is Margaret you mourn for.		15

—Gerard Manley Hopkins

CHAPTER 8

SEMANTICS: THE MEANING OF A PHRASE OR SENTENCE

8.1 Introduction

When we combine words into phrases and sentences, our purpose, of course, is to create meaning. In this chapter, we will briefly survey the meaning (semantics) of NPs, sentences, and modifiers.

8.2 The Semantics of NP

Noun phrases (*the house on the corner, a woman I met, the price of eggs*) refer to *entities*—people, places, things, or ideas.[1] Semantically, NPs fall into two classes: definite NPs (*the red house*) and indefinite NPs (*a woman I met*).

The class of *indefinite NPs* consists of (1) indefinite pronouns (*somebody, anybody, anything, one*), (2) NPs with no determiner (*We saw stars everywhere*), and (3) NPs with indefinite determiners (*a(n) apple, some money, any luck, every student, a few good ideas*). Indefinite NPs introduce persons, places, things, or ideas whose identity is not yet known to the hearer or reader.

The class of *definite NPs* includes (1) proper names (*Bill*), (2) personal pronouns (*he, she, it, they*), (3) common nouns with definite determiners (*the moon, this week, these earrings, that scarf, those people*), and (4) NPs with possessive specifiers (*my brother, your house, our parents' house,* and so forth). Definite NPs refer to entities whose identity is already known. For example, the definite NP *the old barn* can be used appropriately only if both speaker and hearer already know which old barn is under discussion.

EXERCISE 1.

a. Find the NPs in the following passage from "Little Red Cap" (better known as "Little Red Riding Hood") from *The Complete Fairy Tales of the Brothers Grimm*. Classify each NP as definite or indefinite, and explain why the writer has chosen a definite (or indefinite) NP.

> *Once upon a time there was a sweet little maiden. Whoever laid eyes upon her could not help but love her. But it was her grandmother who loved her most. She could never give the child enough. One time she made her a present, a small, red velvet cap, and since it was so becoming and the maiden insisted on always wearing it, she was called Little Red Cap.*

---

[1]NP$_{pred}$'s such as *a genius* in the sentence *You're a genius!* are different from other NPs, as we noted earlier. They do not introduce entities into the discourse, but describe entities that have already been introduced; from a semantic point of view, they are more like AdjPs than NPs.

    b. Young children are notorious for their overuse of definite NPs (because they are egocentric, and believe that other people have access to the same information that they have). Find definite NPs whose referent is not clear in "My Nightmare" and "My Favorite Puppy" (Appendix Section 2).

    c. Modern fiction writers sometimes use definite NPs in an unconventional way at the beginning of a story—as if the reader were already familiar with the characters and setting of the story. Find instances of this unconventional use of definite NPs in the passage from Hemingway's "Hills Like White Elephants" in Appendix Section 1. (Note that this is the first paragraph of the story.) What is the purpose of this convention?

8.3 The Semantics of a Sentence. The meaning of a sentence is organized by the verb. The verb indicates the occurrence, either real or hypothetical, of an event or state of affairs with a certain number of participants or *role players*. Verbs characteristically require a particular number of participants, which may be represented by NPs or PPs:

Table 8.3a Identification of Role Players

Verb	No. of role players	Example
play	1	*The children* were playing.
choose	2	*Sarah* chose *a green vegetable*.
give	3	*Sarah* gave *Bill* *a hug*.
		Sarah gave *two dollars* *to Bill*.

Each participant is assigned a particular role, as shown in table 8.3b.[2]

    EXERCISE 2. List the verb and the role-players in each of the example sentences in table 8.3b; then say which role each role-player is assigned. For example, for the sentence *Sally looked at Jane*, you would say that the verb is *look*. This verb calls for two participants—in

---

[2]This list of semantic roles should be sufficient for our purposes, but as you work through the exercises, you may conclude that there are other possible roles as well.

Table 8.3b Roles of Participants

\<agent\>	The deliberate doer of an action.	*We tried to win.* *Sally looked at Jane.*
\<instrument\>	The entity used by an agent to carry out an action.	*I broke the window with a hammer.* *I used a pencil to mark the place.*
\<patient\> or \<theme\>	The participant whose state, condition, or location is indicated or changed.	*Lightning hit the tree.* *Sue gave him a dollar.* *Bill was sitting at the table.* *The flowers will grow.*
\<result\>	The result of an action.	*We built a house.* *Her comment caused a lot of resentment.*
\<source\>	The location from which something comes.	*We got a dollar from Sue.* *The paint fumes gave me a headache.*
\<goal\>	The person or place toward which something goes or is directed.	*I threw the ball into the yard.* *Sue gave Bill a dollar.*
\<experiencer\>	The experiencer of an emotion, thought, or perception.	*I hear you.* *The decision infuriated me.* *I understand what you're saying.*
\<stimulus\>	The object of an emotion or perception.	*She saw stars.* *Jane likes ice cream.*
\<location\>	The place where something is.	*They sat at home.*
\<possessor\>	The one who has or owns something.	*Bill has a car.* *The car belongs to Bill.*

this sentence, *Sally* and *Jane*. Sally has the role of **<agent>** (the deliberate doer of an action) and Jane has the role of **<goal>** (the person or place towards whom Sally's look is directed).

The semantic roles are assigned by the verb,[3] as shown in the following diagrams for the verbs *look, see,* and *give*. The roles each verb characteristically assigns are listed in order beneath it. For example, the roles for the verb *look* are **<agent>**, which is assigned to the subject, and **<goal>**, which is assigned to the complement; the roles for the verb *see* are **<experiencer>,** which is assigned to the subject, and **<stimulus>,** which is assigned to the complement:

look:

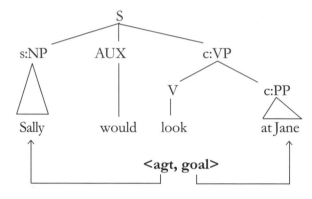

see:

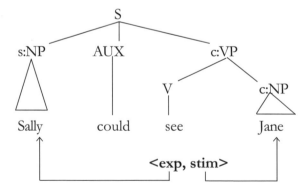

---

[3] Semantic roles can be assigned in other ways, as well, not just by the verb. For example, the role of **<possessor>** is assigned by the possessive suffix in the phrase *Bill's car*. However, we are concerned here with the assignment of semantic roles at the sentence level, rather than inside NPs. At the sentence level, semantic roles are assigned by the verb or by the predicate complement (see section 8.3 below).

give:

When we know the meaning of a verb, we know, among other things, how many participants the verb calls for and what semantic roles it assigns to them.

EXERCISE 3.

a. Notice that, contrary to what you may have learned in school, the subject of the sentence is not always the "doer of an action" (= **<agent>**.) Many verbs assign the role of **<agent>** to their subject, but there are also verbs like *see, receive, die,* and *undergo* whose subjects receive other roles. What roles?

b. The sensory-perception verbs *look* and *see; listen* and *hear, touch* and *feel* go in pairs: In each pair, there is one verb that assigns the role of <**agent**> to its subject and one whose subject is an <**experiencer**>. Which is which?

c. Verbs of emotion and perception assign the roles of <**experiencer**> and <**stimulus**> in different directions: For verbs like *see,* the subject is the experiencer and the complement is the stimulus (*I see you*). For other verbs, such as *frighten,* the subject is the stimulus and the complement is the experiencer (*The thunder frightened the cat*). Specify the role assignment for the following verbs: *hear, like, astonish, surprise, perceive, annoy, irritate, please, bore.* (Young children sometimes mix up the role assignment for these verbs and make statements like *I'm so boring!* when they mean *I'm so bored!*).

8.3 Linking Verbs

Linking verbs do not assign semantic roles; in sentences with linking verbs it is the predicate complement, rather than the verb itself, that assigns a semantic role to the subject. For example, in the sentences below, the subject NP *the instructor* receives the role of <**experiencer**> in (a), from the predicate AdjP *excited*, and the role of <**patient**> in (b), from the predicate AdjP *taller:*

1. *The instructor grew more excited.*

              \<experiencer>

2. The instructor grew taller.

              \<patient>

EXERCISE 4. Find the predicate complement in each sentence below, and say what semantic role it assigns to the subject.

    a. *Some of us had grown sleepy.*
    b. *The children seemed bored.*
    c. *The children seemed boring.*
    d. *Ferdinand Magellan was a daring explorer.*

EXERCISE 5. Fictional characters are sometimes assigned rather consistent roles, sentence by sentence, throughout a story; one character is consistently an **\<agent>**, another is a **\<patient>** (things always happen to him or her), and another is an **\<experiencer>** or a **\<possessor>**. Look over the fictional selections in Appendix Section 1 and, keeping in mind that this is only a very brief segment of the story, identify the roles that are assigned, so far, to each character. Be sure to say what verb, adjective, or preposition is assigning each role. Also include the inanimate "characters." An inanimate object may be assigned not only the role of **\<patient>**, but also, sometimes, that of **\<agent>** or **\<experiencer>**, or some other role.) If you have read the entire story, you might think about whether the character remains in the same role(s) throughout the story.

8.5 When Nouns Assign Semantic Roles. Nouns that are semantically related to verbs or adjectives (they are called *nominalizations*) also assign semantic roles. For example,

Sentence			NP		
We	*enjoyed*	*the movie.*	*Our*	*enjoyment*	*of the movie*
	\<exp, stim>			**\<exp, stim>**	

In academic and bureaucratic writing, there is an unfortunate tendency to substitute nominalizations for verbs and adjectives; this gives the sentence a more formal style but makes it much more difficult to follow. Consider the following contrasts pointed out by Williams (1994), pp. 43-51:

    a. *The police conducted an **investigation** into the matter.*
        vs. *The police **investigated** the matter.*

    b. *We request that on your **return** you should conduct a **review** of the data and provide an immediate **report.***
        vs. *When you **return**, please **review** the data and **report** immediately.*

    c. *The first step was a **review** of the **evolution** of the dorsal fin.*
        vs. *First, we **reviewed** how the dorsal fin **evolved**.*
        or *First, we **reviewed** the **evolution** of the dorsal fin.*

While nominalizations are an efficient way of referring to an event or situation that is already familiar [as, for example, the second nominalization in (c) above], the overuse of nominalization can obscure the meaning of the sentence, making it difficult to identify the roles and role players. It is always easier to understand who is doing what to whom when the semantic roles are assigned by a verb or predicate complement rather than a noun.

EXERCISE 6.

a. Revise the following sentences by changing the boldfaced nominalizations to verbs or adjectives. Notice how much more clearly the role players emerge:[4]

    i.   *We received an **order** from the doctor for an **analysis** of the blood sample.*
    ii. *The President's **impeachment** by the Senate did not lead to his **removal** from office.*
    iii. *Sally's **disagreement** with her employer was the cause of her **dismissal**.*
    iv. *There were **charges** by the panel regarding **misappropriation** of funds on the company's part.*
    v. *The camp's **inability** to enforce safety regulations led to its **closure** by the Department of Health.*
    vi. ***Written cancellation** of the student's housing application by August 15 will result in **forfeiture** of the deposit only, with no additional charge.*

[4] This exercise is patterned after an exercise in Williams, 1994, 50-51.

      vii. *Our **recommendation** is for **completion** of the core curriculum by the end of the second year.*

     viii. *Ms. Bush was given a $600 **fine** for the **use** of someone else's ID for the **purchase** of alcohol.*

      ix. *This office has the **responsibility** for making prompt **responses** to inquiries from prospective students.*

  b. Look over the passage from the University of New Hampshire catalog (chapter 2, exercise 7). How many nominalizations can you find? (I counted nine.) Can you find ways to eliminate any of these?

  c. Look over the Samuel Eliot Morison passage in Appendix Section 1. Can you find any nominalizations in this passage? (I couldn't.) Try changing some of Morison's verbs to nominalizations and see what happens.

  d. Look for nominalizations in your own writing sample. (Choose a piece of expository writing.) Are you satisfied with your own use of nominalizations?

8.6 Modifiers. Modifiers introduce information that is not essential to the grammatical structure of the sentence. The presence of modifiers, if not overdone, adds to the interest of a piece of writing.

8.6.1 Noun Modifiers. Consituents that appear in modifier (*m*) position in a NP are called *noun modifiers*:

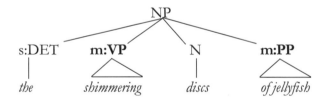

EXERCISE 7.

  a. Look for noun modifiers in the children's writing samples in Appendix Section 2. Write out the NP in which each modifier appears. You should find that the use of noun modifiers increases as the children grow older and their writing becomes more sophisticated. (*Caution:* Don't count predicate complements; these are *complements,* not modifiers, and they are present in speech and writing at all levels. What you are looking for in this exercise is modifiers that are inside NPs.)

  b. Which of the professional writers in Appendix Section 1 uses the most noun modifiers?

8.6.2 Adverbials. Modifiers of V and AUX are called *adverbials*. (Don't confuse this term with the term *adverb*. The term *adverb* names a syntactic category, while *adverbial* names a syntactic function (modifier of V or AUX). AdvPs, NPs, PPs, and subordinate clauses can all function as adverbials. For example, in the sentence below, the AdvP *wildly* and the PP *with her handkerchief* are both adverbials:

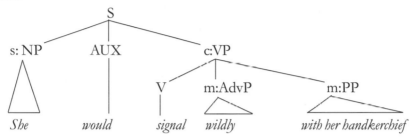

Adverbials are classified, roughly, into the semantic categories that are set out in table 8.6 on the following page.

EXERCISE 8. Consider the underlined adverbials in the following literary passages from Appendix Section 1. Say what semantic category each adverbial belongs to, and relate the semantic categories of the adverbials to the overall content of the passage. For example, why does one passage contain more manner and purpose adverbials than the other? The double underline indicates that there is an adverbial *inside* an adverbial.

The hills across the valley of the Ebro were long and white. On this side there was no shade	1
and no trees and the station was between two lines of rails in the sun. Close against the side	2
of the station there was the warm shadow of the building, and a curtain, made of strings	3
of bamboo beads, hung across the open door into the bar, to keep out flies. The American	4
and the girl with him sat at a table in the shade, outside the building. It was very hot and	5
the express from Barcelona would come in forty minutes. It stopped at this junction for two	6
minutes and went on to Madrid.	7

—Ernest Hemingway, "Hills Like White Elephants"

Ants are so much like human beings as to be an embarrassment. They farm fungi, raise	1
aphids as livestock, launch armies into wars, use chemical sprays to alarm and confuse	2
enemies, capture slaves. The families of weaver ants engage in child labor, holding their	3
larvae like shuttles to spin out the thread that sews the leaves together for their fungus	4
gardens. They exchange information ceaselessly. They do everything but watch television.	5

—Lewis Thomas, *The Lives of a Cell*

Table 8.6 Semantic Categories of Adverbials

manner:	*awkwardly, frugally, well, lengthwise, like an expert, with great courtesy, the same way I did, as if they meant it*
degree:	*very much, completely, absolutely, enormously, scarcely, kind of, almost, more or less, barely, practically*
purpose:	*for dinner, to get some bread, for your mother*
instrument:	*with a key, by car, by pressing this button, microscopically*
accompaniment:	*with a friend*
place:	*in Massachusetts, somewhere*
time:	*last night, on Sunday, the next day, later, now, tomorrow, during the week, three years ago, eventually, once upon a time*
duration:	*for three weeks, since September*
frequency:	*once a week, every Sunday, usually, often, occasionally, frequently*
attitude of subject:	*deliberately, intentionally, accidentally, reluctantly, eagerly, fervently, carefully, enthusiastically*
judgement of speaker:	*surprisingly, tragically, luckily, fortunately, regrettably, hopefully, apparently, truly, in fact, certainly, probably, possibly, obviously frankly, to be honest, personally, apparently, in my opinion, wisely, understandably*
connective:	*first, secondly, finally, in conclusion, however, nevertheless, moreover, consequently, hence, incidentally, on the other hand, in other words*

8.6.3 Position of Adverbials. Adverbials occur in the positions marked 1, 2, 3, and 4 in the diagram below:

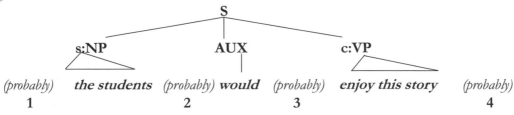

Adverbials that occur only in positions 3 and/or 4 are presumed to be verb modifiers; that is, they belong to the VP and can't move outside it. Adverbials that occur in positions 1 and/or 2 (and perhaps 3 and 4, as well) must be sentential modifiers (modifiers of AUX); their extra mobility comes from the fact that they are attached to S rather than VP.[5]

EXERCISE 9. Determine the syntactic position of each of the semantic classes of adverbials (manner, degree, purpose, etc.), and use this information to determine whether the semantic class in question is a modifier of V or sentential modifier (= modifier of AUX). *Procedure:* Find a sentence in which the adverbial makes sense. (Use one of the sentences below, or make up a sentence of your own.) Draw a tree diagram of the sentence showing only NP, AUX, and VP, as in the example above. Then try the adverbial in each adverbial position—1, 2, 3, and 4—to see where it will fit. Use this evidence to classify the adverbial as a verb modifier or a sentential modifier.

    a. *The people were discussing the performance.*
    b. *Somebody will buy the house.*
    c. *Bill has been living in Chicago.*
    d. *The band would strike a wrong note.*
    e. *The students had finished the assignment.*

Changing the position of an adverbial modifier may create subtle differences in emphasis, as in the examples below:

    a. ***In August,*** *the troops will begin moving.*
       vs. *The troops will begin moving* ***in August.***

    b. *The suspect was* ***illegally*** *detained.*
       vs. *The suspect was detained* ***illegally.***

    c. *The contents should be* ***carefully*** *examined.*
       vs. *The contents should be examined* ***carefully.***

The positioning of adverbials is something to be aware of as you edit your own writing; try moving adverbials from one place to another to see how the clarity and feel of the sentence are affected.

[5]Sometimes the meaning changes as an adverbial moves from one position to another. For example,
    a. *Carelessly, he put the key in the drawer.* (= It was careless of him to put the key in the drawer.)
    b. *He put the key in the drawer carelessly.* (= He did so in a careless manner.)
    a. *Regretfully, she had to decline your invitation.* (= I regret that she had to decline your invitation.)
    b. *She had to decline your invitation regretfully.* (= She had to decline your invitation in a regretful manner.)
Apparently, some adverbials belong to two different categories — the manner category, which are V-modifiers, and the attitude-of-subject category, which are sentential modifiers (modifiers of AUX).

CHAPTER 9
TENSE, ASPECT, VOICE, AND MODALITY

9.1 Introduction

Traditional descriptions of the tense system of English identify three tenses—past, present, and future—each of which can be combined with the *perfect* and *progressive aspects*, as shown in Tables 9.1a and 9.1b. The verb forms in Table 9.1a are in *active voice*; their *passive* counterparts are given in Table 9.1b. Tables 9.1a and 9.1b follow traditional terminology in identifying the *will* form as *future tense;* however, it is more accurate, for English, to speak of the *modal* form, because the other modals can occupy the same position as *will*[1]. For example, corresponding to the "future" form *they will try,* we can create the modal forms *they would try, they can try, they could try, they should try, they may try, they might try,* and *they must try.*

EXERCISE 1.
a. Give the full name of each form in Tables 9.1a and 9.1b; for example, *It has been being repaired* is in the present perfect progressive passive form.
b. In order to see for yourself that the other modals occupy the same position as *will,* try substituting the modals *would, can, could, should, may, might,* and *must* for the modal *will* in Tables 9.1a and 9.1b. (You can also try the modal *shall,* but it will not work well; this modal has a very restricted distribution in Modern English.)
c. To practice the names of the tense forms, start with the sentence *The cat chased the mouse.* What form is this? Then follow the directions below:
  * Change to the simple present.
  * Change to a modal form.
  * Change to the present progressive.
  * Change to the past progressive.
  * Change to a modal progressive form.
  * Change to the present perfect.
  * Change to the past perfect.
  Change to a modal perfect form.
  Change to the present perfect progressive.
  Change to the past perfect progressive.

---

[1]Other languages that you may have studied—French, Spanish, and Italian, for example—have a real future form, which is created by adding a suffix to the verb. English doesn't actually have a future tense, though, like all other human languages, we have ways to referring to the future—the modal forms that are mentioned in the text, forms with *going to* (*They are going to try*), and so forth.

Change to a modal perfect progressive form.
Change to the simple present passive.
Change to the simple past passive.
Change to a modal passive form.
Change to the present perfect passive.
Change to the past perfect passive.
Change to a modal perfect passive form.
Change to the present progressive passive.
Change to the past progressive passive.
Change to a modal progressive passive form.
Change to the present perfect progressive passive.
Change to the past perfect progressive passive.
Change to a modal perfect progressive passive form.

Table 9.1a The Active Voice

	Past	**Present**	**Future**
Simple	They **tried.**	They **try.**	They **will try.**
Perfect	They **had tried.**	They **have tried.**	They **will have tried.**
Progressive	They **were trying.**	They **are trying.**	They **will be trying** (to finish).
Perfect progressive	They **had been trying** (to finish).	They **have been trying** (to finish).	They **will have been trying** (to finish).

Table 9.1b The Passive Voice

	Past	**Present**	**Future**
Simple passive	It **was repaired.** repaired.	It **is** (often) repaired.	It **will be repaired.**
Perfect passive	It **had been repaired.**	It **has been repaired.**	It **will have been repaired.**
Progressive passive	It **was being repaired.**	It **is being repaired.**	It **will be being repaired.**
Perfect progressive passive	It **had been being repaired.**	It **has been being repaired.**	It **will have been being repaired.**

Table 9.2a Table of the Verb Forms

Sentence	Name of Construction
She **plays** the piano.	simple present
They **lived** in Maine.	simple past
You **should enjoy** yourself.	modal[2]
The building **is sinking**.	present progressive (or present continuous)
We **were listening**.	past progressive (or past continuous)
You **should be studying**.	modal progressive (or modal continuous)
Things **have changed**.	present perfect
Nobody **had noticed**.	past perfect
You **should have said** something.	modal perfect
Things **have been deteriorating**.	present perfect progressive
Nobody **had been listening**.	past perfect progressive
They **may have been sleeping**.	modal perfect progressive
The toaster **is broken**.	present passive
The money **was stolen**.	past passive
The patient **should be examined**.	modal passive
The patient **is being examined**.	present progressive passive
The ideas **was being considered**.	past progressive passive
The idea **may be being considered**.	modal progressive passive
The jewels **have been stolen**!	present perfect passive
The jewels **had been stolen**!	past perfect passive
The jewels **might have been stolen**!	modal perfect passive
The idea **has been being considered**.	present perfect progressive passive
The idea **had been being considered**.	past perfect progressive passive
The idea **should have been being considered**.	modal perfect progressive passive

[2]If the modal is *will*, the form is traditionally called *the future*.

Ingredients				
modal	have_{perf}	be_{prog}	be_{pass}	MV
				plays
				lived
should				*enjoy*
		is		*sinking*
		were		*listening*
should		*be*		*studying*
	have			*changed*
	had			*noticed*
should	*have*			*said*
	have	*been*		*deteriorating*
	had	*been*		*listening*
may	*have*	*been*		*sleeping*
			is	*broken*
			was	*stolen*
should			*be*	*examined*
		is	*being*	*examined*
		was	*being*	*considered*
may		*be*	*being*	*considered*
	have		*been*	*stolen*
	had		*been*	*stolen*
might	*have*		*been*	*stolen*
	has	*been*	*being*	*considered*
	had	*been*	*being*	*considered*
should	*have*	*been*	*being*	*considered*

Table 9.2b Fill in the Blanks

Sentence	Name of Construction
The birds **are singing.**	
Birds **sing.**	
The leaves **were falling.**	
The leaves **had been falling.**	
No one **knew** the answer.	
You **should be studying.**	
Somebody **must have been listening.**	
Everybody **likes** ice cream.	
The car **had disappeared.**	
Nobody **can sing** "The Star Spangled Banner."	
They **will have left.**	
The noise **has stopped.**	
The lights **had been turned** out.	
The roof **was blown** off.	
The prisoner **is being questioned.**	
The prisoner **has been questioned.**	
The prisoner **should be questioned.**	
The prisoner **was questioned** very carefully.	
The police **will have questioned** the prisoner.	
The police **are questioning** the prisoner.	
The police **have questioned** the prisoner.	

Ingredients				
modal	have$_{perf}$	be$_{prog}$	be$_{pass}$	MV

9.2 The Formation of the Verb String

The verb string is created by combining the following elements, in the order specified, where MV stands for *main verb*:

$$\left\{ \begin{array}{l} \text{MODAL} \\ \text{[tense/agreement marker]} \end{array} \right\} \quad (have_{\text{perf}}) \quad (be_{\text{prog}}) \quad (be_{\text{pass}}) \quad \text{MV}$$

The only obligatory elements are the main verb (MV) and either a modal or a tense/agreement marker. The tense/agreement marker appears on the first item in the string. The full set of possibilities is set out in table 9.2a, on pages 156-157.

EXERCISE 2.

a. Find and identify the tense/agreement marker in each verb string of table 9.2a. Your choices are [modal], [general present tense], [3rd sg. present tense], or [past tense].

b. Fill in the blanks in table 9.2b.

Some dialects of English do not use an agreement marker; for example, some English speakers say *He don't know* instead of *He doesn't know*. For speakers of these dialects, the Standard English rule can be very confusing (see chapter 11 for a further discussion of this point). However, some constructions, with subject NPs whose number (singular or plural) is unclear, are confusing even for speakers of Standard English. The most reliable rule is to depend on *meaning*: if the subject refers to more than one entity, use [general present]; if it refers to *one* entity, use [3 sg. present]. The examples below are from Lunsford and Connors, 1995, 236:

a. *Tony and his sister commute every day from Louisville.*
AUX = [general present] because the subject, *Tony and his sister,* refers to more than one person.

b. *Drinking and driving remains a major cause of highway fatalities.*
AUX = [3 singular present], because the subject, *drinking and driving,* is intended to refer to a situation in which drinking and driving occur together, as a single event.

Reminder: To find the subject of a statement, change the statement into a *yes/no* question. The string of words between the two AUX positions is the subject of the sentence:

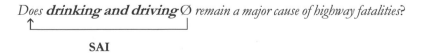

Does **drinking and driving** Ø *remain a major cause of highway fatalities?*

SAI

EXERCISE 3.

a. Identify the subject and the agreement marker in each sentence below, and explain the agreement relationship, following the model above. If you do not like the agreement marker that is used here, explain the source of your discomfort. Notice that in some sentences, more than one choice is possible, depending on exactly what the speaker means:

   i.   *Bacon and eggs is still one of our most popular breakfasts.*

   ii. *A group of Mainers were thwarted in their attempt to transport medical supplies bound for Cuba across the Canadian border.*

   iii. *Pastors for Peace has been given a license to transport supplies.*

   iv. *Every Tom, Dick, and Harry has his own ideas about how this should be handled.*

   v.   *Ten gallons of oil was pumped out of the bilge.*

   vi. *Last year at this time, the couple was headed for the altar.*

   vii. *Now the same couple have decided on divorce.*

   viii. *Ham and Swiss has always been my favorite sandwich.*

   ix. Seven Gothic Tales *is a collection of short stories by Isak Dinesen.*

   x.   *The law firm of Dewey, Cheatam, and Howe, who have brought you this program, are the legal advisors for the radio show "Car Talk."*

b. Indefinite pronouns and determiners are a particular problem. We are sometimes advised that in formal writing we should say *Every one of the students was present* and *None of the pies was hot,* but in informal writing and speech many of us say *Every one of the students were present* and *None of the pies were hot.* Why is there confusion in the choice of agreement marker for this form? Think about what pronoun you would use if you went on to say something else about the students or the pies. Consult at least one usage manual for advice on this matter and compare your findings with those of your classmates.

c. Some statements have an unusual word order, with the subject buried somewhere inside the sentence, rather than in its normal position at the beginning. To find the subject of an inverted statement, convert the sentence to a *yes/no* question: The word order will normalize automatically, and the subject will become apparent.

For example, *Down the hill come the skiers* is an inverted sentence, with the subject NP (*the skiers*) at the end of the sentence. To find the subject, turn the sentence into a *yes/no* question:

   Do the skiers Ø come down the hill?
   ↑_____|

The subject of the sentence—*the skiers*—is the string of words that is framed by the two AUX positions. Use the *yes/no*-question form to identify the subject and AUX in each of the following sentences. Once you have identified the subject, explain the choice of agreement marker:

   i.   *Near the intersection was a small cross.*

   ii. *Attached to the cross were the dog tags of the soldiers who were buried there.*

9.3 The Syntactic Position of the Auxiliaries

We have seen in previous chapters that a modal occupies the head position in the sentence (=AUX):

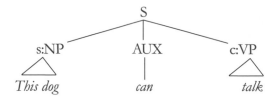

To support this analysis, we observed that the negative particle *not* goes right after the modal:

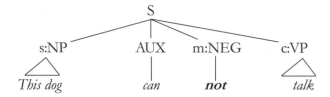

We also observed that sentence adverbs like *probably* and *certainly* can go before or after the modal:

An intelligent dog	***probably***	*can*	*talk.*
An intelligent dog		*can*	***probably***	*talk.*

And, we observed that the modal is moved to the left of the subject in *yes/no* questions:

Subject-AUX Inversion

The auxiliary verbs *have*$_{perf}$, *be*$_{prog}$, and *be*$_{pass}$ can also occupy AUX position, as shown below:

***have*$_{perf}$:**

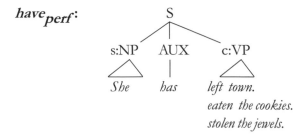

be$_{prog}$:

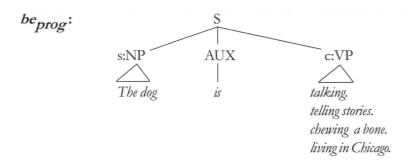

Sentences with the auxiliary *be*$_{pass}$ undergo a transformation called *Passive Movement*, as shown in the following diagram. This transformation moves what would normally be the direct object of the verb out of the VP into subject position. Sentences with *be*$_{pass}$ always undergo this transformation:

bc$_{pass}$:

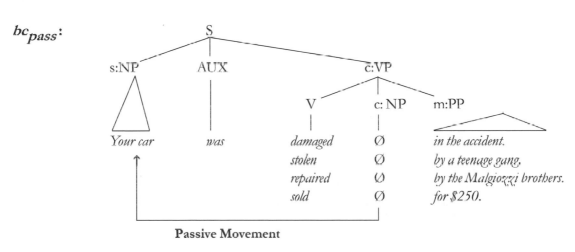

In sentences with more than one auxiliary, the first auxiliary occupies the AUX position (that is, it is the head of the sentence), the second is the head of the VP complement, and so on down the line:

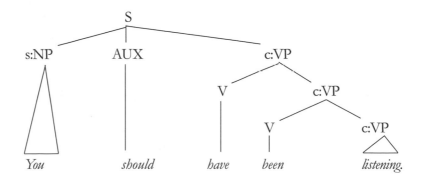

EXERCISE 4. Use *not, probably,* and subject-AUX Inversion to verify the occupant of AUX in the following sentences:

  a. *She has left town.*
  b. *The dog is talking.*
  c. *Your car was damaged in the accident.*
  d. *You should have been watching.*

We have observed that the first member of the verb string carries the tense/agreement marker. The inflectional form of each subsequent element is determined by the auxiliary that precedes it:

After a modal, the verb is in base form:	*George should* **go**.
After be_{prog} the verb is in present participle form:	*George is* **going**.
After $have_{perf}$ the verb is in prefect participle form:	*George has* **gone**.
After be_{pass} the verb is in passive participle form:	*George was* **fired**.

Tables 9.3a and 9.3b provide analyses of more complex verb strings.

EXERCISE 5. Choose five verb strings from table 9.2b. For each verb in the string, determine (a) its inflectional form, and (b) why it has that form. Set out this information in a chart like the ones in Tables 9.3a and 9.3b. *Caution:* Before doing this exercise, please review the names of the inflectional forms in figure 3.1b at the end of chapter 3.

9.3.a Dialect Differences. Except for problems with the choice of agreement marker, native speakers of English follow the verb-string formula without error. We do not make mistakes such as putting the auxiliaries in the wrong order (**We are having sung* for *we have been singing*) or using the wrong inflectional form (**We have finishing* for *We have finished*). However, dialects may differ in how they make the inflectional forms for some verbs. For examples, some dialects use the form *kilt* rather than *killed* as the perfect participle of *kill*: *We had* **kilt** *a spider* where Standard English *says We had* **killed** *a spider*. Verb strings that seem nonstandard are generally the result of this kind of difference.

There are also some dialects that allow two modals: *We might could go*. African-American Vernacular English has some additional auxiliaries that are not found in Standard English; these will be discussed in chapter 11.

Table 9.3a Analysis of a Verb String

Example:	*should*	*have*	*been*	*studying*
What is it?	modal	*have*$_{perf}$	*be*$_{prog}$	MV
What is its inflectional form?	base	base	perfect participle	present participle
Why is it in that form?	Modals have only one form, the base form.	It follows a modal.	It follows *have*$_{perf}$	It follows *be*$_{prog}$

Table 9.3b Analysis of a Verb String

Example:	*was*	*being*	*renovated*
What is it?	*be*$_{prog}$	*be*$_{pass}$	MV
What is its inflectional form?	3 sg. past tense	present participle	passive participle
Why is it in that form?	When there is no modal, there must be a tense/agreement marker on the first item of the string. *Was* carries the tense marker [past tense] and the agreement marker [3rd sg.], to agree with the subject NP, *the building*.	It follows *be*$_{prog}$.	It follows *be*$_{pass}$

9.4 The Semantics of AUX

The auxiliary system makes four contributions to the meaning of the sentence:

time reference	past, present, or future
aspect	whether an event is already completed, or is in progress, or is habitual
modality	degree of certainty or strength of obligation
voice	active or passive

9.4.1 Time Reference. One purpose of the auxiliary system is to assign a situation or event to past, present, or future time. Past and present time are usually indicated by the past and present tense markers:

Present time:	*People have mixed feelings about Hilary Clinton.* (general present tense)
Past time:	*Marie and Pierre Curie discovered radium.* (past tense)

Modals characteristically refer to the future (*It **may** rain tomorrow; nobody **will** hear you; you **should** take your umbrella*).

However, time reference is more complex than is generally acknowledged. First, the forms that are called past, present, and future *tense* do not always refer to past, present, and future *time*:

*If I **had** a hammer right now, I would …*	(past tense referring to present time)
*If I **won** the lottery next week, I would …*	(past tense referring to future time)
*The plane **leaves** at 10 o'clock tomorrow.*	(present tense referring to future time)
And while I'm standing here, this guy **comes** *in and* **says** *…*	(present tense referring to past time)
*The male of the species **will** sometimes* **guard** *the nest while …*	(the modal *will* referring to a habitual occurrence in the present)

Secondly, we have other conventional expressions, apart from the auxiliary system, to indicate time:

*She **used to** smoke.*	(past habitual)
*We're **about to** leave.*	(immediate future)
*It's **fixin'** to rain.*	(immediate future)
*I'm **going to** tell her.*	(future)

EXERCISE 6.

a. Change the Hemingway, Joyce, and Morrison passages (Appendix Section 1) from past tense to present tense.

Caution 1: In each verb string, change *only* the element that carries the present or past tense marker (the first element of the verb string). Otherwise, leave the verb string as it is. For example, you would change the verb string

> *had been crying*

to   *has been crying*

Caution 2: Present and passive participles remain unchanged. For example, you would change

> *Encouraged by her test results, she applied to graduate school.*

to   *Encouraged by her test results, she applies to graduate school.*

    b. The Rachel Carson and Lewis Thomas passages (also in Appendix Section 1) are written in present tense; change them to past tense.

Time clauses are a special case in that they do not accept future forms but, instead, use present tense to refer to the future:

> *When she* **comes in,** *we'll jump out and sing "Happy Birthday."*   (*when she **will come in**)
> *Before we* **know** *it, it'll be summer.*   (*before we **will know** *it*)
> *After they* **leave,** *we'll clean up the mess.*   (*after they **will leave**)

EXERCISE 7. Change the time reference of the passage from "Araby" by James Joyce (Appendix Section 1) to future, and observe what happens in the time clauses.

9.4.2 Aspect. The auxiliaries *be*$_{prog}$ and *have*$_{perf}$ are called *aspect markers.* They indicate that an action is in progress or has already been completed at the time that is indicated by the tense marker. English also has other aspect markers such as *be about to,* which indicates an incipient event, and *used to,* which indicates a habitual occurrence in the past.

    By combining present and past tense with modals and aspect markers, we are able to differentiate past, present, and future time *within a particular time framework*, as when telling a story that takes place in the past. The diagram in figure 9.4 illustrates some of the possibilities; for example, under the heading **PAST**, you will find such forms as the following:

> *The band* **was playing.**   (present with respect to a point in the past)
> *The band* **had been playing** *for an hour.*   (past with respect to a point in the past)
> *The band* **was about to** *play.*   (immediate future with respect to a point in the past)
> *The band* **would play** *the next day.*   (future with respect to a point in the past)

Figure 9.4 shows that similar distinctions can be made within a present or future time framework.

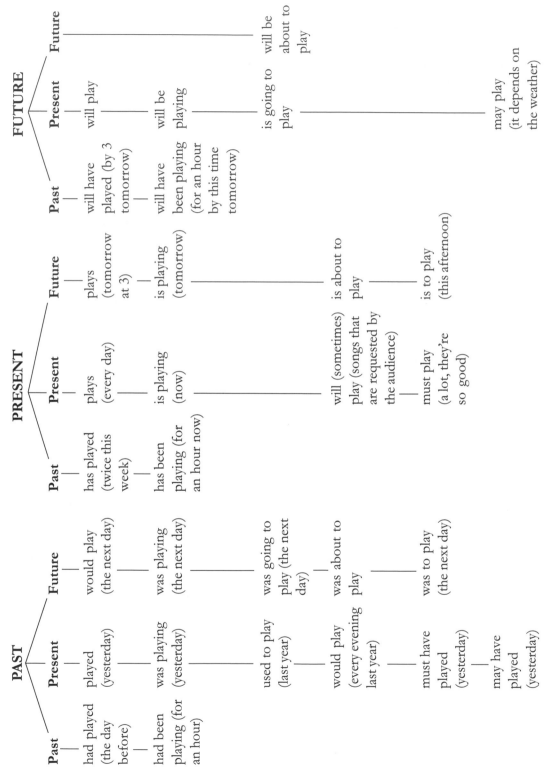

Figure 9.4. Distinguishing past, present, and future *within* a past, present, or future time frame.

EXERCISE 8. In the following selection from James Joyce's story "The Dead," the central character, Gabriel, reflects on the past, present, and future. Set out these references in a chart like the one that is started for you at the end of this exercise, and observe the grammatical forms that Joyce uses to make these time distinctions, all within a past time framework.

> *Gabriel, leaning on his elbow, looked for a few moments unresentfully on her tangled hair and half-open mouth, listening to her deep-drawn breath. So she had had that romance in her life: a man had died for her sake. It hardly pained him now to think how poor a part he, her husband, had played in her life. He watched her while she slept as though he and she had never lived together as man and wife. His curious eyes rested long upon her face and on her hair: and, as he thought of what she must have been then, in that time of her first girlish beauty, a strange friendly pity for her entered his soul. He did not like to say even to himself that her face was no longer beautiful but he knew that it was no longer the face for which Michael Furey had braved death.*
>
> *Perhaps she had not told him all the story. His eyes moved to the chair over which she had thrown some of her clothes. A petticoat string dangled to the floor. One boot stood upright, its limp upper fallen down: the fellow of it lay upon its side. He wondered at his riot of emotions of an hour before. From what had it proceeded? From his aunt's supper, from his own foolish speech, from the wine and dancing, the merry-making when saying good-night in the hall, the pleasure of the walk along the river in the snow. Poor Aunt Julia! She, too, would soon be a shade with the shade of Patrick Morkan and his horse. He had caught that haggard look upon her face for a moment when she was singing Arrayed for the Bridal. Soon, perhaps, he would be sitting in that same drawing-room, dressed in black, his silk hat on his knees. The blinds would be drawn down and Aunt Kate would be sitting beside him, crying and blowing her nose and telling him how Julia had died. He would cast about in his mind for some words that might console her, and would find only lame and useless ones. Yes, yes: that would happen very soon.*

The beginning of an answer to Exercise 8:

Past from Gabriel's point of view	Present from Gabriel's point of view	Future from Gabriel's point of view
	Gabriel looked on her hair and mouth	
She had had that romance in her life.	*It hardly pained him now to think [about it].*	
A man had died for her sake.		

Past from Gabriel's point of view	Present from Gabriel's point of view	Future from Gabriel's point of view
He, her husband, had played a poor part in her life.		
	He watched her while she slept.	
	His eyes rested upon her face and hair.	
He and she had lived together as man and wife.		
	Pity for her entered his soul.	
She must have been beautiful.		
Her face was no longer beautiful.		
Michael Furey had braved death for her face.		

9.4.3 Modality. *Modality* (degree of certainty or strength of obligation) is usually expressed by modal auxiliaries.

1. A modal may indicate some degree of obligation; this is called the *deontic* meaning of the modal:

> *You **will** do as I say.*   requirement
> *You **must** do as I say.*   obligation
> *You **should** do as I say.*   weaker obligation
> You **may** leave now.   permission
> *I **will** help you.*   promise

2. Modals can also be used to indicate the degree of certainty of an event or situation; this is called the *epistemic* meaning of the modal:

> *That **will** be George now.*   logical deduction
> *That **must** be George now.*   logical deduction
> *That **may** be George now.*   less certain logical deduction
> *It **will** certainly snow in December.*   future certainty
> *It **may** snow in November.*   future possibility

3. Epistemic modality (doubtfulness) can also be expressed by the past tense marker. Compare the following:

> *If I* **win** *the lottery, I will buy a vacation home in the Bahamas.*
> > (The present tense indicates that I think I have a good chance.)
> *If I* **won** *the lottery, I would buy a vacation home in the Bahamas.*
> > (The past tense indicates that I'm not optimistic about my chances.)

Past tense forms are used after the verb *wish* to indicate the unreality of the wished-for event:

> *I wish I* **knew** *the answer to the question you are asking.*   (I don't.)
> *I wish I* **had finished** *the assignment.*   (I didn't.)

Compare *hope*, which is more optimistic:

> *I hope I* **know** *the answers to the questions they will ask me.*
> *I hope I* **have finished** *the assignment correctly.*

Both present and past tense modals refer to the future, but past tense modals express less certainty about the outcome:[3]

> *They* **will** *leave.*
> *They* **would** *leave (if they could).*
> *I* **can** *help you.*
> *I* **could** *help you (if I had the right tools).*
> *It* **may** *rain tomorrow.* (That's what the forecasters are predicting.)
> *It* **might** *rain tomorrow.* (But we think the rain will pass to the south of us.)

Past tense modals combine with the auxiliary *have*$_{perf}$ to create a *counterfactual*:

> *You* **should have** *said something.*   (But you didn't.)
> *I* **would have** *said something.*   (But I didn't get the chance.)
> *I* **could have** *danced all night.*   (If only the musicians hadn't gotten tired and gone home.)

---

[3]We have not been treating the modals *would, could,* and *might* as "past tense" forms, but facts like these suggest that *would* is, in some sense, the past tense of *will, could* the past tense of *can,* and so forth.

EXERCISE 9.

a. The Samuel Eliot Morison passage (Appendix Section 1) moves back and forth between past and present tense forms. Write out the verb string that is in present tense. What governs the alternation between present and past?

b. At three points in the Morison passage, the author uses the past perfect form. Write out these three verb strings and explain, in each case, why Morison uses this form. (*Hint:* There are two different reasons.)

c. Find an example of the *modal + have*$_{perf}$ construction in the Morison passage. What does this form indicate?

9.4.4 Voice. Changes of tense, aspect, and modality do not affect the assignment of semantic roles. The verb distributes its semantic roles in the same way, without regard to tense (past or present) or the presence of auxiliaries. For example, in all the sentences below, the verb *eat* assigns the role of **<agent>** to its subject and the role of **<patient>** to its complement:

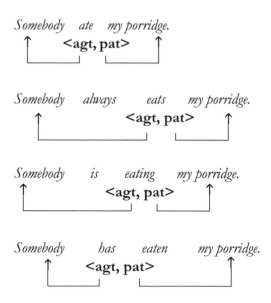

EXERCISE 10. Name the verb form in each sentence above. For example, the first sentence (*Somebody ate my porridge*) is in the past tense form.

The passive is the one exception to the generalization that changing the form of the verb does not affect the assignment of semantic roles. A verb in the passive participle form loses the semantic role that would normally be assigned to its subject; instead, the subject receives the semantic role that would normally be assigned to the verb's complement:

Active Form   **Passive Form**

Somebody has eaten my porridge.   My porridge has been eaten.
⤒   **\<agt, pat\>**   ⤒   ⤒   **\<pat\>**
└_____┘   └____┘   └_____┘

My grandparents built this house in 1930.   This house was built   in 1930.
⤒   **\<agt, result\>**   ⤒   ⤒   **\<result\>**
└_____┘   └____┘   └_____┘

George Washington slept in this bed.   This bed was slept in (by George Washington).
⤒   **\<pat, loc\>**   ⤒   ⤒   **\<loc\>**
└_____┘   └____┘   └_____┘

EXERCISE 11.

a. Change the tense of the following sentences from present to past or past to present, and observe that the assignment of semantic roles remains unchanged:

   i. *Horror movies frighten   some children.*
       ⤒   **\<stim, exp\>**   ⤒
       └_____┘   └_____┘

   ii. *Somebody   took   the coffee urn from the office.*
       ⤒   **\<agt, pat, source\>**   ⤒   ⤒
       └_____┘   └_____┘
                  └_____┘

   iii. *Someday   someone will   discover a cure for AIDS.*
           ⤒**\<exp, result\>**   ⤒
           └____┘   └_____┘

b. Insert a modal auxiliary, or the auxiliary *be*_{prog} or *have*_{perf} into the sentences of (a) and notice that the assignment of semantic roles remains unchanged.

c. Change the sentences of (a) to passive and show what happens to the assignment of semantic roles.

Students are sometimes advised to avoid passive voice, as being *weaker* than the active (because of its suppression of the **<agent>** role). In fact, however, passive voice is common in some styles of writing, particularly expository writing. Contrary to what you may have been told, good writers do not avoid the passive voice in expository writing, though they take care to use it appropriately. Because the subject position is associated, in most cases, with the role of **<agent>**, one purpose of the passive is to avoid mentioning the doer of an action—sometimes because this information is already known, sometimes because it is unnecessary or uninteresting, and sometimes because it might be embarrassing. The examples below are from Williams 1994, 72:

> *Valuable records should always be **kept** in a fireproof safe.*
> (We already know who should do this.)
> *Once this design was **developed** for our project, it was quickly **applied** to others.*
> (We already know who developed it, and we don't really care who applied it elsewhere.)
> *Those who are **found** guilty can be **fined.***
> (We know who will do this—the court.)

EXERCISE 12. Find the passive participle in each sentence below and say, in each case, what **<agent>** has been suppressed by the use of the passive, and why:
a. *The President has been criticized for his decision.*
b. *Although the windows had been left open, no one entered the premises.*
c. *No decision has been made yet about George.*
d. *Children are raised differently in other parts of the world.*
e. *Although we had not been invited to the meeting, we went anyway.*

EXERCISE 13. You should be able to find eleven passive participles in the following excerpt from "The Rats on the Waterfront," by Joseph Mitchell. Be prepared to say something about why the passive voice is appropriate in each case. *Hint:* In order to find all the passive participles in the passage, you will need to be aware that passive participles appear not only as complements to *be*~pass~, but also as noun modifiers, as in line 5 below: *tightly **packed** clay.*

> *The brown rat is distributed all over the five boroughs [of New York City]. It customarily* 1
> *nests at or below street level—under floors, in rubbishy basements, and in burrows. There are* 2
> *many brownstones and red-bricks, as well as many commercial structures, in the city that have* 3
> *basements or sub-basements with dirt floors; these places are rat heavens. The brown rat can* 4
> *burrow into the hardest soil, even tightly packed clay, and it can tunnel through the kind of cheap* 5
> *mortar that is made of sand and lime. To get from one basement to another, it tunnels under* 6
> *party walls; slum-clearance workers frequently uncover a network of rat tunnels that link all the* 7
> *tenements in a block. Like the magpie, it steals and hoards small gadgets and coins. In nest* 8

chambers in a system of tunnels under a Chelsea tenement, workers recently found an empty 9
lipstick tube, a religious medal, a skate key, a celluloid teething ring, a belt buckle, a shoehorn, 10
a penny, a dime, and three quarters. Paper money is sometimes found. When the Civic Repertory 11
Theatre was torn down, a nest constructed solely of dollar bills, seventeen in all, was discovered in 12
a burrow. Exterminators believe that a high percentage of the fires that are classified as "of 13
undetermined origin" are started by the brown rat. It starts them chiefly by gnawing the insula- 14
tion off electric wires, causing short circuits. It often uses highly inflammable material in building 15
nests. The majority of the nests in the neighborhood of a big garage, for example, will invariably 16
be built of oily cotton rags. 17

CHAPTER 10
INTERROGATIVES, EXCLAMATIVES, AND IMPERATIVES

10.1 Introduction

English, like other languages, has four types of sentences, classified according to function, as shown in table 10.1.

Table 10.1 Types of Sentences, According to Function

Declaratives	*Today is Tuesday.*
Imperatives – Giving orders.	*Close the window.*
Exclamatives	*What big teeth you have, Grandmother!*
Interrogatives *yes/no* questions	*Would you like another cookie?*
WH-questions	*What are you doing?*

Up to now, we have confined our attention to declarative sentences. In this chapter, we turn to interrogatives, imperatives, and exclamatives.

10.2 *Yes/No* Questions

As we have seen, *yes/no* questions are formed by a transformation called *Subject-AUX Inversion* (SAI) which moves the head of the sentence (the AUX) to a position before the subject, identified here as C:

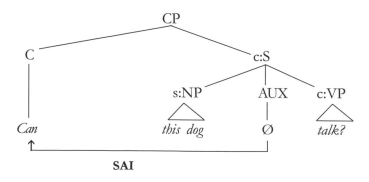

176

What is new in this diagram is the claim that the auxiliary moves into a position called *C*, which is the head of a higher-level constituent called *CP*. Note that the CP follows the normal phrase structure for English, in that it consists of a headword *C* plus its complement *S* (a somewhat defective *S* with a Ø where its AUX used to be).

Students often ask why this higher-level phrase is called *CP*. This notation developed in recognition of the similarity between the structure of a question and that of a dependent or subordinate clause:

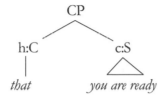

A dependent clause is called *CP* because its head word is a *C* (subordinating conjunction). Because questions are structurally similar to dependent clauses, they are also identified as CPs.

EXERCISE 1. Draw tree diagrams of the following interrogative sentences, following the model shown on p. 176:
   a. *Can you find an answer?*
   b. *Has the jury reached a verdict?*
   c. *Is your refrigerator running?*
   d. *Were the paintings stolen?*

10.3 The Main Verb *be*
The normal position for the verb is inside the VP, as in the sentence below, where the tense marker has joined the verb by the transformation of Tense Hopping:

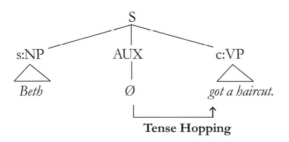

The verb *be* is an exception. If the main verb is *be* and there is no overt auxiliary, then the *verb* moves into the AUX position by a transformation called *Be* Raising:

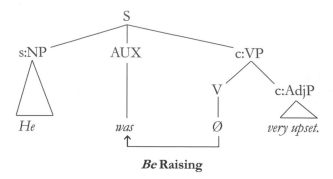

***Be* Raising**

EXERCISE 2. Give evidence to show that the verb has moved into the AUX position in the sentence above. (*Hint:* Consider the position of sentential modifiers like *probably*; then, create the emphatic and negative forms of this sentence, and explain what they tell you about the identity of AUX.)

10.4 *Yes/No* Questions Again

Interrogative sentences with ordinary verbs are created with the aid of the dummy auxiliary *do*, which is inserted by the transformation of *Do* Support:

Yes/No Question:

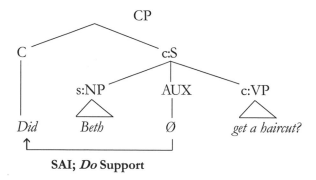

SAI; *Do* Support

With the main verb *be*, in contrast, the interrogative is not formed with *do*; instead the verb is raised to the AUX position by *Be* Raising and then to the C position by SUBJ-AUX Inversion:

Yes/no Question:

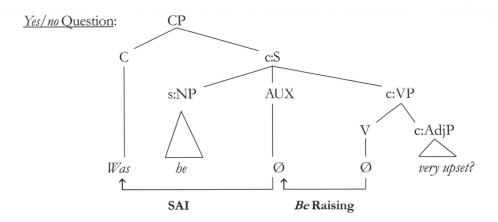

EXERCISE 3. Draw tree diagrams for the following sentences, showing the effects of *Be* Raising and Subject-AUX Inversion:

    a. *This is obviously a serious mistake.*

    b. *Is this a serious mistake?*

    c. *This is not a serious mistake.*

10.4.a Historical note. In most Indo-European languages, *all* verbs behave like the verb *be* in English. For example, in French and Spanish questions, the main verb moves to AUX and then to C.

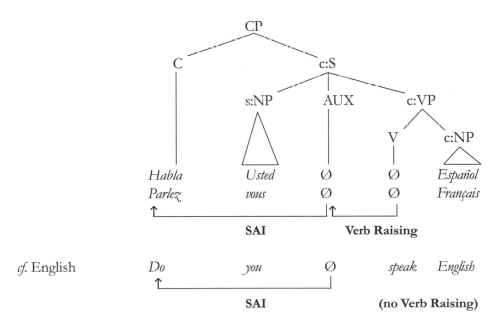

In French, the same point (that the main verb moves into the AUX position) can be made with the negative:

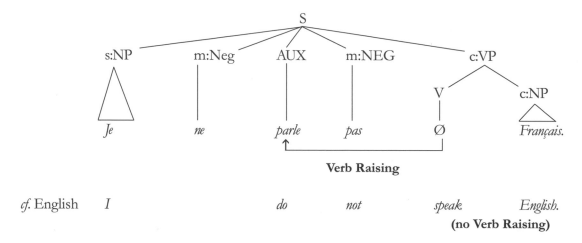

Verb Raising

cf. English   I   do   not   speak   English.

(no Verb Raising)

English was once like French and Spanish; that is why, in older versions of English, we find the negative particle *not* after the main verb, as in Patrick Henry's words:

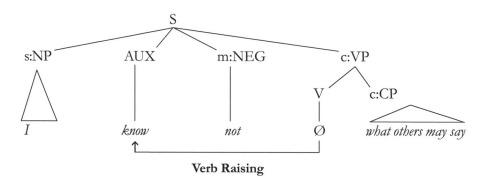

Verb Raising

(but as for me, give me liberty or give me death.)

The verb then moved to the front in questions, as in the following question from the *King James Bible* (Jesus speaking to Peter):

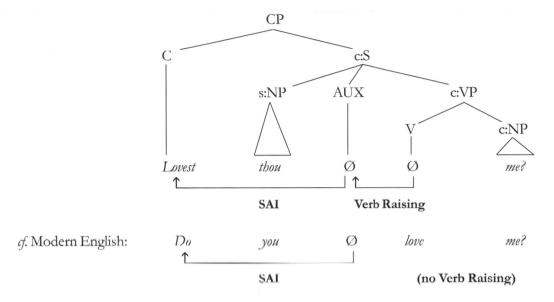

cf. Modern English:

The British maintain the old system with the main verb *have* as well as the main verb *be*; thus, where Americans say

> *Do you have the time?*   and   *I don't have the time.*

the British say

> *Have you the time?*   and   *I haven't the time.*

EXERCISE 4.

a. Draw tree diagrams for the British and American sentences above: *Have you the time? Do you have the time? I haven't the time. I don't have the time.*

b. Draw tree diagrams for the following sentences, showing what transformations have taken place. The transformations are as follows: *Be* Raising, Subject-AUX Inversion, Tense Hopping, *Do* Support, and Contraction.

i.	*Should we go?*	vi.	*I don't hear you.*
ii.	*Have they finished?*	vii.	*Do you hear me?*
iii.	*Will they have finished?*	viii.	*We are ready.*
iv.	*They will not have finished.*	ix.	*We are not ready.*
v.	*I hear you.*	x.	*Are we ready?*

181

10.4 WH-Questions

WH or *information* questions contain *WH-words* such as *who, whom, whose, what, which, where, why,* and *how.* In one type of WH-question, called an *echo* question, the WH-phrase maintains its normal position in the sentence:

> *You went* **where**?
> *You borrowed* **whose** *car?*
> *She said* **what**?
> *Your grandmother is* **how** *old?*

Echo questions are used to express puzzlement or dismay at what someone has just said.

Neutral WH-questions—simple requests for information—have a different structure: Here, the WH-phrase (the phrase containing the WH-word) is required to occupy initial position in the sentence:

> **Where** *did you go?*
> **Whose car** *did you borrow?*
> **What** *did she say?*
> **How old** *is your grandmother?*

If this requirement is not met by the normal word order,[1] then the WH-phrase must be *moved* to the front, by a transformation called *WH Fronting*, and the AUX must be moved, as well, to create a CP for the WH-phrase to move into:

---

[1] If the WH-phrase is the subject of the sentence, then the requirement that it must occupy first position is met automatically, and no transformation is needed:

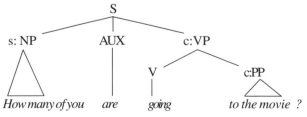

182

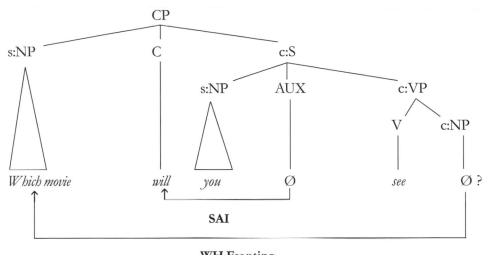

WH Fronting

In the example above, the WH-phrase is a NP that originates as the complement of the verb *see*. However, AdjPs, AdvPs, and PPs can be moved, as well, as in the examples below:

WH-phrase = AdjP:

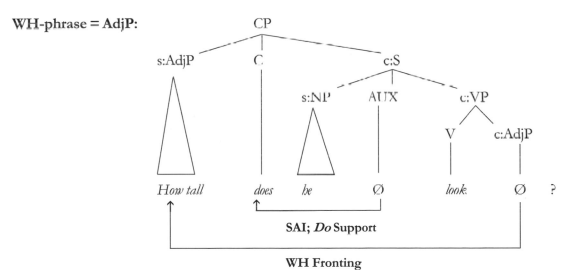

WH Fronting

WH-phrase = AdvP:

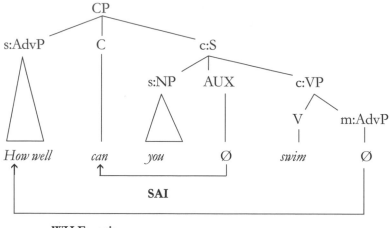

WH-phrase = PP:

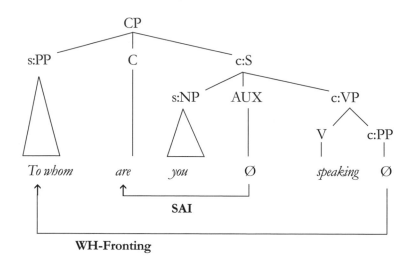

It is more common, in conversational English, to front just the *complement* portion of the PP, leaving the preposition *stranded*:

WH-phrase = NP:

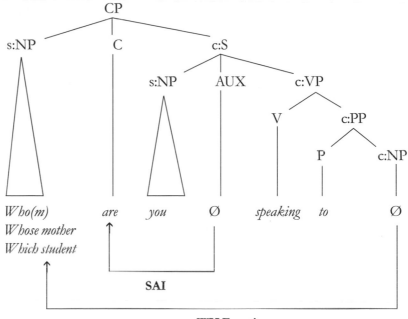

EXERCISE 5.

a. Draw tree diagrams of the following sentences, which have undergone WH Fronting and SUBJ-AUX Inversion:

    i.   *Who(m) should the parents call?*

    ii. *How old does he seem?*

    iii. *Who(m) will you stay with in Chicago?*

    iv. *What did Terry find?*

    v. *What are you looking at?*

    vi. *What verdict did the jury reach?*

    vii. *What time is it?*

    viii. *How many hot dogs do you want?*

    ix. *What grade is she in?*

    x. *How reliable are you?*

b. In very formal language, the *case* of the WH-word (*who* vs. *whom*) is determined by its original position. If the WH-word comes from subject position, choose *who*; if it comes from a complement position, choose *whom*.[2] If the WH-phrase is the subject of the

---

[2]The predicate complement is an exception to this generalization.

        It is I. (Formal)   *It's me.* (Informal)   *Who is it?* (All registers)

sentence, then the requirement that it must occupy first position is met automatically, and no transformation is needed:

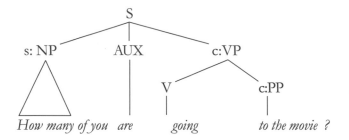

Why is it possible to use *whom* in sentences (i) and (iii) above? Why can't we use *whom* in the sentence *Who do you think will call me first?*

10.6 Exclamatives

Exclamatives such as *What big teeth you have, Grandmother!* also undergo WH-Fronting, but not Subj-AUX Inversion. Exclamatives have a "silent" C which we will represent as Ø:

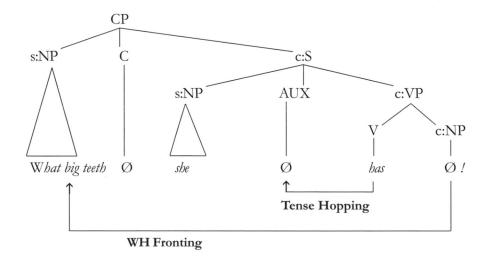

EXERCISE 6. Draw tree diagrams of the following exclamative sentences:

    a. *What a nice job you did with this report!*

       (Caution: The *did* in this sentence is the past tense form of the main verb *do*.)

    b. *How discouraged he looks!*

    c. *How quickly they grow up!*

10.7 Imperatives

Imperatives have the same structure as statements, except that they have a silent AUX, and the subject may be also be silent, in which case it is understood as *you*:

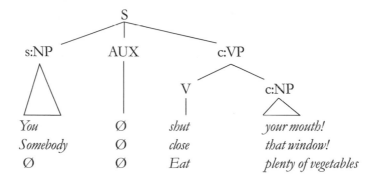

Notice that there is no Subj-AUX agreement in Imperatives; we say *Somebody close that window*, not *Somebody closes that window* (which would be a statement, rather than an imperative).

EXERCISE 7. Draw tree diagrams of the following imperative sentences:
- a. *Have another cookie.*
- b. *Give the man the money.*
- c. *Everybody hold up your hands!*

10.8 Speech Acts: The Semantics of Declaratives, Interrogatives, Exclamatives, and Imperatives

When we speak directly and literally, the sentence-types *declarative, interrogative, exclamative,* and *imperative* are used to carry out the *speech acts* that are shown in table 10.8a.

Table 10.8a Sentence Types and Speech Acts

Sentence Type	Speech Act	Example
Declarative	Stating a fact	*Christmas comes but once a year.*
Interrogative	Asking a question	*Do you live on campus?*
Imperative	Giving a command	*Close the door.*
Exclamative	Making an emotional comment	*What nice children you have!*

There are other speech acts, such as giving permission, making a request, giving a compliment, making a promise, and so forth, which are not linked to particular sentence structures.

When a speech act is performed by a sentence of the designated type—for example, when the interrogative sentence *Do you have a ballpoint pen?* is used to ask a *yes/no* question—the utterance is called a *direct speech act*. But in real conversation sentences are often used *indirectly*, to perform speech acts other than the ones they represent literally. For example, if you tell me that you couldn't turn in your paper because your printer is not working, I might use the sentence *Do you have a ballpoint pen?* not as a question, but as a suggestion that there are alternative methods for producing a paper. This is called an *indirect speech act*. Because my sentence isn't intended as a request for information, I don't expect you to respond with a *yes* or *no* answer, but with an apology for having made so little effort to carry out your assignment. The contrast between direct and indirect speech acts is illustrated in table 10.8b below:

Table 10.8b Direct and Indirect Speech Acts

Purpose of Speech Act	Direct Speech Act	Indirect Speech Act
To ask the time	*What time is it?*	*I wonder what time it is.*
		Do you know what time it is?
To ask someone to pass the salt	*Please pass the salt.*	*Can you reach the salt?*
		Is there any salt?
		I wonder if I could have the salt.
To state a fact	*There are 4617 islands in Maine.*	*Did you know that there are 4617 islands in Maine?*

EXERCISE 8. Give the literal meaning of each sentence in the Indirect Speech Act column in table 10.8b. For example, the sentence *I wonder what time it is* is literally a statement indicating that a certain thought is present in my consciousness.

Indirect speech acts are a puzzling phenomenon. If I want to ask you what time it is, why don't I just say *What time is it?* And if I ask *Do you know what time it is?*, how are you supposed to know that I will not be satisfied with the answer, *Yes, I do?* In the theory developed by the philosopher John Searle, our ability to use and understand indirect speech acts derives from our knowledge of a set of *appropriateness conditions* that define when each speech act can be performed. Some appropriateness conditions for statements are listed below:

> Appropriateness conditions for stating a fact
> *(S = speaker; H = hearer)*
> 1. S knows this fact to be true.
> 2. The fact is relevant to the conversation.
> 3. S believes H does not know this fact.
> 4. S believes H will be interested.

Thus, for example, if I (the speaker) state that there are 4617 islands in Maine, then, by Condition 1, you (the hearer) have a right to assume that I have obtained this information from some reliable source—in other words, I know what I am talking about. Furthermore, by Condition 2, the statement is relevant to our conversation—I can't make a statement like this right out of the blue. Condition 3 says that you, the hearer, are not an expert on Maine islands, since in that case you would know this fact already, and I would have no business telling it to you. However, by Condition 4, you must have some sort of interest in islands or in the state of Maine—otherwise I would have no *reason* to tell you.

Some appropriateness conditions for questions and commands are listed below:

> Appropriateness conditions for asking a question
> 1. S does not know the answer to the question.
> 2. S believes H knows the answer.
> 3. S believes that H is willing to tell him/her.
> 4. S wants to know the answer.
> 5. S would like H to tell him/her.

> Appropriateness conditions for giving a command
> 1. S has authority over H with respect to this matter.
> 2. S believes H is capable of carrying out the command.
> 3. S wants H to do this.

EXERCISE 9. Following the models above, list appropriateness conditions for two other speech acts: giving permission and making a request.

Following Searles's (1974) theory, we can explain an indirect speech act as an attempt to avoid one or more of the appropriateness conditions for the speech act that the speaker intends to perform. For example, if I ask *Do you know what time it is?* instead of *What time is it?,* that may be because I am uneasy about Appropriateness Conditions 2 (*S believes that H knows the answer*) and 4 *(S wants H to tell him/her)*; I don't want to put you on the spot by demanding information that you cannot give me. By asking a *yes/no* question, instead, I make it possible for you to give an appropriate answer (*No, I don't*) even if you don't have the information I want.

Turning now to the other participant in the conversation, how do you know that when I ask, *Do you know what time it is?* I really mean *What time is it?* In other words, how do you know to respond *It's three o'clock* rather than *Yes, I do?* The answer lies, again, in the appropriateness conditions for questions. According to Appropriateness Condition 4, I would not *really* ask a question unless I wanted to know the answer. But why would I care whether you know the time or not? The only reason I would be interested in this information is that I want to know whether you can tell me the time. So, you conclude, that is the information I really want, and you respond accordingly: *Yes, it's three o'clock.*

EXERCISE 10.

a. The imperative form can seem abrupt and rude, and even a *request* may seem somewhat demanding in American culture, where people are normally expected to accede to requests. Thus we are likely to speak indirectly when giving commands or making requests, using a question or statement that the hearer *interprets* as a command or request. All the following sentences can be interpreted as commands or requests. For each sentence, explain first the literal meaning of the sentence, then the request that the sentence can be understood to make and how H knows to interpret the sentence as a request. For example, sentence (i) is literally a *yes/no* question inquiring about H's ability to reach the salt, but it can be understood as a request to pass the salt. The reason is that sentence (i) does not meet Appropriateness Condition 4 for questions: The information is of no possible interest unless S wants H to pass the salt.

   i.   *Can you reach the salt?*
   ii. *It's awfully hot in here.*
   iii. *You've already had three beers.*
   iv. *The garbage is full.*
   v.   *Would it be out of your way to stop by the grocery store?*

b. Sometimes a question acts indirectly as a statement, or a statement acts indirectly as a question. For the following sentences, specify the literal meaning of the sentence, its *understood* meaning, and what the speaker gains by speaking indirectly. In other words, if I want to inform you as to how many islands there are in Maine, why not do so directly, by using a declarative sentence?

   i. *Did you know that there are 4617 islands in Maine?*
   ii. *I wonder what time it is.*

c. What is the literal meaning of the sentence below, and how is it understood in conversation? Why do you think the speaker chose to speak indirectly?

   Have another piece of cake! (as he passes you the plate)

d. Since the usual purpose of a question is to gain information, one of the appropriateness conditions for a question is that the speaker does not know the answer. However, this condition is sometimes violated. One thing children have to learn when they go to school is that *teachers* often ask questions whose answers they already know; these are not real questions, but rather a teaching technique that many teachers use. What is the purpose of the questions in the Samuel Eliot Morison passage in Appendix Section 1?

10.9 The Cooperative Principle of Conversation

When people communicate with one another, they follow a *cooperative principle* which, according to the philosopher H. Paul Grice (1975), includes a tacit understanding between speaker and hearer that the speaker will be truthful, relevant, concise, and clear, and will give all the information that is necessary for the situation. In addition, speakers and hearers usually cooperate by taking turns as they converse, by being as agreeable as they can, and by trying to understand and respond to the speaker's *intended* meaning, rather than what he literally said. (That is why, when someone asks you *Do you know what time it is?*, you cannot answer simply *Yes, I do.* You have to answer *Yes, I do; it's three o'clock* or *No, I'm sorry, I don't.*)

EXERCISE 11. Read through the conversation from Hemingway's "Hills Like White Elephants" in Appendix Section 5. Although the participants in this conversation do take turns, as they should, their conversation is not very cooperative in other respects. Something is clearly wrong between them.

Go through the conversation to find instances where the speakers do or do not respond cooperatively to one another. For the responses that you identify as uncooperative, say what is uncooperative about them, and suggest what the speaker might have said if he/she were in a more cooperative mood.

CHAPTER 11
VARIATION IN ENGLISH

11.1 Introduction

In this chapter, we will take a short break from our investigation of English syntax in order to apply the concepts that we have already covered to the topic of *variation* in English—including differences between spoken and written English, and differences among regional and social dialects. We will return to our syntactic analysis in chapter 12, which deals with compound and complex sentences.

11.2 Dialects

Language changes over time, as we have seen, because of changes in culture, influences from other languages, and, most of all, because of the adjustments children make as they acquire the language, generation after generation. When speakers of a language are in close contact with one another, changes made by one group spread to other groups as well, so that the language remains uniform despite historical change. However, if two groups become separated, then as time goes on they develop separate dialects, and if they continue to be separated, then they eventually develop separate languages. That is what happened when Indo-European divided into Celtic, Germanic, Italic, Hellenic, and so forth, and again when Germanic split into Danish, Swedish, Norwegian, German, Dutch, and English.

Whether two varieties are classified as distinct dialects or distinct languages depends, in principle, on whether they are mutually intelligible: If two speakers can understand one another, then they are speaking the same language. In real life, however, the classification of language varieties is partly a political decision. For example, Swedish and Norwegian are largely mutually intelligible, but they are classified as separate languages because they are identified, politically, with two different countries. And many of us have met speakers of English whose speech was almost unintelligible to us but whom we consider, nevertheless, to be speaking a dialect of English.

11.3 Regional Dialects

One source of dialect differences is geographical separation. American English differs from British English and Australian English, and there are further differences *within* each of these countries. These dialects differ in pronunciation, vocabulary, and syntax. For example, American English differs from British English in that (except along the East Coast) Americans pronounce [r] after a vowel, as in *car*, *poor*, and *over*. American English also exhibits a pronunciation regularity called the *flap rule* which causes [t] to be pronounced as [d] between a stressed and an unstressed vowel. Thus the words *latter* and *ladder*, *waited* and *waded*, *otter* and *odder* are homophones in American English but not in British English.

American and British English also differ in vocabulary; for example, what Americans call *gasoline,* the British call *petrol,* and what Americans call an *apartment* the British call a *flat.* Finally, there are some syntactic differences between British and American English; for example, the words *ought* and *used* can undergo Subject-AUX Inversion in British English:

Ought *we* Ø *to go?*   **Used** *you* Ø *to smoke?*

Also, the main verb *have* acts as an AUX (that is, it undergoes the rule of *Be* Raising, which we discussed in Chapter 10):

Have *you* Ø Ø *the time?*   (*cf.* Am. Eng   **Do** *you* Ø *have the time?*)

EXERCISE 1.

a. Listen to a speaker of British English in person, in a film, or on TV, and identify one or two additional differences between British and American English.

b. There are some *spelling* differences (introduced by Noah Webster) between British and American English. Give examples.

c. Translate these British vocabulary items into American English. If necessary, use your dictionary or consult a friend:

lorry	*spanner*	*bonnet* (of a car)	*knock up*
loo	*bobby*	*boot* (of a car)	*biro*
biscuits	*nappy*	*chemist's shop*	*dustbin*
pram	*pub*	*trunk call*	*cinema*

There are also regional differences *within* American and British English. People from different parts of the U.S.—Southerners, New Englanders, New Yorkers, Chicagoans, Wisconsinites, Californians—are often recognizable by their pronunciation. Those of us who live on the East Coast tend to *r*-drop, like the British. A New Yorker may make a three-way distinction among the vowel sounds [ô] *law,* [ä] *father,* and [ŏ] *box,* while a Californian pronounces all three vowels exactly the same. Southerners and Midwesterners often treat *pen* and *pin, hem* and *him* as homophones (that is, they merge the vowel sounds [ĕ] and [ĭ] before nasal consonants). For Chicagoans, the vowel sound [ă] of *bad* closely approaches the pronunciation other Americans give to the [ĕ] of *bed.* Wisconsinites have a distinctive pronunciation of the vowel sounds [ā] and [ō].

Regional dialects also differ in vocabulary; whether you say *sneakers* or *tennis shoes, a sack of groceries* or *a bag of groceries* depends primarily on where you live. If you have traveled to other regions of the country, then you can probably add examples of your own. However, American regional dialects show very little variation when it comes to syntax. A few examples that can be observed are the use of double modals in Appalachian English (*I **might could** go*), a second person plural pronoun (*y'all*) in Southern dialects, and the short answer *so don't I* instead of *so do I* in eastern New England.

EXERCISE 2.

a. Use a dictionary and/or your own experience to identify the geographical locations in which the following expressions are used:

    i. *tennis shoes* vs. *sneakers*

    ii. *a sack of groceries* vs. *a bag of groceries*

    iii. *a bubbler* vs. *a water fountain*

    iv. *a cabinet* vs. *a frappe* vs. *a milkshake*

    v. *hose* vs. *stockings* vs. *nylons*

    vi. *a teeter-totter* vs. *a see-saw*

    vii. *an elastic* vs. *a rubber band*

    viii. *lightning bugs* vs. *fireflies*

    ix. *fixin' to* vs. *about to*

    x. *sprinkles* vs. *jimmies*

    xi. *a belly buster* vs. *a belly flop*

b. List six additional regional differences that you are aware of in American English.

In Britain, with its much longer history as an English-speaking nation, rural communities were isolated for many centuries, so that regional differences had a greater opportunity to develop and become established. British regional dialects differ dramatically in pronunciation and vocabulary. Furthermore, unlike the situation in the United States, there are significant differences in syntax from one region to another. For example, some speakers in the north and west of England still use the old second person singular pronouns *thou, thee,* and *thy*, though these pronouns have disappeared in most other areas; in southwestern dialects, the pronouns *he, she, we,* and *they* can be used as objects of verbs, while the pronouns *him, her,* and *us* can be used as subjects:[1]

> *John saw **they**.*
> *Bill gave it to **she**.*
> ***Us** be a-goin.*
> ***Her** don't like it.*

---

[1] This information on British traditional regional dialects is taken from Trudgill (1999) and Trudgill and Chambers, eds. (1991). The examples of the Devonshire dialect are from Harris (1991); the examples of the Somerset dialect are from Ihalainen (1991).

The examples below, from the southwestern county of Devon, illustrate a set of demonstrative determiners that are rather different from Standard English:

> *I came down here to live in* **thease** [this] *little street.*
> **Theys** [these] *places be alright if you know where you'm goin to.*
> *What makes all* **they** [those] *hills look so well?*
> *I traveled* **thicky** [that] *old road four year.*
> *I expect* **thicky** [those] *nine was all one man's sheep.*

Many dialects have nonstandard subject-verb agreement:

He **like** *her.*	East Anglia (eastern England)
She **want** *some.*	
I **wants** *it.*	western and northern England
We **likes** *it.*	
We **putten** 'We put'	Staffordshire (west central England)
They cutten 'They cut'	
I **likes** *everybody.*	Somerset (southwestern England)
He's older than what I **be.**	
Where **be** *I to?* 'Where am I?'	
He [the spade] **were** *like that, see, a long handle on un.*	

They also exhibit nonstandard past tense and past participle forms:

> *He* **done** *that wrong.*
> *I* **give** *her a birthday present yesterday.*
> *I* **writ** *a letter yesterday.*
> *Is that the car I* **see/seed/sawed/seen**?

and nonstandard auxiliary forms:

Cost *lend us a quid? No, I* **conna.**	Straffordshire
'Can you (canst thou) lend me a pound? No, I can't.'	
I **anna** *done it*	
'I haven't done it.'	
I **divent** *knao—I* **might could** *do it.*	Northumberland (northern England)
'I don't know—I might be able to do it.'	
The girls usually make me some, but they **mustn't could've** *made any today.*	
'The girls usually make me some, but they must not have been able to make any today.'	

As you can see, there is far greater regional variation in British English than in American English, especially in syntax. In American English, syntactic differences tend to be associated with social class rather than with region. (See section 11.5 below.)

11.4 Spoken English *vs.* Written English

[handwritten: → more careful b/c there's no instant feedback.]

Spoken English is quite different from written English, and forms that are acceptable in the one are not necessarily acceptable in the other. For example, the following sentences would be decidedly odd in spoken English:

> *To whom have you given the money?*
> *They had, although they were hungry, refused all food.*
> *Behind me were my mother and my mother's friend.*
> *The quick, brown fox jumped over the lazy dog.*
> *While very hot indeed, the temperature never rose over 106°.*

Conversely, lexical expressions and syntactic constructions that are used in spoken English are not always acceptable in formal writing (unless the writer is trying to *represent* spoken English). For example, as we have seen, sentence fragments are very common in conversation, but they are not always acceptable in writing. Written English also avoids slang expressions such as *awesome* 'very good' and colloquial expressions such as the word *pretty* used as an intensifier (*The play was* **pretty** *good*). One pervasive difference between the two varieties is the use of contractions. In spoken English, the negative particle *not* is almost always contracted onto the AUX:

	will	*not*	→	*won't*
You do the rest:	*would*	*not*	→	
	should	*not*	→	
	must	*not*	→	
	is	*not*	→	
	are	*not*	→	
	has	*not*	→	
	had	*not*	→	

The AUX (if not contracted with *not*) is contracted onto the subject:

	she	*will*	→	*she'll*
You do the rest:		*would*	→	
		is	→	
		has	→	
		had	→	
	they	*will*	→	
		would	→	
		are	→	

they	*have*	$\rightarrow$
	had	$\rightarrow$

The AUX may also be contracted onto a preceding WH-word:

who	*will*	$\rightarrow$	*who'll*
You do the rest:	*would*	$\rightarrow$	
	is	$\rightarrow$	
	has	$\rightarrow$	
what	*will*	$\rightarrow$	
	is	$\rightarrow$	

and the auxiliary verb *have*$_{perf}$ is contracted onto a preceding modal:[2]

will	*have*	$\rightarrow$	*will've*
would	*have*	$\rightarrow$	
could	*have*	$\rightarrow$	
should	*have*	$\rightarrow$	
might	*have*	$\rightarrow$	

You do the rest (for *would*, *could*, *should*, *might*).

In casual spoken English, we often use other *informal contractions* which have no standard spelling. The infinitive particle *to* may be contracted onto the preceding verb:

have to	[hăft´ə]
has to	
want to	
going to	
got to	

A pronoun may be contracted onto a preceding verb:

I told	*him*	[ĭm]
	her	
	them	
	you	

and a pronoun may be contracted onto a preceding AUX:

---

[2]Because the contracted *have* sounds like *of*, students sometimes write *would of* and *could of* instead of *would have* and *could have*.

Will	*he*	[wĭľ ē]
	you	
Did	*he*	
	you	

Short function words, including *and*, *or*, *can*, and *of*, tend to be *reduced*:

black **and** *white*	[n]
men **or** *women*	[ər]
I **can** *go*	[kĭn]
cup **of** *coffee*	[ə]

and unstressed *ing* may be pronounced as [ĭn]:

| *something* | [sʌm´ thĭn] |
| *running* | [rʌn´ ĭn]. |

Another common phenomenon in conversational English is the deletion of AUX, and sometimes the subject pronoun *you*, in questions:

Are you going?	→	*You goin'?* or *Goin'?*
Do you want another pancake?	→	*Want another pancake?*
Did you catch any fish?	→	*Catch any fish?*
Have they gone yet?	→	*They gone yet?*
Where are you going?	→	*Where you goin'?*

EXERCISE 3.

a. Listen to the recording you made of a short conversation (Appendix Section 4). What contracted forms do you hear? Do you hear any examples of AUX Deletion in questions? What other characteristics (colloquial vocabulary and sentence structure, use of fragments, and so forth) mark your sample as spoken rather than written English?

b. Consider the literary representations of conversation by Poe and Hemingway in Appendix Section 5. What makes each representation realistic or unrealistic? You will notice, of course, that Hemingway's dialogue is more realistic than Poe's. But is the Hemingway passage completely realistic? If you recorded an actual conversation between two people, would it look exactly like this? If not, how would it differ?

c. What adjustments would you make in your recorded conversation (Appendix Section 4) if you wanted to include it as a piece of dialogue in a novel or short story you were writing?

11.5 Social-Class Dialects

Geography is not the only thing that separates people; we are separated by social boundaries as well as geographical ones. Each social group has its own way of speaking. As children, we acquire the language of the group to which we belong, and unless we choose to change our station later in life, we maintain that dialect in adulthood; this is one of the ways we proclaim our identity. As we noted earlier, social-class dialects are characterized not only by a distinctive pronunciation and vocabulary, but also, particularly, by syntax. The syntactic constructions listed below are characteristic of working-class dialects in both American and British English.

It is important to keep in mind that there is nothing inherently wrong or illogical about any of these constructions: All dialects of English follow a consistent set of rules that make sense from a linguistic point of view; otherwise, children couldn't learn to speak them! The judgements we make about these constructions are social judgements, not linguistic ones. Remember, also, that these are spoken dialects, not written ones; many people *speak* nonstandard dialects but use Standard English for writing. And many of us are bi-dialectal even in speech, switching back and forth between a standard and a nonstandard variety depending on the situation.

11.5.1 Some characteristics of working-class American dialects.

a. Use of the third-person pronoun *them* as a determiner: *them shirts* for SAE *those shirts*. Standard American English (SAE) uses first- and second-person plural pronouns as determiners: *us kids, you students,* and so on, but does not accept third-person pronouns as determiners.

b. Lack of subject-AUX agreement, especially in the negative forms, as shown in table 11.5:[3]

c. Use of *ain't* where Standard English uses *am not, is not, are not, have not, has not:*
    She **ain't** *here.*
    He **ain't** *come in yet.*
Ain't was originally a contraction for *am not,* but has been extended, in some dialects, to include *is not, are not, have not,* and *has not.* It is now severely stigmatized and is no longer used in Standard English even with its original meaning, *am not.* This is unfortunate, since we *need* the contraction *ain't* in tag questions such as "I'm here, _____ I?" The banishment of *ain't* from Standard English has left us with no satisfactory way to complete this sentence—a fitting punishment for our snobbery!

d. Negative Concord
    Use of *no, none, nothing, nobody, no one, never* in negative contexts where SAE uses *any, anything, anybody, anyone,* and *ever:*

---

[3]Nonstandard subject-AUX agreement in the negative forms is a marker of social class; nonstandard subject-AUX agreement in the affirmative forms is more common in ethnic dialects (section 11.6).

Table 11.5 Subject-AUX Agreement in Standard and Nonstandard English

Standard American English (SAE)	Nonstandard English		
I know	*I know*	*or*	*I knows*
You know	*You know*	*or*	*You knows*
He/she/it knows	*He/she/it know*	*or*	*He/she/it knows*
We know	*We know*	*or*	*We knows*
You know	*You know*	*or*	*You knows*
They know	*They know*	*or*	*They knows*
I don't smoke	*I don't smoke*		
You don't smoke	*You don't smoke*		
He/she/it doesn't smoke	*He/she/it don't smoke*		
We don't smoke	*We don't smoke*		
You don't smoke	*You don't smoke*		
They don't smoke	*They don't smoke*		

*They didn't do **nothin** to **nobody**.*	vs.	*They didn't do **anything** to **anybody**.*
*He ain't **never** gonna say it to his face.*	vs.	*He isn't **ever** going to say it to his face.*
*We can't do **nothin**.*	vs.	*We can't do **anything**.*

While the rule of Negative Concord is highly stigmatized in English, it is the standard method of forming negatives in many languages, including French and Spanish:

French: *Je **ne** sais **rien**.* Lit., 'I don't know nothing.'

Spanish: ***No** se **nada**.*

e. Nonstandard past tense or perfect participle

*Finally, she **come** in.*	(*come*, rather than *came*, as the past tense of *come*)
*He **brang** me one.*	(*brang*, rather than *brought*, as the past tense of *bring*)
*I **seen** him.*	(*seen*, rather than *saw*, as the past tense of *see*)
*She's already **went**.*	(*went*, rather than *gone*, as the past participle of *go*)

f. Homonymy between adjectives and adverbs that are distinguished in SAE

*You did **good**.*

*He talks too **slow**.*

SAE uses *fast* as either an adjective or an adverb (*A **fast** car goes **fast***), but uses *good* and *slow* only as adjectives; the adverb forms are *well* and *slowly*.

g. Object-case pronouns in subject position
> **Him** and **me** *are good friends.*

Native speakers of English have no intuitions about the assignment of case in coordinate structures (NPs joined with *and* or *or*). We tend to use the object-case forms (*him* and *me*) as children, and this is the form that persists in many dialects, but in communities that speak Standard English, we are told by our parents and teachers to say **He and I** *are good friends.* We accept this correction but then make the opposite error: *This is between* **he and I.**

EXERCISE 4. The characters in the following excerpts speak English that is marked by both regional and social-class features. Discuss the representation of dialect in these passages. (*Caution:* In analyzing literary dialogue, keep in mind that you are dealing not with actual speech, but with a writer's representation of speech; thus it would be appropriate to comment not only on the dialect itself, but also on how the author chooses to *represent* that dialect.)

Anse keeps on rubbing his knees. His overalls are faded: on one knee a serge patch cut out of a	1
pair of Sunday pants, worn iron-slick. "No man mislikes it more than me," he says.	2
"A fellow's got to guess ahead now and then," I say. "But come long and short, it won't be	3
no harm done either way."	4
"She'll want to get started right off," he says. "It's far enough to Jefferson at best."	5
"But the roads is good now," I say. "It's fixing to rain tonight, too. His folks buries at New	6
Hope, too, not three miles away. But it's just like him to marry a woman born a day's hard drive	7
away and have her die on him."	8

> —William Faulkner, *As I Lay Dying*

"Father!" said she.	
The old man pulled up. "What is it?"	1
"I want to know what them men are diggin' over there in that field for."	2
"They're diggin' a cellar, I s'pose, if you've got to know."	3
"A cellar for what?"	4
"A barn."	5
"A barn? You ain't goin' to build a barn over there where we was goin' to have a house,	6
father?"	7
The old man said not another word. He hurried the horse into the farm wagon, and	8
clattered out of the yard, jouncing as sturdily on his seat as a boy.	9

> —Mary E. Wilkins Freeman, "The Revolt of 'Mother'"

11.6 Ethnic Dialects

In addition to regional and social-class dialects, American English also has *ethnic* dialects such as Chicano English, Chinese English, and African-American Vernacular (also called *Black English* or *Ebonics*). Dialects are, of course, cultural, not biological: There are African-Americans who do not speak African-American Vernacular, and members of other ethnic groups who *do* speak this dialect as a result of having lived in an African-American community. Ethnic dialects are also subject to regional variation; for example, the Hispanic English of New York City differs from that of Chicago, but both dialects show evidence of influence from Spanish.

Like other nonstandard dialects, ethnic dialects are primarily *spoken* dialects; most English speakers use Standard English for writing. Speakers of nonstandard dialects often *speak* Standard English, as well, in formal situations outside their own community. However, within the community the dialect is an important cohesive force; we establish our membership in a community by using the language of the community, whether it is a regional dialect, an ethnic dialect, college slang, or Standard American English. English teachers have a responsibility to teach their students Standard English, especially for writing, but they should not try to replace the students' home dialect—the language that connects them to their family and friends. The school's job is to give the child access to a *second* dialect (or a second language, if the child speaks another language at home) which will open the door to opportunities in the world outside his or her own community.

Ethnic dialects have a somewhat different history than other dialects, in that they have their source in the English spoken by speakers of another language. For example, Chicano English was created by speakers of Mexican Spanish. As time went on, however, the dialect took on a life of its own; children growing up in the Chicano community learn Chicano English as their mother tongue even if they themselves do not speak Spanish.

African American Vernacular is believed to have originated as a *creole* spoken by African slaves on American plantations. There may also have been an influence from Irish plantation overseers, who spoke a nonstandard dialect of English. The African people who were brought to this country as slaves spoke many different languages (Wolof, Malinke, Temne, Yoruba, and Luba, to name just a few), but they had to use English to communicate with their white masters and even with one another, when speakers of different languages were mixed together on a single plantation. The first step, in such circumstances, is the development of a *pidgin*—a simple linguistic system that allows speakers of different languages to communicate with one another for business purposes. However, when children are born into the community and hear the pidgin more than any other language, they adopt it as their mother tongue, expanding and regularizing it as they go, so that it develops the vocabulary and structure of a full-fledged language. A language that is created in this way, by a generation of children, is called a *creole*.

Creoles arose all over the world in the eighteenth and nineteenth centuries as colonialism, with its plantation economies, brought in laborers from different language backgrounds to work together. Some important English-based creoles are

Jamaican Creole	Tok Pisin (Melanesia)
Bahamian Creole	Hawaiian Creole
Belizean Creole	Krio (Sierra Leone)

There are also French-based creoles, including Haitian Creole and Louisiana (Cajun) French, and Portuguese-based creoles such as Cape Verde Creole, spoken in the Cape Verde Islands and by immigrants from Cape Verde to Massachusetts and California.

The English-based creole that was used on American plantations is called *Gullah,* and remnants of this creole are still spoken on the sea islands off the coast of Georgia and South Carolina. The following is an excerpt from a Gullah folktale collected by C.C. Jones in 1888 and reprinted in Loreto Todd's (1984) *Modern Englishes: Pidgins and Creoles*:

> *Buh Elephant, [Brother Elephant] him bin know Buh Rooster berry well. Dem blan [used to] roam togerrur, an Buh Rooster blan wake Buh Elephant duh mornin, so eh kin hunt eh bittle befo de jew dry.*
>
> *Dem bin a talk togerrur one day, an Buh Elephant, him bet Buh Rooster say him kin eat longer ner him. Buh Rooster, him tek de bet, an dem tun in nex mornin, wen de sun jis bin a git up, fuh see who gwine win de bet.*

— C.C. Jones

African American or Black English Vernacular (AAEV or BEV) is the *de-creolized* English dialect that developed when speakers of the plantation Creole began to interact more closely with the surrounding English-speaking population. Some characteristics of BEV, especially its distinctive aspectual system, are apparently derived from Gullah, but other features are found in Southern American English generally. These features were not noticeable as long as American blacks remained in the South, but drew more attention when they migrated to northern cities in great numbers after the Second World War. Some characteristics of BEV are as follows:

11.6.1 Pronunciation.

a. Substitution of [t] and [d] for initial [th] and [*th*]

| *thing* | → | [tĭng]; | *this* | → | [đis] |

Substitution of [t] and [v] for final [th] and [*th*]:

| *mouth* | → | [mouf]; | *bathe* | → | [bāv] |

b. Simplification of consonant clusters

most	→	[mōs];	*field*	→	[fēl];
told	→	[tōl] or [tō];	*ask*	→	[ăs] or [ăks];
help	→	[hĕp]			

c. [r]-dropping:

| *car* | → | [kä]; | *over* | → | [ōv́ə]; |
| *here* | → | [hĭə] | | | |

d. Pronunciation of [ī] as [ä]:

| *I* | → | [ä]; | *mine* | → | [män] |

11.6.2 Syntax

a. Deletion of contracted AUX or *copula* (the main verb *be*):[4]

Standard English	**Black English Vernacular**
I'll do it in just a minute.	**I** do it in just a minute
We're on tape.	**We** on tape.
He's gonna try to get up.	***He** gon try to get up.*

b. Use of invariant *be* to indicate habitual or durative aspect

*The office **be** closed on weekends.*

*Everyday when I come home, I **be** scared.*

*But the teachers don't **be** knowing the problems like the parents do.*

*Everybody **be** tired from the heat.*

*He **be** hiding when he know she's mad.*

c. *Done + past participle* to indicate perfective aspect

*She **done** lost her keys.*

*We **done** told him about these pipes already.*

*It don't make no difference, cause they **done** used all the good ones by now.*

*Boy, you **done** done it now.*

This construction sometimes occurs as the complement of uncontracted *be*

*They **be done** left.*

*I **be done** bought my own radio by then.*

d. Inversion of a negative auxiliary with an indefinite subject pronoun (to satisfy a requirement that indefinite negative pronouns must be preceded by the negative particle *not* or *n't*)

***Ain't** nobody seen it.*

***Didn't** nobody see it.*

e. *It* as a "dummy" subject where standard English uses *there*

***It's** a lot of people here.*　　　　(cf. SAE ***There's** a lot of people here.*)

EXERCISE 5. Discuss the following representations of Black English Vernacular, the first from a novel by Zora Neale Hurston first published in 1937 and set in Florida, and the second from a short story by James Baldwin, first published in 1957 and set in New York City. Find specific constructions and/or pronunciations that identify the character as a

---

[4]As we saw above, Standard English speakers also delete certain auxiliaries in questions, so that *Are you going?* → *You goin'?*

speaker of BEV. Be sure, also, to say something about the writer's method of *representing* this dialect:

"Come to yo' Grandma, honey. Set in her lap lak yo' use tuh. Yo' Nanny wouldn't   1
harm a hair uh yo' head. She don't want nobody else to do it neither if she kin help it.   2
Honey, de white man is de ruler of everything as fur as Ah been able tuh find out. Maybe   3
it's some place way off in de ocean where de black man is in power, but we don't know   4
nothin' but what we see. So de white man throw down de load and tell de nigger man tuh   5
pick it up. He pick it up because he have to, but he don't tote it. He hand it to his   6
womenfolks. De nigger woman is de mule uh de world so fur as Ah can see. Ah been prayin'   7
fuh it tuh be different wid you. Lawd, Lawd, Lawd."   8

—Zora Neale Hurston, *Their Eyes were Watching God*

"Oh, honey," she said, "there's a lot that you don't know. But you are going to find   1
out." She stood up from the window and came over to me. "You got to hold on to your   2
brother," she said, "and don't let him fall, no matter what it looks like is happening to him   3
and no matter how evil you gets with him. You going to be evil with him many a time. But   4
don't you forget what I told you, you hear? . . . You may not be able to stop nothing from   5
happening. But you got to let him know you's **there**.*"*   6

—James Baldwin, "Sonny's Blues"

EXERCISE 6. Here are two other ethnic varieties to discuss—first, the Yiddish influenced English of Jewish immigrants in New York City and then the Chinese-influenced English of the character Kwan from Amy Tan's novel *The Hundred Secret Senses:*

"What do we need all this for?" he would ask loudly, for her hearing aid was turned   1
down and the vacuum was shrilling. "Five rooms" (pushing the sofa so she could get into the   2
corner) "furniture" (smoothing down the rug) "floors and surfaces to make work. Tell me,   3
why do we need it?" And he was glad he could ask in a scream.   4
"Because I'm use't."   5
"Because you're use't. This is a reason, Mrs. Word Miser? Used to can get unused!"   6
"Enough unused I have to get used to already . . . Not enough words?" turning off the   7
vacuum a moment to hear herself answer. "Because soon enough we'll need only a little closet,   8
no windows, no furniture, nothing to make work for but worms. Because now I want room   9
. . . Screech and blow like you're doing, you'll need that closet even sooner . . . Ha, again!"   10
for the vacuum bag wailed, puffed half up, hung stubbornly limp. "This time fix it so it   11
stays; quick before the phone rings and you get too important-busy."   12

—Tillie Olsen, *Tell Me a Riddle*

"I was just making a—ah, forget it. What's a secret sense?"   1
"How I can say? Memory, seeing, hearing, feeling, all come together, then you know   2

something true in you heart. Like one sense, I don't know how say, maybe sense of tingle.	3
You know this: Tingly bones mean rain coming, refreshen mind. Tingly skin on arms,	4
something scaring you, close you up, still pop out lots a goose bump. Tingly skin top a you	5
brain, oh-oh, now you know something true, leak into you heart, still you don't want believe	6
it. Then you also have tingly hair in you nose. Tingly skin under you arm. Tingly spot in	7
back of you brain—that one, you don't watch out, you got a big disaster come, mm-hm.	8
You use you secret sense, sometimes can get message back and forth fast between two people,	9
living, dead, doesn't matter, same sense."	10

—Amy Tan, *The Hundred Secret Senses*

EXERCISE 7. In a story with several characters, there may be a linguistic contrast between the characters. Discuss the following excerpts, which represent conversations between two people. In both examples, one character is white and one is black. First, identify the differences in their speech; then say whether you think these differences are realistic and, if not, what the author is trying to accomplish with his representation. [For example, in the passage from *Huckleberry Finn*, Huck and Jim are represented as having different pronunciations of the suffix –*ing*. Jim says *fool'n* (line 3), but Huck says *nothing* (line 6). Is this realistic? If not, why does Twain give them different pronunciations?]

"Le's land on her, Jim."	1
But Jim was dead against it, at first. He says:	2
"I doan' want to go fool'n 'long er no wrack. We's doin' blame well, en we better let	3
blame' well alone, as de good book says. Like as not dey's a watchman on dat wrack."	4
"Watchman your grandmother," I says; "there ain't nothing to watch but the texas	5
and a pilot-house; and do you reckon anybody's going to resk his life for a texas and a pilot-	6
house such a night as this, when it's likely to break up and wash off down the river any	7
minute?" Jim couldn't say nothing to that, so he didn't try. "And besides," I says,"we might	8
borrow something worth having, out of the captain's stateroom. Seegars, I bet you—and	9
cost five cents apiece, solid cash. Steamboat captains is always rich, and get sixty dollars a	10
month, and they don't care a cent what a thing costs, you know, long as they want it . . ."	11

—Mark Twain, *Huckleberry Finn*

'Howdy, Dave! Whutcha want?'	1
'How yuh, Mistah Joe? Aw, Ah don wanna buy nothing. Ah jus wanted t see if yuhd	2
lemme look at tha ol catlog erwhile.'	3
'Sure! You wanna see it here?'	4
'Nawsuh. Ah wans t take it home wid me. Ahll bring it back termorrow when Ah	5
come in from the fiels.'	6
'You plannin on buyin something?'	7
'Yessuh.'	8

'Your ma letting you have your own money now?'	9

—Richard Wright, "The Man Who was Almost a Man"

EXERCISE 8. Characters sometimes change their speech from one point to another in a story (just as in real life). What changes do you see in Sula's speech from line 3 to line 6 in the passage below, and what causes the change?

When Sula opened the door [Eva] raised her eyes and said, "I might have knowed	1
them birds meant something. Where's your coat?"	2
Sula threw herself on Eva's bed. "The rest of my stuff will be on later."	3
"I should hope so. Them little old furry tails ain't going to do you no more good than	4
they did the fox that was wearing them."	5
"Don't you say hello to nobody when you ain't seen them for ten years?"	6
"If folks let somebody know where they is and when they coming, then other folks can	7
get ready for them . . ."	8

—Toni Morrison, *Sula*

EXERCISE 9. It can also be interesting to compare the language of the characters with the language of the narrator. Discuss the following passages from that point of view:

. . . [Fred Henry] pushed his coarse brown moustache upwards, off his lip, and	1
glanced irritably at his sister, who sat impassive and inscrutable.	2
"You'll go and stop with Lucy for a bit, shan't you?" he asked. The girl did not	3
answer.	4
"I don't see what else you can do," persisted Fred Henry.	5
"Go as a skivvy," Joe interpolated laconically.	6
The girl did not move a muscle.	7
"If I was her, I should go in for training for a nurse," said Malcolm, the youngest of	8
them all. He was the baby of the family, a young man of twenty-two, with a fresh, jaunty	9
museau.	10
But Mabel did not take any notice of him. They had talked at her and round her for	11
so many years, that she hardly heard them at all.	12

—D.H. Lawrence, "The Horse Dealer's Daughter"

Now and then there was a quivering in the thicket. Old Phoenix said, "Out of my way,	1
all you foxes, owls, beetles, jack rabbits, coons and wild animals! . . . Keep out from under	2
these feet, little bob-whites . . . Keep the big wild hogs out of my path. Don't let none of those	3
come running my direction. I got a long way.' Under her small black-freckled hand her cane,	4
limber as a buggy whip, would switch at the brush as if to rouse up any hiding things.	5

On she went. The woods were deep and still. The sun made the pine needles almost too   6
bright to look at, up where the wind rocked. The cones dropped as light as feathers. Down   7
in the hollow was the mourning dove—it was not too late for him.   8

    The path ran up a hill. 'Seem like there is chains about my feet, time I get this far,"   9
she said, in the voice of argument old people keep to use with themselves. "Something always   10
take a hold of me on this hill—pleads I should stay."   11

                        —Eudora Welty, "A Worn Path"

CHAPTER 12
COORDINATION AND SUBORDINATION

12.1 Introduction

In this chapter, we will return to our survey of the syntactic structure of English in order to extend our analysis to compound and complex sentences.

12.2 Coordination

Coordinate or *conjoined* structures are formed by joining two or more constituents of the same category with a coordinating conjunction such as *and* or *but*, as indicated by the formula below, where the symbol $\propto$ stands for "any syntactic category," and the subscript n means "any number from one on up":

$$\propto \ \Rightarrow \ \propto_n \ \text{CONJ} \ \propto$$

The formula says that if we conjoin two or more instances of any category with a conjunction such as *and*, the result is an instance of the same category. For example, if we conjoin two NPs, the result is a NP:

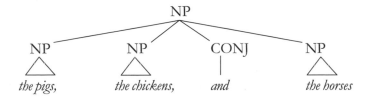

As the formula indicates, a conjoined structure can contain more than two members:

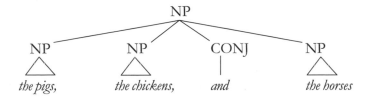

A conjoined constituent can occupy the same syntactic positions as any other member of that category; for example, a conjoined NP occupies NP positions such as the subject of a sentence or the complement of a verb.

A conjoined NP as the subject of a sentence:

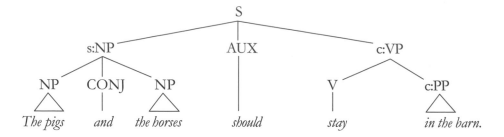

A conjoined NP as the complement of a verb:

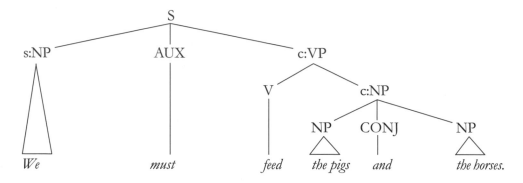

Other categories can be conjoined in the same way as NPs; in each case, the result is a member of the same category as the constituents that were conjoined:

S:

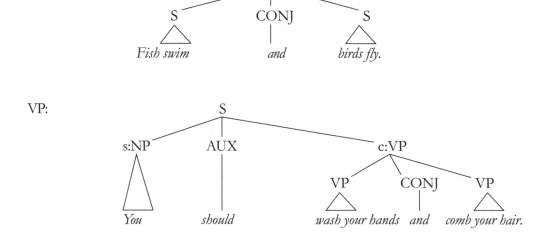

PP:

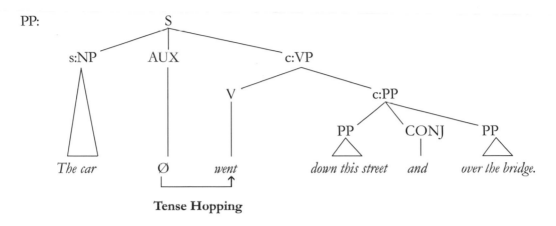

Tense Hopping

Lexical categories can be conjoined, also, as in the examples below:

N:

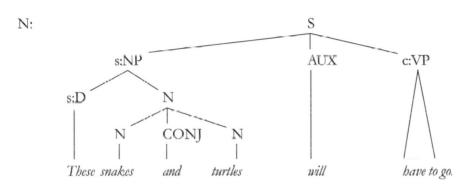

V:

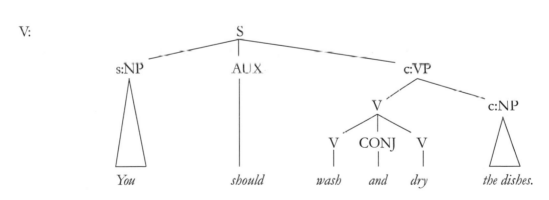

P:

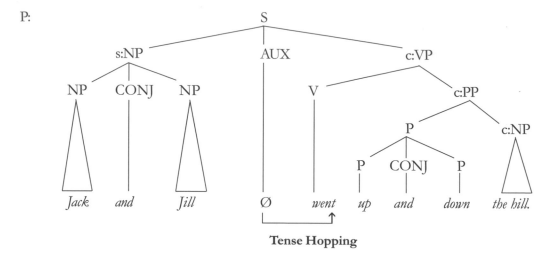

Tense Hopping

EXERCISE 1. Draw tree diagrams of the following sentences, which contain coordinate (*conjoined*) structures:

a. *The guests drank soda or beer.*
b. *The plane will land at the airport and taxi to the terminal.*
c. *I walked down the stairs and out the door.*
d. *We landed on the island and made a fire.*
e. *I just can't stand these snakes and turtles.*
f. *Spring will come and the gardens will flourish.*

Coordination is very common in spoken English, but in writing, particularly formal writing, we rely more heavily on *subordination* (the use of dependent clauses introduced by subordinate conjunctions such as *if, when, although, as,* and so forth). Subordinating conjunctions provide a more explicit statement of the relationship between ideas, while the coordinating conjunctions, especially *and,* leave it to the reader or listener to work out the connection. Compare the examples below:

> With coordinating conjunction:
> *The sun rose, **and** the birds began singing all around us.*

> With subordinating conjunction:
> ***As** the sun rose, the birds began singing all around us.*

Children acquire coordinating conjunctions early, especially *and*; see, for example, the speech of the child "Eve" in Appendix Section 6. When children first begin to write, they follow the pattern to which they are accustomed in speech, stringing chains of sentences together with *and* or *and then*.

As their writing matures, they move toward the adult pattern, with less coordination and more subordination. The grammar of subordinating conjunctions will be discussed in sections 12.3 and 12.4 below.

EXERCISE 2.

a. Look for coordinate (conjoined) structures in the speech of Eve at 27 months (Appendix Section 6). What coordinating conjunctions does she know, and what syntactic categories (NP, S, VP, and so on) does she conjoin?

b. As we noted above, children rely heavily on coordination in their writing as well as their speech. Look for examples of conjoined structures in the children's writing samples in Appendix Section 2, especially examples where a more mature writer would not have used coordination. Are there changes in the children's use of coordination vs. subordination as they grow older?

c. Some mature writers continue to rely heavily on coordination. Discuss Hemingway's use of coordination in the selection from "Hills Like White Elephants" (Appendix Section 1). Begin by locating the conjunctions in the passage and saying what constituents are joined by each conjunction. Then comment on the stylistic effect of coordination in Hemingway's writing. Why does he use so many coordinating conjunctions, and what is the effect of this choice?

Conjoined constituents normally belong to the same category, as we have seen, and must have the same grammatical function (s, h, c) within the clause. In the case of Vs and VPs, they must also be in the same inflectional form (that is, all past tense or all in the *–ing* form, and so on). This is called *parallel structure*. Failure to use parallel structure is a serious writing fault. Consider the following example:

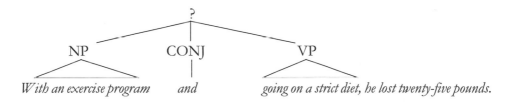

The first member of the above structure (*an exercise program*) is a NP, but the second (*going on a strict diet*) is a VP. The structure could be made parallel in either of the following ways:

a. Change the first conjunct to a VP:

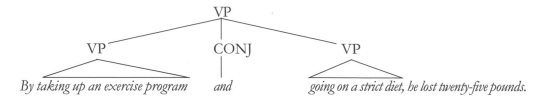

(two VPs, both complements of the preposition *by*)

b. Change the second conjunct to a NP:

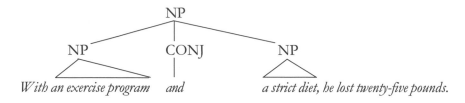

(two NPs, both complements of the preposition *with*)

EXERCISE 3. Find and correct the nonparallel structures in the following sentences, following the examples in the diagrams above. Explain what you did to correct each sentence.

    a. *I enjoy swimming, jogging, and to take long walks.*
    b. *In spring, summer, and in winter, I like to be outside.*
    c. *On a university campus, drunkenness can lead to expulsion or even being arrested.*
    d. *During the summer, we worked at the restaurant, went to the beach, and a few parties.*
    e. *Dialects can be classified into three types: regional, social class, and ethnicity.*

The *correlative conjunctions* listed in the tree below have two parts, which surround the first member of the conjoined structure:

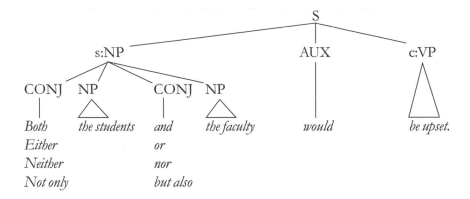

As with simple conjoined structures, two constituents that are joined with a correlative conjunction must match one another in category and function. For example, the following sentence is ungrammatical, because the first conjunct is a PP, while the second is an NP:

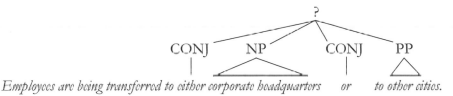

Again, we can correct the sentence in either of two ways.

1. Change the first conjunct to a PP (by moving the first part of the correlative conjunction to a different position):

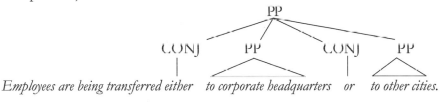

2. Change the second conjunct to an NP:

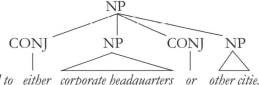

EXERCISE 4.

a. Find the correlative conjunctions and correct the nonparallel structures in the following sentences, following the model above. Explain what you did to correct each sentence.

    i.   *You can either talk to her mother or to her father.*

    ii.   *This is a time not for words, but action.*

    iii.   *Either you must do as he says or take the consequences.*

    iv.   *The students were not only given the questions, but also the answers,*

    v.   *Some guys came into the restaurant neither wearing shoes nor shirts.*

b. The following sentence seems to me to be grammatical, but it should not be grammatical according to our rule. Can you give an explanation for this exception?

    We should be able to express ourselves both orally and in writing.

A second issue that arises in coordinate structures is the choice of case for pronouns. When a pronoun appears alone in an NP, English speakers have no difficulty with case. A pronoun in subject position has subject case:

    We *know the answer.*

A pronoun that is the specifier of a noun has possessive case:

    Your *niece is here.*

And a pronoun in complement position has object case:[1]

*We gave **her** the money.*	(complement of verb: indirect object)
*We saw **her**.*	(complement of verb: direct object)
*We will go with **them**.*	(object of preposition)

Speakers of Standard English never make mistakes with these pronouns. For example, we are not even slightly tempted to say ***Us** will go with **they***. However, pronouns inside coordinate structures are a different matter. Coordination, for some reason, interferes with our intuitions about case; we are uncertain whether to use the subject or the object form, and we make mistakes in both directions:

---

[1]There is one exception to this statement. In formal register, the complement of the verb *be* takes subject case rather than object case:

    *It was **I** who cut down the cherry tree.*   *This is **she** now.*   *It's **I**.*

However, many speakers find this choice too stilted, and use object case instead—*This is **her** now; It's **me**.* (If you feel uneasy about this, notice that the French do the same thing: they say *C'est moi,* not **C'est je.*)

Bill and **me** *went to the movies.*
>   (object case *me* wrongly chosen for subject position)

This information will be strictly between you and **I**.
>   (subject-case *I* wrongly chosen for object of preposition *between*)

EXERCISE 5. Try the following sentences. You can find the correct form simply by eliminating the other member of the conjoined structure; once the pronoun is alone in its NP, your native-speaker intuition will choose the correct form for you. However, because this is a course in English grammar, I would like you, in addition, to explain *why* a particular case form (subject or object) is required. For example, for sentence a. you should say that the subject pronoun *I* must be chosen for the first blank because the NP *Helen and I* is the subject of the clause *Helen and I had to stay after school*.

  a. *Helen and ____ had to stay after school because ____ and ____ were passing notes. I, me; she, her; I, me)*
  b. *Nobody except Ann and ____ voted for Louisa and ____. (I, me; he, him)*
  c. *Between you and ____, I don't think Greg is as cute as Bill. (I, me)*
  d. *The dog comes to ____ and ____ whenever we call it. (he, him; I, me)*
  e. *The answer will be the same whether you ask Laura or ____ . (I, me)*

12.3 Subordination

   A *subordinate* or *dependent* clause is a sentence or near-sentence that functions as a subject, complement, or modifier within a larger sentence. There are two types of subordinate clauses—*finite* clauses (e.g., *if it rains*) and *nonfinite* clauses (e.g., *for you to leave now*).

12.3.1 Finite Clauses. Finite clauses are ordinary sentences that begin with a subordinating conjunction (C) such as *that, when, although,* or *because.* The internal structure of a finite clause is the same as for an independent sentence—that is, it has a subject, AUX, and VP, and the AUX is a modal or tense marker. There are two types of finite clauses: ordinary CPs and WH-CPs.

a. Ordinary CPs

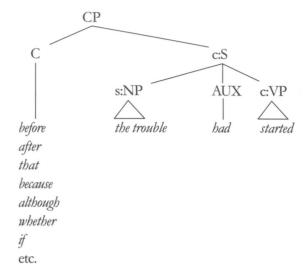

Some clauses have a *silent* C (Ø) which is interpreted as *that:*

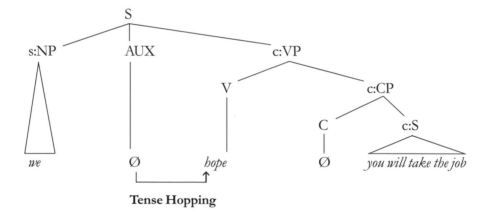

Tense Hopping

EXERCISE 6.

a. Put brackets around the subordinate clauses in the examples below, and identify the subordinating conjunction (C) in each clause. (Remember that it may be Ø):

i. *Columbus thought he had reached the Indies.*

ii. *Nobody told me that the faucet was broken.*

iii. *That enrollment is increasing is also a consideration.*

iv. *The fact that enrollment is increasing is also a consideration.*

v. *Before I say anything, I should know all the facts.*

vi. *I will talk to you after I look at the facts.*

vii. *If it rains, we won't go.*

viii. *I'm glad it isn't raining.*

  ix. *We can't leave until I find my keys.*

  x. *The engine overheated because the radiator was leaking.*

 b. Choose two clauses from the sentences in (a), and draw tree diagrams like those at the beginning of this section, so as to illustrate their internal structure.

 c. Explain why each of the CPs above qualifies as a finite clause (in other words, find the AUX position in each clause and say whether it is a modal or a tense marker).

---

b. *WH*-CPs. In addition to ordinary CPs, English also has *WH*-CPs in which a *WH*-phrase has been moved out of its inherent position by *WH* Fronting:

                CP

      s:XP^2 C   c:S

I wonder	*who(m)*	Ø	*you met*	Ø	*at the mall*
	whose friends	Ø	*you talked to*	Ø	
	what	Ø	*you bought*	Ø	*for Bill*
	which movie	Ø	*you saw*	Ø	
	where	Ø	*you went*	Ø	*last night*
	why	Ø	*you left*	Ø	
	how quickly	Ø	*you can get them*	Ø	
	how tall	Ø	*she is*	Ø	*now*
	when	Ø	*they got here*	Ø	

WH Fronting

There are two Øs in each tree above: The first Ø is the subordinating conjunction, which in *WH*-CPs is always Ø. The Ø inside the clause is the *underlying* position of the *WH*-phrase (the position it occupied before *WH* Fronting): *You met who(m) at the mall; you saw which movie; you got there when; you went why,* and so on.

 In Standard English, the C position in a *WH*-CP is always Ø, as we just noted. However, there are English dialects, including Irish English and African-American Vernacular, in which Subject-AUX Inversion is allowed to apply in *WH*-CPs:

---

^{2}*XP* is an abbreviation for *any* phrase; as the examples show, the constituent that moves to this position may be a NP, AdjP, or AdvP.

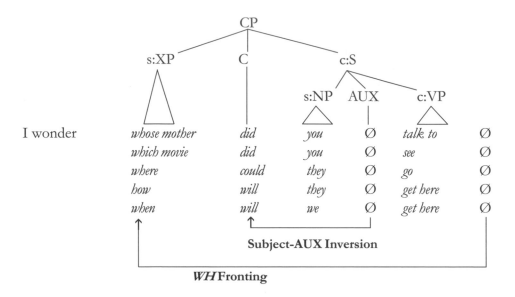

EXERCISE 7.

a. Bracket the *WH*-CP in each of the following sentences. Then underline the *WH*-phrase (the phrase that was moved by *WH*-Fronting), and mark its underlying position with Ø.

    i. *I wonder how tall she is.*

    ii. *We asked Bill when he would be ready.*

    iii. *The detectives were shocked by what they found in the cellar.*

    iv. *Beethoven could not hear how his compositions sounded.*

    v. *Whoever goes out last should turn out the lights.*

    vi. *Whatever you decide will be O.K. with me.*

    vii. *Why she did it, I can't imagine.*

b. Choose two of the *WH*-clauses from (a) above and draw tree diagrams, following the model above, to illustrate their internal structure.

c. Say why each of the *WH*-clauses in (a) counts as *finite* (that is, identify the AUX in each clause and say whether it is a modal or a tense marker).

12.3.2 *Nonfinite* Clauses. English also has several types of *nonfinite* or *near* clauses: infinitives, *WH*-infinitives, present participle or *ing*-clauses, passive participles, and absolute or *verbless* clauses. Nonfinite clauses have no modal or tense marker, and the subject position is often empty.[3]

---

[3]Non-finite clauses with Ø subjects (e.g., [*Ø Holding her hands behind her*], *she strode into the boardroom; We'll try* [*Ø to find a solution*]) are traditionally called *phrases*, rather than *clauses,* because they have no overt subject. However,

a. Infinitives

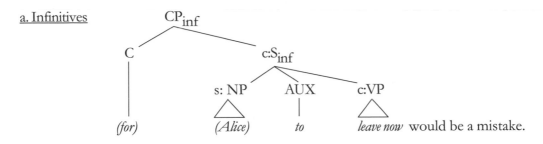

(for) ... *(Alice)* ... *to* ... *leave now* would be a mistake.

The AUX position in an infinitival clause is occupied by the particle *to*.[4]

   When the subject of an infinitive is not overtly expressed (that is, when it is Ø), it is interpreted from the context; for example, in the sentence below the Ø is identified with the subject of the main clause, *we*:

   We wanted [Ø to stay home].

and in the sentence below, the Ø is interpreted as *us, you,* or *anyone*:

   [Ø to stay home] would be a mistake.

Adult speakers of English have no difficulty in interpreting the Ø subject of an infinitival clause, but children find this confusing; for example, a seven-year-old, given the instruction *Donald asked Mickey Ø to turn around* may think that it is *Donald* rather than Mickey who is going to turn around.

   1. WH-Infinitives. A *WH*-infinitive is an infinitival clause which contains a *WH*-phrase. As always in English, the *WH* phrase will have moved to the specifier-of-C position by the transformation of *WH*-Fronting:

modern grammarians generally treat them as clauses, on the grounds that (1) they sometimes do have overt subjects ([**Your** *holding your hands behind you*] *was what tipped off the police*), and (2) even when the subject is not overtly expressed, it can still be understood; for example, in the sentence [Ø *Holding her hands behind her*], *she strode into the boardroom*, we understand that *she* is the person who is holding her hands behind her. There is an extensive linguistic literature on the question of when the subject of a nonfinite clause can or must be Ø, as well as the system we follow in determining the identity of a Ø subject.

[4]There are also infinitival clauses without *to*, called *bare* infinitives: *We watched the children* [Ø *cross the street*]; [Ø *Sail around the world*] *is what we'd like to do.* The internal structure of bare infinitives is not entirely clear, but we will assume here that they have the usual sentence structure, with Øs in subject and AUX position.

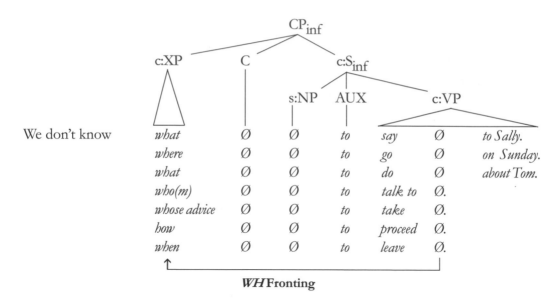

WH Fronting

There are three Øs in these diagrams: The first is the subordinating conjunction (C), which is always silent in a *WH*-infinitive. The second is the subject of the clause, which is also silent. The third is the underlying position of the *WH*-phrase: *to say* **what** *to Sally; to go* **where** *on Sunday,* and so on.

2. *ing*-Clauses. *ing*-clauses have a Ø in AUX position, with the VP in present participle *(-ing* form):

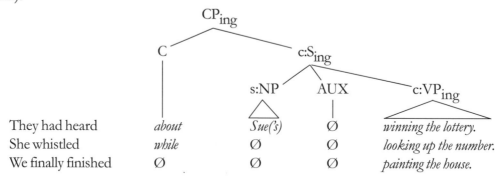

If the clause has an overt subject (that is, not Ø), it is often in possessive case (***Sue's*** *winning the lottery*) rather than object case (***Sue*** *winning the lottery*), especially in formal writing. However, the subject can also be Ø, as in the second and third examples above.

b. Passive Participles

Passive participles have a Ø in AUX position, with the VP in passive participle form:

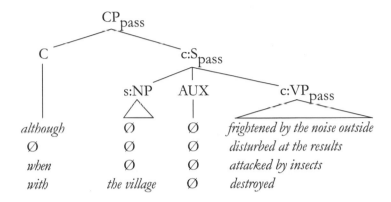

although	Ø	Ø	*frightened by the noise outside*
Ø	Ø	Ø	*disturbed at the results*
when	Ø	Ø	*attacked by insects*
with	*the village*	Ø	*destroyed*

c. Absolute or Verbless Clauses

Absolute clauses have an overt subject but no tense or modal and no verb; that is why they are sometimes called *verbless* clauses. The presence of the subject is particularly important in a verbless clause; if the subject were empty, there would be no reason to call the construction a clause rather than a PP, AdjP, or NP.

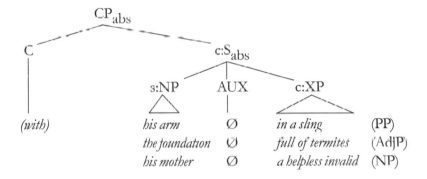

(with)	*his arm*	Ø	*in a sling*	(PP)
	the foundation	Ø	*full of termites*	(AdjP)
	his mother	Ø	*a helpless invalid*	(NP)

EXERCISE 8.

a. Find the nonfinite clauses in the sentences below, and say what type of clause each one is [an infinitive, a *WH*-infinitive, an *ing*-clause, a passive participle, or an absolute (verbless) clause].

    i. *Everybody likes to feel important.*

    ii. *I asked the children to pick up their toys.*

    iii. *The time to plant garlic is in the Fall.*

    iv. *She went to the store to get some bread.*

    v. *To open the door, you should press this knob.*

    vi. *What I want is for you to put on your coat.*

vii. *Nobody knew what to say.*

viii. *How to break the news to her parents was a difficult question.*

ix. *For you to come for Christmas would make your parents very happy.*

x. *They had finally saved enough money to buy a house.*

xi. *They like living in New Hampshire.*

xii. *We caught Bill sneaking out the door.*

xiii. *Everyone was surprised at Sue('s) taking such a strong stand.*

xiv. *Living in an apartment on the beach, we could watch the sunrise over the ocean every morning.*

xv. *The window got broken in the storm.*

xvi. *Driven to madness by her English grammar class, she had to spend the rest of her life in an asylum.*

xvii. *The person chosen for this job must be able to handle pressure.*

xviii. *Although terribly discouraged by the outcome, they refused to give up.*

xix. *Her heart in her mouth, she slowly turned the key.*

xx. *With the engine roaring, he zoomed out of the driveway.*

xxi. *My hands shaking, I reached towards the window.*

b. From the sentences above, choose one infinitive, one *WH*-infinitive, one *ing*-clause, one passive participle, and one verbless clause and draw a tree diagram for each one (just the clause, not the entire sentence), following the models provided earlier in this section.

12.3.3 The Functions of Subordinate Clauses. A subordinate (dependent) clause functions as a subject, complement, or modifier within larger phrase, as shown in tables 12.3a–12.3h.

Table 12.3a Subject of Sentence

CP   [*That you gave up so soon*] *surprised everybody.*

CP_{WH}   [*What she wanted*] *remained a mystery.*

CP_{inf}   [*(For you) to give up now*] *would be a mistake.*

CP_{wh-inf}   [*What to do next*] *is a difficult question.*

CP_{ing}   [*Phil('s) giving you the answer*] *was dishonest.*

Table 12.3b Complement of V

CP	*We know [(that) you'll understand].*
CP_{WH}	*I wonder [why she said that].*
CP_{inf}	*We'll try [to understand].*
CP_{wh-inf}	*We wondered [what to do next].*
CP_{ing}	*The children enjoyed [singing madrigals].*
CP_{pass}	*The mail carrier got [bitten by a dog].*

Verbs that take clauses as complements usually require a particular type of clause; for example, the verb *wonder* takes a CP_{WH}: *I wonder why she said that*; the verb *enjoy* takes a CP_{ing}: *Do you enjoy studying grammar?*; the verb *try* takes either a CP_{inf} or a CP_{ing}: *We tried to open the window; we tried opening the window*. A complete list of VP patterns, including verbs that take clauses as complements, is provided in table 12.5 located at the end of this chapter.

Table 12.3c Complement of P

CP_{WH}	*(We wondered) about [what they were doing].*
CP_{wh-inf}	*(We thought) about [where to go next].*
CP_{ing}	*(The plans called) for [going on to Miami].*

Table 12.3d Complement of N

CP	*our belief [that the earth is round]*
CP_{WH}	*no idea [who committed the crime]*
CP_{inf}	*our attempts [to understand]*
CP_{wh-inf}	*no idea [what to do next]*

Table 12.3e Complement of Adj

CP	*afraid* [*(that) we can't help you*]
CP$_{WH}$	*curious* [*why she said that*]
CP$_{wh\text{-}inf}$	*puzzled* [*what to do next*]
CP$_{inf}$	*eager* [*to understand*]

Table 12.3f Sentential Modifier

CP	[*If you read the letter*] *you'll understand.*
	We bought it [*because it was on sale*].
	[*Since you've been away*], *everything has changed.*
	[*After you left*], *things changed a lot.*
CP$_{WH}$	[*When he took off his hat*], *everybody cheered.*
	[*Whenever you eat Chinese food*], *you always feel thirsty afterward.*
CP$_{inf}$	[*To understand the issue*], *you should first read the letter.*
CP$_{ing}$	[*Singing and carrying candles*], *they marched through the campus.*
CP$_{pass}$	[*Painted green*], *the shutters wouldn't look so bad.*

Table 12.3g Modifier of V

CP	*(I) called* [*until he came*].
CP$_{WH}$	*Do it* [*however you like*].
CP$_{inf}$	*Go to the store* [*to buy some bread*].
CP$_{ing}$	*(She) sat* [*knitting a sweater*].

It is not always easy to distinguish between a modifier of V and a sentential modifier. The criterion used here is that a sentential modifier can appear at the beginning of the sentence, not just at the end: If a clause prefers to stay at the *end* of the sentence, inside the VP, then it is a modifier of V.

Table 12.3h Modifier of N

CP	*the information [(that) we sent for]*
	the people [(that) you talked to]
	the day [(that) we met]
	the reason [(that) I called you]
CP_{WH}	*the information [(which) we sent for]*
	the information [(for which) we sent]
	the students [(who(m) we met]
	the student [whose roommate we met]
	the day [when we met]
	the place [where we met]
	the reason [why I called you]
CP_{inf}	*a goal [(for us) to strive towards]*
CP_{ing}	*the child [standing near the stairs]*
CP_{pass}	*the banners [carried by the demonstrators]*

EXERCISE 9.

a. Choose one sentence from each of the tables above, and draw a tree diagram, using a triangle for the subordinate clause. The purpose here is not to illustrate the *internal* structure of the clause, but to be sure you understand where the clause goes in the matrix sentence.

b. Find the dependent (subordinate) clauses in the sentences below and identify their type (ordinary CP, CP_{WH}, infinitive, *WH*-infinitive, *ing*-clause, passive participle, or absolute) and function (subject, complement, or modifier of . . .). For example, for the first sentence, you will say that the clause is *that he had reached the Indies*, that it is an ordinary CP, and that it is the complement of the verb *thought*.

    i. *Columbus thought that he had reached the Indies.*

    ii. *Nobody told Bill that the faucet was broken.*

    iii. *That enrollment is increasing is also a consideration.*

    iv. *Nobody liked the speech he made.*

    v. *I wonder how tall she is.*

    vi. *Students who have finished the assignment should turn it in now.*

    vii. *We asked Susan when she would be ready.*

    viii. *The detectives were shocked by what they found.*

    ix. *Beethoven could not hear how his compositions sounded.*

x.   *Whoever goes out last should turn out the lights.*

xi.   *Whatever you decide will be O.K. with me.*

xii. *The fact that enrollment is increasing is also a consideration.*

xiii. *Everybody likes to feel important.*

xiv. *I asked the children to pick up their toys.*

xv.   *My first attempt to grow garlic was a complete failure.*

xvi. *The bus to take is Number 17.*

xvii. *She went to the store to get some bread.*

xvii. *To open the door, please press this knob.*

xix. *What I want is for you to put on your coat.*

xx.   *For you to come home for Christmas would make your parents very happy.*

xxi. *They like living in New Hampshire.*

xxii. *The clothes hanging on the line should be dry by now.*

xxiii. *We caught Bill sneaking out the door.*

xxiv. *Everyone was surprised at Sue('s) taking such a strong stand.*

xxv. *Sue('s) taking such a strong stand surprised everyone.*

xxvi. *Living in an apartment on the beach, we could watch the sunrise over the ocean every morning.*

xxvii. *The window got broken in the storm.*

xxvii. *Driven to madness by her English grammar class, she had to spend the rest of her life in an asylum.*

xxix. *We have a lot to work to do.*

xxx. *The person we hire must be able to handle a lot of pressure.*

xxxi. *Although terribly discouraged, we refused to give up.*

xxxii. *Her heart in her mouth, she quietly turned the key.*

xxxiii. *With the engine on fire, he leapt out of the car.*

xxxiv. *My hands shaking, I reached towards the window.*

EXERCISE 10. Combine the sentences below, following the instructions given below each set of input sentences. Sentence-combining exercises are usually done without conscious attention to grammatical structure, as a way to practice forming longer, more complex sentences. However, because this is a course in English grammar I have asked you, in this exercise, to be aware of the grammatical structures you are creating. This first one is done for you as an example.

a. i.   *Tom called the chickens.*

   ii. *They came to him.*

   iii. *They squawked and flapped their wings.*

Change (i) into a *WH*-clause that acts as a sentential modifier. Change (iii) into an *ing*-clause that acts as a sentential modifier.

Answer: *When Tom called the chickens, they came to him, squawking and flapping their wings.*

   b. i.   *Rachel's supervisor walked into her cubicle.*
       ii. *She quickly turned off the computer game.*
       Change (i) into a *WH*-clause that acts as a sentential modifier.
   c. i.   *Rachel turned off the computer game.*
       ii. *She had been playing the computer game.*
       Change (ii) into an ordinary CP that modifies the noun *computer game.*
   d. i.   *Why did he chase the alligator in the first place?*
       ii. *I don't understand this.*
       Change (i) into a *WH*-clause that acts as the complement of the verb *understand.*
   e. i.   *Aunt Esmeralda leapt onto the coffee table.*
       ii. *She shrieked with fear.*
       Change (ii) into an *-ing* clause and attach it to (i) as a sentential modifier.
   f. i.   *Here is the house.*
       ii. *The murder occurred here.*
       Change (ii) into a WH-clause that modifies the noun *house.*
   g. i.   *Rodney the beaver was nestled safely in his lodge.*
       ii. *Rodney the beaver had no clue about this.*
       iii. *What would the impending spring bring?*
       Change (iii) into a *WH*-clause that acts as the complement of the preposition *about.*
       Change (i) into a passive participle that functions as a sentential modifier.
   h. i.   *Their quarrel was finished*
       ii. *Cecelia kissed Brad right in front of the whole crowd.*
       Change (i) into an absolute clause and attach it to (ii) as a sentential modifier.
   i. i.   *What makes these boots so dangerous?*
       ii. *It is this.*
       iii. *The soles are five inches thick.*
       Change (i) into a *WH*-clause that acts as the subject of the sentence. Change (iii) into an ordinary CP that functions as the complement of the verb *is.*
   j. i.   *Other topics for gossip ran out.*
       ii. *We returned to the subject of Joan's strange marriage.*
       Change (i) into a *WH*-clause that acts as a sentential modifier.
   k. i.   *Hedwig the woodchuck burrowed under the fence.*
       ii. *By this method, he gained access to the succulent snap peas.*
       Change (i) into an *ing*-clause that acts as the complement of the preposition *by.*
   l. i.   *He raced back to his computer.*
       ii. *He only found this.*
       iii. *He had forgotten all his wonderful ideas.*
       Change (iii) into an ordinary CP that functions as the complement of the verb *find.*
       Change (ii) into an infinitive that functions as a modifier of the verb *raced back.*
   m. i. *Someone might underestimate her capacity for mischief.*
       ii. *It would be a big mistake.*

Change (i) into an infinitive that functions as the subject of the sentence.

n. i.   *She had invented the story about alien abduction.*

  ii.   *The police were quite sure of this.*

Change (i) into an ordinary CP that acts as the complement of the adjective *sure*.

o. i.   *They were married.*

  ii.   *They told me so.*

  iii.   *What should I say?*

  iv.   *I had no idea.*

Change (i) into an ordinary CP that functions as the second complement of the verb *told*.

Change (ii) into a *WH*-clause that functions as a sentential modifier.

Change (iii) into a *WH*-clause that functions as the complement of the noun *idea*.

Exercise 11.

a. Draw a tree diagram of each sentence in the James Joyce passage in Appendix Section 1, showing the position and function of each subordinate clause. Do *not* show the internal structure of the subordinate clauses; use the triangle notation.

b. (For the very ambitious student) Do the same with the Toni Morrison passage.

12.4 The Semantics of Subordinate Clauses

12.4.1 Noun Clauses. Finite clauses in subject or complement position are traditionally called *noun clauses*. Like the sentences to which they correspond, noun clauses can be classified semantically as declarative, interrogative, exclamative, or imperative:

Declarative clauses represent statements, facts, or states of affairs. They have the subordinating conjunction *that* or Ø.

> *I can see* [*that you're o.k.*]
> *I'm glad* [Ø *you're o.k.*]
> [*That you're o.k.*] *is a great relief to me.*

Interrogative clauses represent questions. Interrogative clauses that correspond to *yes/no* questions begin with the subordinating conjunction *if* or *whether*.

> *She asked* [*if I was o.k.*]
> *His research addresses the question of* [*whether frogs have nightmares*].
> [*Whether frogs have nightmares*] *is the subject of his research.*

Interrogative clauses that correspond to *WH*-questions begin with *WH*-phrases.

We wondered [*what they would serve for dinner*].
[*What they would serve for dinner*] *was the question on all our minds.*

Exclamative clauses represent exclamations. Like independent exclamative sentences (section 10.6), they begin with *WH*-phrases:

See [*what a nice tree I drew*]!
Look [*how tall it is*]!

Imperative clauses represent commands or requirements. They are introduced by the subordinating conjunction *that*, and, like independent imperative sentences (section 10.7), they have no tense or agreement marker. Thus, the verb in the first example below is *be* (base form) rather than *are* (general present tense), and the verb in the second sentence is *arrive* (base form) rather than *arrives* (third person singular present tense).[5]

The university requires [*that all students be tattooed with their I.D. numbers*].
It is essential [*that everyone arrive by 8:00*].

12.4.2 Substantive Clauses. *WH* clauses in subject or complement position may designate *entities* (person, places, real or abstract things), rather than questions or exclamatives. Clauses of this type are called *substantive clauses.*

I'll talk to [*whoever answers the phone*].	(a person)
We liked [*what we saw*].	(a thing)
[*Whatever you decide*] *will be o.k. with me.*	(an abstract thing)
[*What you did*] *was disgraceful.*	(an abstract thing)
If you read the letter, you'll see [*what I mean*].	(an abstract thing)

12.4.3 Nonfinite Clauses in Subject and Complement Position. *Ing*-clauses, infinitives, and *WH*-infinitives can also be used as subjects or complements. *Ing*-clauses in these positions are traditionally called *gerunds*, but there is no special name for infinitives that function in this way. (They are just called *infinitives*.)

---

[5] This verb form is called the *mandative subjunctive*. (The adjective *mandative* is built from the root *mand*, which also appears in the words *mandatory* and *command*.) See section 10.7 for a discussion of the structure of independent imperative sentences.

231

Nonfinite clauses as subjects
[*Making mistakes*] *is how we learn.*
[*To err*] *is human.*
[*What to do next*] *was the question on all our minds.*

Nonfinite clauses as complements

We learn by [*making mistakes*].	(Complement of the preposition *by*)
I hate [*to make mistakes*].	(Complement of the verb *hate*)
We have no idea [*what to do next*].	(Complement of the noun *idea*)

Both *ing*-clauses and infinitives represent events or situations; however, *ing*-clauses represent real or likely events or situations, while infinitival clauses represent events or situations that are potential or imaginary.

Ing-clauses
We enjoy [*walking on the beach*].
Some people were surprised by [*the police arresting the driver*].
[*Swimming fifty laps*] *is good exercise.*

Infinitives
We would like [*to walk on the beach*].
Everybody was expecting [*the police to arrest the driver*].
[*To swim fifty laps*] *would be good exercise.*

WH-infinitives have an interrogative meaning:
We wondered [*what to do next*].
[*Which candidates to interview*] *will be decided by the committee.*
The committee will decide [*how to proceed*].
The committee will decide [*how quickly to proceed*].

12.4.4 Relative Clauses. Clauses that modify nouns are traditionally called *relative clauses* or *adjectival clauses*. Relative clauses are descriptive in meaning—they ascribe some property to the person, place, or thing that is named by the noun the clause modifies (the head noun).

What allows a clause to describe a noun is the fact that it contains a Ø (an empty space) that is identified with that noun. If the clause is a *WH*-clause, then this correspondence is established through the *WH*-phrase at the front of the clause: For instance, in the first example below, the *WH*-phrase is *which*, which corresponds to the head noun *informatio*n and to the Ø inside the CP. It is this chain of corresponding constituents that allows us to make the semantic connection between the clause and the head noun (*we sent for the information*).

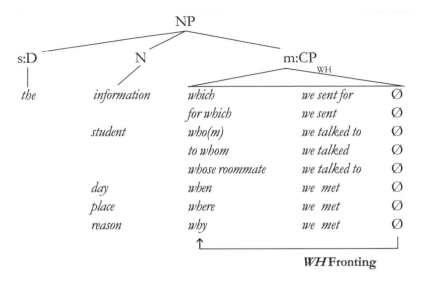

Relative clauses with no WH-phrase also have a Ø somewhere in the clause which corresponds to the noun that the clause modifies; for instance, in the first example below, the clause contains a Ø which we understand to mean *the information*.

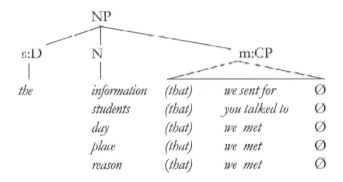

12.4.5 Nonfinite Clauses as Relative Clauses. Infinitives, *WH*-infinitives, *ing*-clauses, and passive participles can also serve as noun modifiers (relative clauses). Like the finite relative clauses of the preceding section, these clauses also contain a Ø which is identified with the noun that the clause is modifying:

WH-infinitive

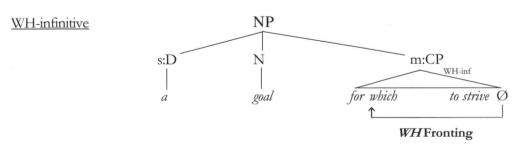

Infinitive

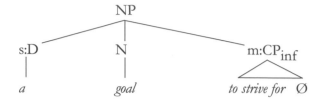

Ing-clause

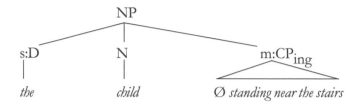

Passive participle

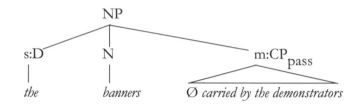

EXERCISE 12. Combine the sentences below by forming relative clauses as indicated. Put brackets around the relative clause *and* around the NP that contains the relative clause. The first one is done for you as an example.

a.   i.   *Sarah met her boyfriend in the dorm.*
    ii. *You lived in that dorm last year.*
    Change (ii) into a *WH*-clause (CP$_{WH}$) that modifies the noun *dorm*.
    Answer: *Sarah met her boyfriend in [the dorm [where you lived Ø last year]].*

b.   i.   *A person was crammed into the armchair.*
    ii. *The person was Madeline.*

    Change (i) into a passive participle (CP$_{pass}$) that modifies the noun *person*.

c.   i.   *When Raoul finished talking, Steve let out a loud cough.*
    ii. *It sounded oddly like "jerk."*
    Change (ii) into a *that*-clause (CP) that modifies the noun *cough*.

d.   i.   *He was remembering the glories of earlier days.*
    ii. *Then his back was not yet bent with the toil of the years.*
    Change (ii) to a CP$_{WH}$ that modifies the noun *days*.

e.   i.   *Jackie had sensed the terrible thing.*
    ii. *Her warning had been shrugged off as the ranting of a hysterical woman.*
    iii. *It was waiting out there in the darkness.*

Change (ii) into a CP$_{WH}$ that modifies the noun *Jackie*. Change (iii) into an *ing- clause* that modifies the noun *thing*.

f. i.   *Calvin went right ahead with his plan.*
    ii. *He didn't let common sense stand in his way.*
    iii. *He wasn't that sort of person.*

Change (ii) into an infinitival clause that modifies the noun *sort (of person)*.
Change (iii) into a *WH*-clause that modifies the noun *Calvin*

g. i.   *A broker can skin the bear market.*
    ii. *He trades this way.*
    iii. *We trade this way.*

Change (iii) into a *that*-clause that modifies the noun *way*.
Change (ii) into a WH-clause that modifiers the noun *broker*.

h. i.   *Here is a porch light.*
    ii. *Lovers can linger under it.*

Change (ii) into an infinitival clause (CP$_{inf}$) that modifies the noun *porch light*.

12.4.6 Relative Clause or Complement? As we have seen, a clause that follows a noun may be either a *modifier* (relative clause) or a *complement* of that noun:

a. *the belief* [*that the earth is flat*]	Complement of the noun *belief*
b. *the belief* [*that we defend most strongly*]	Modifier of the noun *belief* (= relative clause)
c. *an attempt* [*to climb Mount Everest*]	Complement of the noun *attempt*
d. *an attempt* [*to tell your children about*]	Modifier of the noun *attempt* (= relative clause)

Here's how to tell one from the other:

1. A noun plus complement is semantically similar to a verb plus complement. Thus (a) above corresponds in meaning to the VP *believe that the earth is flat* and (c) corresponds to the VP *attempted to climb Mount Everest*. There is no VP corresponding to (b) or (d): **believe that we defend most strongly*, **attempted to tell your children about*.

2. Finite relative clauses can begin with *that/Ø* or with *WH*-phrases. Thus, the relative clause of (b) can be changed to *the belief **which** we defend Ø most strongly*. Complements do not have this option: a noun requires a *that*-clause or a *WH*-clause as its complement and will not accept anything else. Thus, the complement of (a) cannot be changed to a *WH*-clause: **the belief **which** the earth is flat.*

EXERCISE 13.

a. Each of the sentences below contains a NP with a clause inside it. Put brackets around the NP and around the clause. Then identify the clause as a modifier (relative clause) or a complement and explain why. The first one is done for you as an example.

    i. *Her claim that she had been abducted by aliens met with some skepticism.*

    Answer: [*Her claim* [*that she had been abducted by aliens*]] *met with some skepticism.*

    The clause is a complement (1) because the NP is semantically similar to a VP: *claimed that she had been abducted by . . .* , and (2) because the subordinating conjunction *that* cannot be replaced by a *WH*-phrase: **her claim <u>which</u> she had been abducted . . . .*

    ii. *Sue reminded us of the fact that alcohol is addictive.*

    iii. *This is certainly a day to remember.*

    iv. *She made an enormous effort to remember.*

    v. *Students who fail to turn in their assignments on time will be shot.*

    vi. *We were disturbed at the suggestion that malingering students might be shot.*

b. Find the relative clauses in the literary passages in Appendix Section 1. *Hint:* There are two in the Toni Morrison passage, one in the Rachel Carson passage, three in the Samuel Eliot Morison passage, and five in the passage from Stephen Hawking. The Hawking passage also contains a finite clause acting as *complement* of a noun; find it. The Hemingway passage has no *finite* relative clauses, but it does have a CP$_{pass}$ functioning as a noun modifier; find it, also.

12.4.7 Clauses of Comparison and Degree. Both finite and non-finite clauses combine with intensifiers such as *so, too,* and *enough* to indicate *degree:*

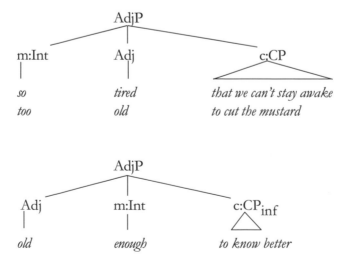

Note that the degree clause is a complement of the intensifier—if the intensifier were not present, then the clause could not be either: *tired that we can't stay awake* or *old to know better*. The intensifier also determines the *type* of clause; *so* requires a finite clause with the subordinating conjunction *that*; *too* and *enough* require infinitives.

The comparative elements *as*, *-er* and *-est* also take complements, traditionally called *comparative clauses*. The choice of subordinating conjunction (*than*, *that*, or *as*) depends on the comparative element: *as* takes an *as*-clause, *-er* takes a *than*-clause, and *-est* wants a clause beginning with *that* or Ø:

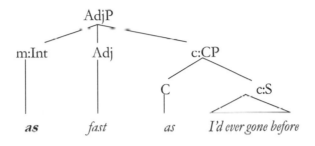

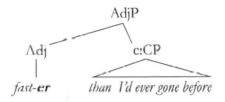

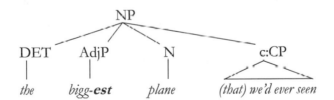

Clauses of comparison and degree are often *truncated*—that is, part of the clause is omitted. For example, the comparative clause *than you are* in the sentence below is truncated—short for (*than*) *you are smart*:

>   *Nobody is smarter* [*than you are*].

EXERCISE 14. Combine the following sentences, following the instructions given:

a. i. *A century ago, something so horrible happened in that house.*
    ii. *Nobody has dared to enter it since.*

Change (ii) to a degree clause that is the complement of the intensifier *so*.

b. i. *The story had been retold too many times.*

ii. *No one could be sure of the truth.*

Change (ii) to a degree clause and insert it into (i) as complement of the intensifier *too*. (Hint: You will have to change *no one* to *anyone*.)

c. i. *She would get them out before the water rose any higher.*

ii. *She knew he had to work quickly enough.*

Change (i) into a degree clause that acts as complement of the intensifier *enough*.

d. i. *Your dad can run fast.*

ii. *My dad can run just as fast.*

Change (i) into a truncated comparative clause and insert it into (ii) as complement of the intensifier *as*.

e. i. *This is the biggest house.*

ii. *I've never seen a bigger house.*

Change (ii) into a truncated comparative clause and insert it into (i) as complement of the superlative suffix *–est*. (*Hint*: You will have to change *never* to *ever*.)

12.4.8 Adverbial Clauses. Both finite and nonfinite clauses can function as sentential modifiers or modifiers of the verb. Clauses that function in either of these ways are called *adverbial clauses*. Adverbial clauses are traditionally divided into the semantic categories shown in table 12.4.

EXERCISE 15. Identify the adverbial clauses in the examples below, and classify each one as a clause of Circumstance, Concession, Condition, Manner, Place, Preference, Purpose, Reason, or Time.

a. *Because the fashion had changed from leopard skin to plaid, Marcia had to re-do her entire wardrobe.*

b. *When the fashion changed from leopard skin to plaid, she was left with a drawer full of unusable clothing.*

c. *The fashion having changed from leopard skin to plaid, she could no longer be seen in last year's outfits.*

d. *She raced to the mall to stock up on the latest fashions.*

e. *Decked from head to toe in the latest plaid patterns, she stepped proudly onto the crowded concourse.*

f. *You wouldn't need new clothing if you didn't go out in fashionable circles.*

g. *Never wear leopard-skin patterns where you know you will be judged for your knowledge of the latest fashions.*

h. *If the fashion changes again, you will have to extend the limit on your credit card.*

i. *Although the fashion had changed from leopard skin to plaid, we continued sporting last season's leopard-spot patterns.*

j. *Rather than purchase an entire new wardrobe, I dyed last season's coat in a stunning plaid pattern.*

Table 12.4 Semantic Categories of Adverbial Clauses

Circumstance	[*The weather having improved*], *we decided to go ahead.*
	[*Being a woman of ingenuity*], *Sue soon rigged a replacement sail.*
Concession	[*Although we hadn't eaten*], *we felt fine.*
	[*Old as he is*], *he's still more agile than you are.*
Condition	[*If you read the letter*], *you'll see what I mean.*
	[*Unless the weather improves*], *we won't be able to go.*
	[*Painted green*], *the shutters wouldn't look so bad.*
Hypothetical Condition	[*If you listened to me*], *you wouldn't make so many mistakes.*
Counterfactual Condition	[*If you had listened to me*], *you wouldn't have made this mistake.*
	[*Had you listened to me*], *you wouldn't have made this mistake.*
Manner	*Do* [*as I do*].
	Do it [*however you like*].
	[*Singing and carrying candles*], *they marched through the campus.*
Place	*They went* [*wherever they could find work*].
Preference	[*Rather than travel by air*], *I took the bus.*
Purpose	*I was hurrying* [*to catch the train*].
	[*To understand what I'm saying*], *you'll have to read the article.*
Reason	*I'm phoning you* [*because I have some rather disturbing news*].
Time	*Buy your ticket* [*as soon as you reach the station*].
	[*When he took off his hat*], *everybody was astonished.*
	[*Whenever you eat Chinese food*], *you always feel thirsty afterward.*
	[*Since you left*], *things have changed a lot.*
	[*After you left*], *things changed a lot.*

12.4.9 Dangling Participles. Because non-finite clauses often have empty subjects (Ø), the listener or reader must be able to identify the subject of a non-finite adverbial clause. *Ing*-clauses and passive participles whose Ø subjects cannot easily be identified are called *dangling participles*. To make the sentence maximally easy to understand, the Ø subject of an adverbial clause should be the same as the subject of the main clause. For example, the passive participle in the sentence below, cited by

Greenbaum1989, is a dangling participle because its Ø subject is not the same as the subject of the main clause (*they*):

[*When Ø delivered*], **they** *found the merchandise to be spoiled.*

The sentence will be much easier to follow if the main clause is reworded so that its subject is the same as the Ø subject of the participle:

[*When Ø delivered*], **the merchandise** *was found to be spoiled.*

Alternatively, the introductory clause could be recast as a finite clause with an overt subject:

[*When* **the merchandise** *was delivered*], *they found it to be spoiled.*

Although usage handbooks tend to concentrate on dangling participles, infinitives are subject to the same problem:

[*Ø To be sure the package will get there in time*], **express mail** *should be used.*
Clearer: [*Ø To be sure the package will get there in time*], **you** *should use express mail.*

Exercise 16. Re-write the sentences below so that the Ø subject can be identified more easily. *Hint*: The general rule is that the Ø subject of the non-finite clause should be the same as the subject of the main clause:

    i. [*Upon Ø getting home from work*], *the dog greeted us at the door.*
    ii. [*Ø Having finally graduated*], *his parents took him out to dinner.*
    iii. [*Upon Ø crossing the finish line*], *the race is over.*
    iv. [*Ø To assemble the apparatus correctly*], *a wrench or a pair of pliers will be needed.*
    v. [*Ø Fearing that it would spoil the children's teeth*], *the candy was kept locked away in a cupboard.*
    vi. [*Ø Originally located in Thompson Hall*], *the move to new office space will accommodate the program's growing staff.*

12.5 Coordination and Subordination: A Summary

In this chapter, we have considered the two devices by which simple sentences consisting of a subject, AUX, and VP are combined into longer, more complicated sentences. By the device of coordination, sentences or sentence parts are joined together with coordinating conjunctions such as *and*, *or*, and *but*. By the device of subordination, one sentence is converted into a dependent clause and inserted into another sentence as a subject, complement, or modifier. English speakers have seven types of subordinate clauses to choose from: ordinary finite clauses (CPs), *WH*-clauses, infinitives, *WH*-infinitives, present participles (*ing*-clauses), passive participles, and absolute clauses.

The extent to which simple sentences are combined into longer sentences and the particular devices that are used to combine them are an important part of a writer's style. The structures of four sentences from the literary passages of Appendix Section 1 are set out in figure 12.5. Sentence (1), from the Hemingway passage, is a compound sentence consisting of two simple sentences conjoined with *and*. The sentence is made more difficult to understand by the fact that the first of the conjoined sentences ends with a conjoined NP (*no shade and no trees*), causing the reader a moment's confusion in locating the boundary between the two sentences. Sentence (2), from the Joyce passage, begins and ends with an adverbial clause, with a very simple sentence (*dusk fell*) at its core. Sentence (3), from the Thomas passage, is a simple sentence beginning with the subject but ending with a long string of conjoined VPs. This sentence is heavily weighted toward the end, unlike the very balanced examples from Hemingway and Joyce. Finally, sentence (4), from the Hawking passage, begins and ends with an adverbial modifier. Like the Thomas sentence, it is weighted heavily towards the end, with a much longer and more complicated PP at the end of the sentence than at the beginning.

Of course, good writers employ a variety of sentence structures; sentence variety is one of the things we look for in a piece of writing. All the same, it is possible to make some generalizations about the structures that are characteristic of a particular writer, and discussions of a writer's style will normally include some observations of this kind.

EXERCISE 17. Choose three of the literary passages in Appendix Section 1, including at least one fiction and one nonfiction passage. To what extent does each author use co-ordination, and at what level? (In other words, does the author conjoin whole sentences or particular constituents within the sentence?) What kinds of subordinate clauses does the author use, and where are they placed? (For example, if there are adverbial clauses, are they placed at the beginning or the end of the sentence?) What is the stylistic effect of these choices? Can you make any generalizations about differences in sentence structure between fiction and nonfiction, or between two writers in the same genre?

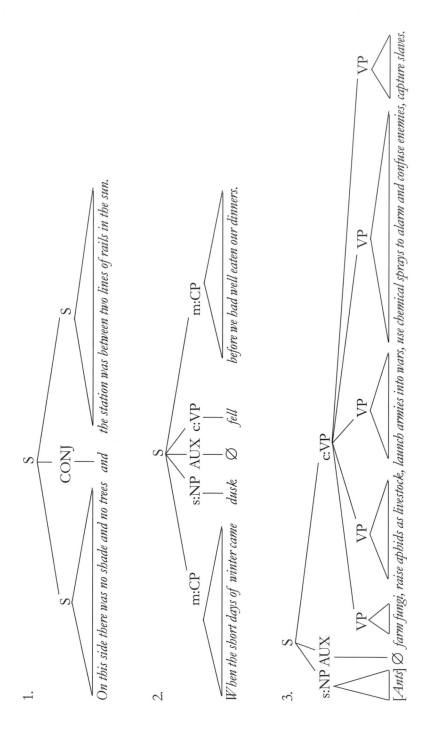

1.

```
            S
   ┌────────┴────────┐
   S       CONJ       S
   │        │         │
On this side there   and   the station was between two lines of rails in the sun.
was no shade and
no trees
```

2.

```
              S
   ┌──────┬────┬─────┬──────┐
 m:CP   s:NP  AUX  c:VP   m:CP
   │      │    │     │       │
When the  dusk  ∅   fell   before we had well
short days of                    eaten our dinners.
winter came
```

3.

```
              S
     ┌────────┴────────┐
  s:NP AUX           c:VP
    │   │    ┌────┬────┬────┬────┐
 [Ants] ∅   VP   VP   VP   VP   VP

   farm fungi, raise aphids as livestock, launch armies into wars, use chemical sprays to alarm and confuse enemies, capture slaves.
```

4.

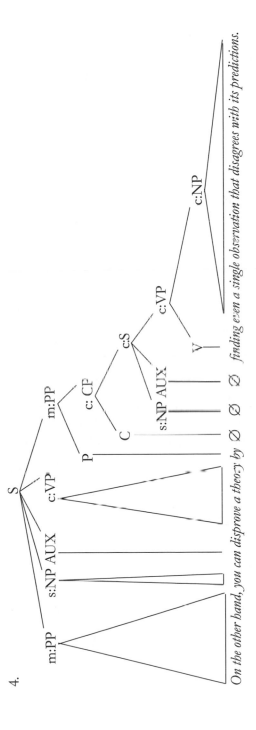

On the other hand, you can disprove a theory by ∅ ∅ ∅ finding even a single observation that disagrees with its predictions.

Figure 12.5 Some sentences from the literary passages in Appendix Section 1.

243

Table 12.5 Complementation Patterns for Verbs

The addition of clauses as complements for verbs gives us several new VP patterns. A complete list of VP patterns is given in this table. The second columns for patterns 12, 13, and 14 are left blank because these patterns have no traditional names.

Pattern	Traditional Name	Examples
1. VP │ V	Intransitive	They *laughed*. They *frowned*. They *sang*. They *left*.
2. VP │ ＼ V c:NP	Transitive: The complement is called the direct object.	I *closed the door*. We *enjoyed the movie* You have *made a mistake*. She is *singing a song*.
3. VP V c:NP c:NP	Ditransitive: The first c:NP is the indirect object; the second is the direct object.	Sue *gave Tom a kiss*. I will *make you a cup of tea*. The children *sang us a song*. Please *pass me the sugar*.
4. VP V c: {AdjP / NP$_{pred}$}	Linking: The AdjP or NP$_{pred}$ is a predicate complement that describes the subject of the clause.	He *is very tall*. She *seems worried*. You *look lovely*. She *became a famous writer*.
5. VP V c:NP c:{AdjP / NP$_{pred}$}	Complex transitive: The first complement is the direct object; the second is a predicate complement that describes the direct object.	We *found the news very disturbing*. I *consider him a friend*. We *elected Bush president*.
6. VP │ ＼ V c:PP	Prepositional	We *looked at the house*. We *listened to the crickets*. They *have decided on an answer*. We *agree with you*.

Table 12.5 Complementation Patterns for Verbs *(continued)*

	Pattern	Traditional Name	Examples
7.	VP V c:NP c:PP	Transitive prepositional	We *gave the books to the children.* They *blamed George for the accident.* We *loaded the wagon with hay.* Tell *us about your sister.*
8.	VP V c:CP	Clausal	I *think (that) you're right.* She *said (that) she'd go.* I *wonder if she's ready.* We don't *know whether she's coming.*
9.	VP V c:NP c:CP	Transitive clausal.	We *told Bill (that) you were here.* I'll *inform the president (that) you're here.* I *asked Sue if she was ready.*
10.	VP V c:CP$_{inf}$	Infinitival	We *tried to open the window.* We *wanted you to open the window.* Birds *like to eat worms.* We *expected it to rain.* We *saw him go.* ("bare" infinitive)
11.	VP V c:NP c:CP$_{inf}$	Transitive infinitival	Please *tell your brother to come in.* They *forced him to attend the meeting.* We *helped him (to) change the tire.*
12.	VP V c:CP$_{ing}$		I *enjoyed playing tennis.* I *like raking leaves.* *Try opening the window.*
13.	VP V c:NP c:CP$_{ing}$		They *have him bagging groceries.* We *found her painting the shutters.* We *heard Bill leaving the house.*
14.	VP V c:CP$_{pass}$		The glass *got broken.* We *had the windows repaired.* We *got the house painted.* They *found the village destroyed.*

CHAPTER 13
SEMICOLONS, COLONS, AND COMMAS

13.1 Semicolons

A semicolon [;] is used to connect two independent clauses that are not joined by a conjunction:[1]

> *There are many basements in the city that have dirt floors; these places are rat heavens.*
> *To get from one basement to another it tunnels under party walls; slum-clearance workers frequently uncover a network of rat tunnels that link all the tenements in a block.*

Be careful with connectives like *however* and *nevertheless*. Although these are *logical* connectives, they are not conjunctions. Clauses that are joined by connectives need a semicolon, as well:

> *It would have been possible to adjust Ptolemy's theory so as to account for the observed facts; however, Copernicus's theory was much simpler.*

> *Composition teachers often frown upon the passive voice as being "weaker" than the active; nevertheless, passives are very common in serious expository writing.*

13.2 Colons

A colon announces a list of examples or some other expansion of what has just been said:

> *Aristotle believed that everything was made out of four elements: earth, air, fire, and water.*
> *A physical theory is . . . only a hypothesis: you can never prove it.*[2]

Note that the sentence is already grammatically complete before the colon is added. A colon should not be placed in the middle of a clause:

> **The four basic elements in Aristotle's theory were: earth, air, fire, and water.*
> **The Indo-European language family includes languages such as: Russian, Hindi, Greek, French, and English.*

Instead, these sentences should be punctuated as follows:

---

[1]These examples are based on sentences from the Mitchell passage found in chapter 9, Exercise 13.
[2]From the Hawking passage found in Appendix Section 1.

The four basic elements in Aristotle's theory were earth, air, fire, and water.
The Indo-European language family includes languages such as Russian, Hindi, Greek,
    French, and English.

13.3 Commas

There are three uses of commas in English—conventional commas, series commas, and modifier commas:

1. Conventional commas. A comma is placed, by convention, in certain positions such as between the day and year in a date: *January 4, 1937* and between the name of a town and its state: *Portland, Oregon.* I will not attempt to list these comma positions here, but I would like to note one common error regarding the use of commas with quotations. A quoted utterance is set off by a comma:

Bill said, "Please pass the sugar."
"This is a most auspicious occasion," Sally oozed.

However, quoted words and phrases that are part of the normal structure of a sentence are not set off with commas. Thus, there is no comma before the quoted material in the following examples:

The word "accommodate" is spelled with two c's and two m's.
According to the article, the public schools of Portland now have "over a thousand ESL students from
    twenty seven different language backgrounds."
Exterminators believe that a high percentage of the fires that are classified as "of undetermined origin" are
    started by the brown rat (Mitchell).

2. Series commas. Commas are used to separate conjoined items or items in a series:

The room was filled with excited men, women, and children.	(Conjoined Ns)
It was a big, mean dog with ugly, pointed teeth.	(AdjPs in series)
The room was hot, noisy, and crowded.	(Conjoined AdjPs)
He pulled out his gun, pointed it at the intruder, and fired.	(Conjoined VPs)

Exceptions:
a. Items that cannot be separated by a pause in speech are not separated by commas in writing:

Near the old brick house was a big red barn.
(No comma between *old* and *brick* or between *big* and *red*.)

b. *Two* constituents that are joined with a coordinating conjunction (*and, or, but*) are normally not separated by a comma:

> *We ordered a hamburger and a coke.*   (Conjoined NPs)
> *The car turned down the street and into an alley.*   (Conjoined PPs)
> *The child was emaciated and very pale.*   (Conjoined AdjPs)
> *The plane landed on the runway and taxied to the terminal.*   (Conjoined VPs)
> *He called her but didn't leave his name.*   (Conjoined VPs)

However, *sentences* conjoined with *and* are separated by commas, even when there are only two:

> *I've never seen a purple cow, and I never hope to see one.*   (Conjoined sentences)

As before, if there would be no pause in pronunciation, there is no comma in writing:

> *Fish swim and birds fly.*

<u>3. Commas to Set Off Modifiers.</u> Modifiers (not subjects or complements) are set off by commas if they would be set off by pauses in speech. Note that modifier commas go in pairs; that is, there is a comma at each end of the modifier:[3]

a.

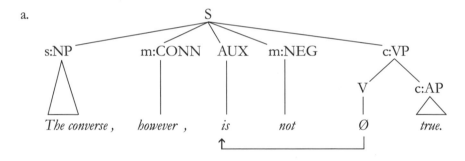

In the example above, the modifier *not* has no surrounding commas because it cannot be surrounded by pauses in speech. The same is true of the modifiers *physical* and *never* in the example below; however, the modifier *which are the basis of scientific reasoning*, which *is* pronounced with pauses, has a comma on either side:

b.

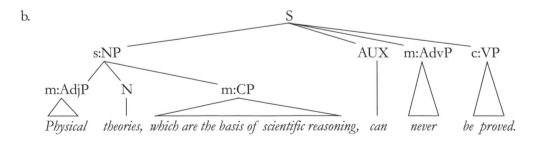

[3]Examples (a), (c), and (d) are based on examples from the Hawking passage found in Appendix Section 1.

If the modifier is at the edge of the sentence, as is the case with the first m:PP in (c) below, only one comma—the inside comma—will appear. The second m:PP in this example is not set off by commas because it would not have a pause before it in speech:

c.

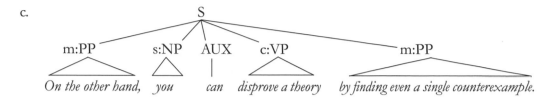

Example (d) illustrates a modifier set off by commas at the *end* of a sentence:

d.

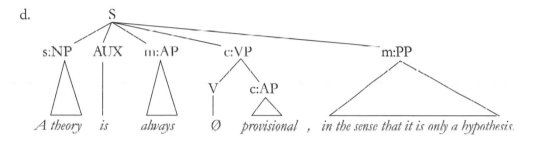

A pause by itself does not justify a comma. For example, sentence (e) below might well be spoken with a pause after the subject (s:NP), but subjects are never set off by commas:

e.

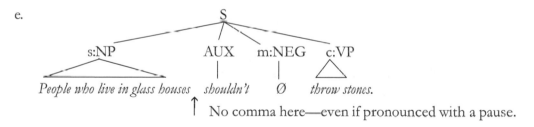

Similarly, in example (f), there might be a pause, in speech, before the c:CP, but a complement can never be set off by a comma:

f.

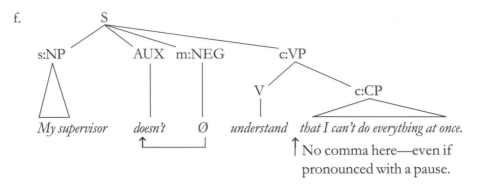

In other words, two conditions are required for a constituent to be set off with commas—the constituent must be a modifier, and it must be set off, in speech, with pauses.

EXERCISE 1. Decide where to put commas in the following sentences, and explain why. Remember that commas require a pause, but that subjects and complements are never set off by commas, even if pronounced with a pause.

    a.   *Jack and Jill went up the hill.*
    b.   *Jack Jill and Rudolph went up the hill.*
    c.   *We washed and dried the dishes.*
    d.   *We washed the dishes but didn't dry them.*
    e.   *Tomorrow I'll cry.*
    f.   *I'll cry tomorrow.*
    g.   *When the bell rang everybody stood up.*
    h.   *Everybody stood up when the bell rang.*
    i.   *Everybody came running although the bell had not yet rung.*
    j.   *The first person to complete the exercise will win the prize.*
    k.   *George Washington who was the first president of the United States wore false teeth.*
    l.   *Students who move into apartments off campus often need to buy a car.*
    m.   *Some of the parts unfortunately did not fit together.*
    n.   *Some of the parts really didn't fit together.*

EXERCISE 2. Punctuate the literary passages below, presented here with all their commas removed. Be able to explain the reason for each comma you put in. Then compare your punctuation with that of the originals (found in Appendix Section 1). Note that fiction writers are sometimes unconventional punctuators. (In expository writing, we are expected to follow the rules more closely.) If you find instances of unconventional punctuation, consider their effect. Is the punctuation effective as it is, or would it have been better if the author had been taken in hand by a stern copyeditor?

The hills across the valley of the Ebro were long and white. On this side there was no   1
shade and no trees and the station was between two lines of rails in the sun. Close against the   2
side of the station there was the warm shadow of the building and a curtain made of strings   3
of bamboo beads hung across the open door into the bar to keep out flies. The American and   4
the girl with him sat at a table in the shade outside the building. It was very hot and the   5
express from Barcelona would come in forty minutes. It stopped at this junction for two   6
minutes and went on to Madrid.   7

—Ernest Hemingway, "Hills Like White Elephants"

When the short days of winter came dusk fell before we had well eaten our dinners.   1
When we met in the street the houses had grown sombre. The space of sky above us was the   2
colour of ever-changing violet and towards it the lamps of the street lifted their feeble   3
lanterns. The cold air stung us and we played till our bodies glowed. Our shouts echoed in the   4
silent street.   5

—James Joyce, "Araby"

Nowhere in all the sea does life exist in such bewildering abundance as in the surface   1
waters. From the deck of a vessel you may look down hour after hour on the shimmering   2
discs of jellyfish their gently pulsating bells dotting the surface as far as you can see. Or one   3
day you may notice early in the morning that you are passing through a sea of microscopic   4
creatures each of which contains an orange pigment granule. At noon you are still moving   5
through red seas and when darkness falls the waters shine with an eerie glow from the   6
phosphorescent fires of yet more billions and trillions of these same creatures.   7

—Rachel Carson, *The Sea Around Us*

Ants are so much like human beings as to be an embarrassment. They farm fungi raise   1
aphids as livestock launch armies into wars use chemical sprays to alarm and confuse enemies   2
capture slaves. The families of weaver ants engage in child labor holding their larvae like   3
shuttles to spin out the thread that sews the leaves together for their fungus gardens. They   4
exchange information ceaselessly. They do everything but watch television.   5

—Lewis Thomas, *The Lives of a Cell*

EXERCISE 3. Now, try the passage that appeared in chapter 9, Exercise 13. Here you will need two semicolons, plus lots of commas.

The brown rat is distributed all over the five boroughs [of New York City]. It   1
customarily nests at or below street level—under floors in rubbishy basements and in bur-   2
rows. There are many brownstones and red-bricks as well as many commercial structures in   3
the city that have basements or sub-basements with dirt floors these places are rat heavens.   4

The brown rat can burrow into the hardest soil even tightly packed clay and it can tunnel   5

through the kind of cheap mortar that is made of sand and lime. To get from one basement   6

to another it tunnels under party walls slum-clearance workers frequently uncover a network   7

of rat tunnels that link all the tenements in a block. Like the magpie it steals and hoards   8

small gadgets and coins. In nest chambers in a system of tunnels under a Chelsea tenement   9

workers recently found an empty lipstick tube a religious medal a skate key a celluloid   10

teething ring a belt buckle a shoehorn a penny a dime and three quarters. Paper money is   11

sometimes found. When the Civic Repertory Theatre was torn down a nest constructed solely   12

of dollar bills seventeen in all was discovered in a burrow. Exterminators believe that a high   13

percentage of the fires that are classified as "of undetermined origin" are started by the   14

brown rat. It starts them chiefly by gnawing the insulation off electric wires causing short   15

circuits. It often uses highly inflammable material in building nests. The majority of the nests   16

in the neighborhood of a big garage for example will invariably be built of oily cotton rags.   17

—Joseph Mitchell, *The Rats on the Waterfront*

Chapter 14
Presenting Information

14.1 Introduction

Not *all* language is intended to communicate ideas and information. The language of a love letter, a pep rally, or a political speech may serve primarily to arouse emotion. And the language of ordinary conversation often has little purpose other than to establish or maintain social relationships. For example, when you greet an acquaintance by saying, "Hi! How are you?" you are not asking for a detailed account of her present situation, but only expressing a friendly interest, and when you go on to say, "Beautiful day, isn't it?" you are not telling her something she did not already know, but only prolonging the greeting a little so as not to seem abrupt. Language of this sort is called *phatic* communication.

Other uses of language *are* intended, at least partly, to convey ideas or information—to give directions, to make a report, to orient an employee to a new job, to tell a story, to bolster an argument, and so on. Such language is often planned in advance, sometimes very carefully and sometimes just by pausing for a moment to get one's thoughts together. In thinking through the presentation, the writer or speaker must make decisions about such questions as the following:

> a. *What are my main points and subpoints, and how can I make these salient to my listener or reader?*
> b. *What information should I include?*
> c. *In what order should I present my ideas and information?*
> d. *What internal organization should I provide in the form of sections and/or paragraphs?*
> e. *What can I do to make the presentation flow clearly from section to section and from sentence to sentence?*
> f. *How can I word each sentence so as to make my meaning as clear as possible?*

Some of these questions are properly the subject of a course in composition rather than one on the structure of English. We do, however, have something to say about those questions that concern the saliency of the topic, the flow of information from sentence to sentence, and the ordering of information within a sentence. These are the issues that will be dealt with in this chapter.

14.2 Coherence: Making It Clear What the Passage Is About

A passage is said to be *coherent* when its *topic* (what the passage is about) is easily identified and when each sentence of the passage relates in a clear and logical way to the development of that topic. In very straightforward passages, such as the selection from Lewis Thomas in Appendix Section 1, the topics of the individual sentences correspond closely to the overall topic of the passage, so that the reader can hardly be confused as to what the passage is about. The Thomas passage is repeated below, with the topics of the individual sentences highlighted in boldface:[1]

> *Ants are so much like human beings as to be an embarrassment. They farm fungi, raise aphids as livestock, launch armies into wars, use chemical sprays to alarm and confuse enemies, capture slaves. The families of weaver ants engage in child labor, holding their larvae like shuttles to spin out the thread that sews the leaves together for their fungus gardens. They exchange information ceaselessly. They do everything but watch television.*

More typically, as in the following example from Williams (1994, 124), the individual sentences and clauses have different topics, but these are few in number and can all be related to one overall theme—in this case, the identification of topics by a reader:

> **Topics** *are crucial to a reader because* **they** *focus attention on particular ideas toward the beginning of sentences and thereby notify readers what a whole passage is "about." If* **a sequence of topics** *seems coherent, then* **readers** *will feel* **they** *are moving through a paragraph from a cumulatively coherent point of view. But if* **topics** *shift randomly through the paragraph, then* **the reader** *has to begin each sentence out of context, from no coherent point of view. When* **that** *happens,* **the reader** *will feel dislocated, disoriented, out of focus.*

EXERCISE 1.

a. Underline the topic of each finite clause in the following passage, and then make a list of the topics you have underlined. Is the passage coherent, in your opinion, with a logical sequence of topics all related to one overall theme? *Note:* When the topic position is occupied by a pronoun such as *which* in line 3, then the topic of that clause is the referent of the pronoun; thus, along with the pronoun *which,* you should list the NP that the pronoun stands for.

> | | |
> |---|---:|
> | *E-mail derives its usefulness from the fact that users are able to choose which incoming* | 1 |
> | *messages to read and respond to. Unfortunately, e-mail is limited by its input and output* | 2 |
> | *devices, a keypad and a screen, which are cumbersome when large and hard to use when* | 3 |
> | *reduced to pocket size. Cell phones have the advantage of being significantly more compact.* | 4 |
> | *Also, spoken messages include intonational clues about the mood of the speaker and so forth,* | 5 |
> | *which are missing from written messages. Unfortunately, incoming calls are often disruptive,* | 6 |

---

[1] The topic of a sentence (what the sentence is about) is usually in subject position, as in the Thomas passage. Some exceptions are sentences such as the following, which have overtly specified topics:

> *As for* **dessert,** *I'm hoping you'll serve your famous Bananas Foster.*
> **Why she said that** *I can't imagine.*

and sentences such as the following, where the logical subject has been moved to a position following the verb:

> *There was* **an enormous vase** *on the table.*
> *It's obvious* **that you don't care for my Bananas Foster.**

> *and voice-mail services are inconvenient to use. What we will see in the future is a combina-*   7
> *tion of these two devices: Messages will be spoken and stored in a voice-mail system but will*   8
> *be displayed and retrieved in a fashion similar to e-mail, in a written list, accompanied by*   9
> *subject lines, so that the user can select which messages to respond to.*   10

    b. Find the string of topics in the Rachel Carson and Samuel Eliot Morison passages in Appendix Section 1, and evaluate the coherence of these passages.

    c. The Stephen Hawking passage from Appendix Section 1 is repeated below, with the string of topics identified in boldface:

> **A physical theory** *is always provisional, in the sense that* **it** *is only a hypothesis:*   1
> **you** *can never prove it. No matter how many times* **the results of experiments**   2
> *agree with some theory,* **you** *can never be sure that the next time the result will not*   3
> *contradict the theory. On the other hand,* **you** *can disprove a theory by finding even a single*   4
> *observation that disagrees with its predictions. As* **philosopher of science Karl**   5
> **Popper** *has emphasized,* **a good theory** *is characterized by the fact that* **it** *makes a*   6
> *number of predictions* **that** *[= the predictions] could in principle be disproved or falsified by*   7
> *observation. Each time* **new experiments** *are observed to agree with the predictions*   8
> **the theory** *survives, and* **our confidence in it** *is increased; but if ever* **a new**   9
> *observation is found to disagree,* **we** *have to abandon or modify the theory.*   10

Some readers have suggested that the coherence of this passage is weakened by the use of *you* (= the reader) as topic in some sentences, because the reader is not really a participant in these events and so is not easily related to the other topics. (i) Do you agree? (ii) Why do you think Hawking used this pronoun? What does he gain by this choice? (iii) Rewrite these sentences to eliminate the topic *you*. For example, the clause at the end of the first sentence could be rewritten as *it can never be proven*. Make a similar change to the clause in line 4. Change the *you* in line 3 to *we* (to match the *we* and *our* which appear as topics in other sentences). Is the passage improved or weakened by these changes, in your view?

14.3 Cohesion: Linking Sentences Together in Connected Discourse

Writers must also pay attention to the connections between sentences. A discourse is said to be *cohesive* when each sentence follows smoothly from the sentence that precedes it. This section will set out some strategies for creating cohesion between sentences.

Strategy 1. Begin each finite clause with information that has been mentioned in an immediately preceding clause or sentence. For example, here are two versions of the same statement—one active and one passive:

    1. *Christopher Columbus discovered America.*
    2. *America was discovered by Christopher Columbus.*

Either of these sentences can be inserted, as a subordinate clause, in the blank space in (3):

> 3. *Everything changed in 1492, when* _____.

Which version I should choose depends on what I have been talking about in previous sentences: If I have been talking about the history of European exploration in the fifteenth century, then I should choose version (1), which begins with Christopher Columbus, one of those explorers:

> 4.*Everything changed in 1492, when* **Christopher Columbus** *discovered America.*

But if I have been talking about the life of Native Americans on this continent, then I should choose version (2), which begins with *America*:

> 5. *Everything changed in 1492, when* **America** *was discovered by Christopher Columbus.*

To give another example, an adverbial modifier can be placed either at the beginning or the end of a sentence:

> 1. *Many of his customers stopped doing business with him* **when he introduced his environmental service fee.**
> 2. **When he introduced his environmental service fee**, *many of his customers stopped doing business with him.*

But in the blank position below, sentence (2) is the better choice, because it begins with information about Rubin's new concern for the environment, which has just been mentioned in the previous sentence:

> 3. Not everyone appreciated Rubin's new concern for the environment. _____

EXERCISE 2.

a. Here are two versions of the same proposition—one active and one passive (from Williams 1994, p. 116). Decide which version, the active or the passive, is more appropriate for the blank space in the following paragraph, and say why:

> i. *A black hole is created by the collapse of a dead star into a point perhaps no larger than a marble.*
> ii. *The collapse of a dead star into a point perhaps no larger than a marble creates a black hole.*
> *Some astonishing questions about the nature of the universe have been raised by scientists exploring black holes in space.* _____
> *So much matter compressed into so little volume changes the fabric of space around it in puzzling ways.*

b. Improve cohesion between the sentences of the following paragraphs by revising each sentence so that it begins with a topic that has been mentioned in an immediately preceding sentence:

    i. *In his address to the committee, Dr. Aaronsen posited that the single biggest influence on the evolution of human intelligence was a dramatic reduction in fertility rates. Diet, environment, or perhaps a virus caused this fertility reduction in pre-humans. Natural selection favored parents who were able to reproduce over a long period of time, because the offspring were born later and less frequently. Intelligence favored a long reproductive lifespan, because intelligent parents were more successful at finding food and avoiding predators. Parents could devote more time to each child, because they had fewer offspring to raise. Thus knowledge, as well as instinct, could be passed along to the children by the parents.*

    ii. *If possible, transport the computer in its original packaging. Computer manufacturers fit the packaging material to the individual computer. During your move, your computer will be held securely by this packaging. Ask the company for similar material if you have not kept the original packaging. Alternatively, you can simply toss the computer into a box, with cables and whatnot still connected, during those last few frantic moments before the moving van arrives.*

Strategy 2: Eliminate unnecessary repetition. For example, the passage below lacks cohesion because it contains repeated NPs:

> *Ireland was once a poverty-stricken nation. But today Ireland is experiencing a comeback, fueled in no small part by American companies. By the end of 1997, almost six hundred American companies had set up offices in Ireland. In 1999 American companies located in Ireland contributed about thirty-two billion dollars of the fifty billion dollars worth of goods and services exported from Ireland. Today Ireland is the fastest-growing nation in Europe, and American companies are reaping the benefits of Ireland's booming economy.*

The passage can be improved by deleting some of the repeated constituents or replacing them with proforms or other substitutes:

> *Ireland was once a poverty-stricken nation. But today its economy is experiencing a comeback, fueled in no small part by American companies. By the end of 1997, almost six hundred of them had set up offices there. In 1999 they contributed about thirty-two billion dollars of the fifty billion dollars worth of the goods and services the country exported. Today Ireland is the fastest-growing nation in Europe, and American companies are reaping the benefits of its booming economy.*

EXERCISE 3. Improve the cohesion of each passage by deleting unnecessarily repeated constituents or by replacing them with proforms or other substitutes. Repeated NPs and VPs are highlighted in the first example:

    a. *Stanley made mistakes just as everyone **makes mistakes**. Unlike other people, however,*

>   *Stanley never apologized for **his mistakes**. Instead, **Stanley** took out his broom, swept up **his mistakes**, and tossed **his mistakes** into the trash. **The mistakes** sat **in the trash** until Tuesday morning. **On Tuesday morning Stanley** took **the mistakes** out to the curb to be picked up by the garbage collector.*

>   b. *The name Rudyard Kipling brings to mind jungles, boarding schools, and English soldiers. That's why many Rudyard Kipling fans are surprised to learn that the only house Rudyard Kipling ever built is located in Brattleboro, Vermont. Rudyard Kipling's wife's family lived in Brattleboro, Vermont. Rudyard Kipling was so fond of the house, which Rudyard Kipling completed in 1893 and called Naulakha, that Rudyard Kipling apparently intended to live in the house for the rest of his life.*

>   c. *Before 1999, most investors looking for mutual funds that invested solely in Internet companies had little to choose from. In 1999, however, Internet mutual funds began proliferating rapidly. A total of nineteen new Internet mutual funds were born in 1999. By three weeks into January of 2000, four more Internet mutual funds had been delivered, and the storks were circling with another eight Internet mutual funds. This population explosion of Internet mutual funds was inspired by an Internet mutual fund that garnered returns of close to 200 percent in both 1998 and 1999.*

>   d. *Do not expose your Elvis Commemorative Plate no. 1367 to direct sunlight. Exposing the plate to direct sunlight will fade the lettering. Do not expose your Elvis Commemorative Plate to extreme temperature fluctuations. Exposing the plate to extreme temperature fluctuations may result in cracking. Wipe your Elvis Commemorative Plate no. 1367 regularly with a dry cloth. Wiping the plate with a dry cloth will discourage mildew. Mildew is caused by dampness. Wiping the plate with a dry cloth will also keep the surface dust free.*

Strategy 3. Use connectives such as *first, secondly, for example, for instance, furthermore, moreover, in addition, similarly, finally, in fact, therefore, as a result, of course, consequently, in other words, yet, however, in contrast, nevertheless,* and *on the other hand,* or evaluative expressions such as *fortunately, in the view of most observers, frankly, briefly put,* and so on. For example, consider the passage below, in which the connectives at the beginning of each sentence have been deleted:

>   *E-mail derives its usefulness from the user's ability to sort incoming messages and respond at will. E-mail is limited by its input and output devices, a keyboard and a screen, which are cumbersome when large and inconvenient when reduced to pocket size. Cell phones are significantly more compact. Spoken messages contain intonational information that cannot be obtained from a written message. Incoming calls are disruptive and voice-messaging devices are inconvenient to use. Spoken messages will be displayed and retrieved in a fashion similar to e-mail, in a written list that allows users to select which messages they wish to retrieve.*

Notice the improvement when connectives are added:

E-mail derives its usefulness from the user's ability to sort incoming messages and respond at will. **However**, *e-mail is limited by its input and output devices, a keyboard and a screen, which are cumbersome when large and inconvenient when reduced to pocket size.* **In contrast**, *cell phones are significantly more compact.* **Furthermore**, *spoken messages contain intonational information that cannot be obtained from a written message.* **Unfortunately**, *incoming calls are disruptive and voice-messaging devices are inconvenient to use.* **Possibly, in the future**, *spoken messages will be displayed and retrieved in a fashion similar to e-mail, in a written list that allows users to select which messages they wish to retrieve.*

EXERCISE 4. Improve the cohesion of the following paragraphs by inserting connectives or connective phrases:

   a. *This short quotation—insightful, amusing, and well written—gives you an idea what you can expect from the rest of the book. The first essay is a clunker. Apart from this one chapter, this is a five-star book.*

   b *The flowering herb Buddleia has many advantages. It is a delicious flavoring for fish. It provides a perfect foil for lavender and black fennel. Butterflies love its blooms. It is often called "butterfly bush."*

   c. *Verre églomisé is the technique of decorating glass by applying gold leaf. The artist etches designs into it. Layers of color are added. Varnish is applied. It's a painstaking process.*

   d. *Chicken makes solid nutritional sense. It is a good souce of protein. Poultry with the skin removed is low in fat. Red meat can be a bit fattier. Many people on a low-fat diet avoid it.*

Strategy 4. Use coordination and parallel structure. (By *parallel structure,* we mean that the second part of a conjoined structure or a series of sentences should mirror the structure of the first part). Consider the following example from Daiker, Kerek, and Morenberg 1982, 290-291:

> *For the Northerners, Lincoln was a hero because he ended slavery and saved the Union. But because he threatened to destroy one of the staples of their economy, Lincoln was regarded as a villain by Southerners.*

As pointed out by Daiker et al., this passage will be stronger if we adjust the second sentence in such a way as to make the two sentences parallel in structure:

> [1]*For the Northerners, Lincoln was a hero because he ended slavery and saved the Union, but* [2]*for Southerners he was a villain because he threatened to destroy one of the staples of their economy.*

EXERCISE 5. Improve the cohesion of the following passages by using coordination and parallel structure:

   a. *If possible, transport the computer in its original packaging. If you have not kept the packaging,*

> *your computer store may be able to supply similar materials. Or the computer can be tossed into a box, with cables and whatnot still connected, during the final frantic moments before the moving van arrives.*
>
> *Hint:* The first sentence is an imperative, while the second and third are declaratives. Make them all the same.

b. *Lao was responsible for transporting the general's servants. He was also responsible for transporting the general's concubines. He was also responsible for transporting the general's visitors. But, like most drivers of that era, he was also expected to keep track of the whereabouts of his charges and the conditions of their coming and going. His performance of these duties was such that he secured a prominent position in Qui's hierarchy of intrigue. But he also gained favor with those whose secrets he was paid to keep.*

c. *E-mail is limited by its input device, the keyboard. It is also limited by its output device, the screen. These are cumbersome at their normal size, and when they are reduced to pocket size they are hard to manipulate. Cellphones are significantly more compact. Unfortunately, incoming calls are disruptive, and cellphone manufacturers have yet to deliver a voice-messaging system that is convenient to use.*

14.4 The Ordering of Constituents in a Sentence

As we have seen in previous sections, concern for the flow of information in a passage often dictates which constituent should be placed at the beginning of a sentence or clause. However, the grammar of English is based on a fixed word order—*SUBJECT AUX VP*—that gives us little choice about which constituent comes first. Fortunately, English has several transformations—called *stylistic* transformations—which give the writer some flexibility.

14.4.1 Transformations That Move Long, Heavy Constituents to the End of the Sentence.

A heavy constituent in the middle of a sentence disrupts the flow of information and makes the sentence difficult or impossible to process. For example, consider the sentences below, all of which contain heavy constituents (enclosed by brackets):

    a. [*That everyone already knew what had happened*] *was obvious.*
    b. [*A Supreme Court ruling* [*that concerns racial preferences in university admissions*]] *has just come out.*
    c. [*A new book* [*on the same topic*]] *has just been published.*
    d. *We had checked* [*every window and door on the ground floor*] *very carefully.*

English has two transformations that move long, awkward constituents to the end of the sentence:

1. *Extraposition* shortens the subject of the sentence by moving a CP or PP out of subject position to the end of the sentence. If the moved constituent *is* the subject (not just part of it), then a "dummy" subject, *it,* is left behind as a place-holder (because English always has to have *something*

in subject position). But if the extraposed constituent is only part of the subject then nothing is left in its place. Extraposition can be used to improve sentences (a), (b), and (c) above:

a. [*That everyone already knew what had happened*] *was obvious.* → *It was obvious that everyone already knew what had happened.*

b. [*A Supreme Court ruling* [*that concerns racial preferences in university admissions*]] *has just come out.* → [*A Supreme Court ruling Ø*] *has just come out that concerns racial preferences in university admissions.*

c. [*A new book* [*on the same topic*]] *has just been published.* → [*A new book Ø*] *has just been published on the same topic.*

2. Heavy Complement Shift moves a long, heavy complement to the end of the sentence. This transformation can be used to improve sentence (d) above:

d. *We had checked* [*every window and door on the ground floor*] *very carefully* → *We had checked Ø very carefully every window and door on the ground floor.*[2]

EXERCISE 6.

a. Find an example of Extraposition in the Toni Morrison passage in Appendix Section 1. What would the sentence look like if Extraposition had not applied?

b. *Advanced.* Find three examples of Extraposition in the following passage from a short story by Henry James. Hint: In order to uncover the basic word order of these sentences, you may want to begin by removing the *parentheticals* that interrupt each sentence. *Parentheticals* are comments by the narrator that are inserted into the middle of the sentence, in adverbial positions; the frequent use of *parentheticals* is characteristic of James's style.

> *It was one of the secret opinions, such as we all have, of Peter Brench that his main success in life would have consisted in his never having committed himself about the work, as it was called, of his friend Morgan Mallow. This was a subject on which it was, to the best of his belief, impossible with veracity to quote him, and it was nowhere on record that he had, in the connexion, on any occasion and in any embarrassment, either lied or spoken the truth.*
>
> —Henry James, "The Tree of Knowledge"

c. *Advanced.* Find two examples of Heavy Complement Shift in the Rachel Carson passage in Appendix Section 1. *Hint:* Begin by locating each verb and trying to find its complement. In two clauses, the complement does not immediately follow its verb, but has been moved to the end of the sentence. Underline the complement and mark its underlying position with Ø.

---

[2]Notice that the complement can move *only* if it is heavy; for example, the complement *every window* cannot be moved to the end of the sentence below:

We had checked [*every window*] *very carefully.* → **We had checked Ø very carefully every window.*

14.4.2 Transformations that Move New Information Away from the Beginning of the Sentence. In general, a sentence should begin with information that orients the hearer or reader. That's why sentences so often begin with time and place adverbials: *Later, when they were at home, . . .* Another option is to begin with information that has already been mentioned in a previous sentence. English has two transformations that rearrange constituents when normal word order would violate this principle:

1. *There* Insertion moves a subject NP that introduces new information to the position following the main verb, leaving a dummy subject called "existential *there*" in its place. Existential *there* at the beginning of a sentence serves to warn the hearer or reader that new information is coming up:

> [*A smudge*] *is on your nose* → *There is a smudge on your nose.*
> [*A note*] *should have been attached to the paper* → *There should have been a note attached to the paper.*
> [*A day*] *came when the king could no longer govern his people.* → *There came a day when the king could no longer govern his people.*

Sometimes a locative complement is fronted, as well. This transformation is called *Locative Fronting*:

> [*A large mole*] *was* [*on her nose*]. → *On her nose there was a large mole.*

2. The Passive Transformation can be used to reverse the order of the subject and the direct object when the subject presents new information that needs to be moved away from the beginning of the sentence. For example, the active sentence in the example below can be converted to the passive form, as shown, so that *America* comes before *Christopher Columbus*:

> *Christopher Columbus discovered America.* → *America was discovered by Christopher Columbus.*

As we observed in section 14.3, the choice between these versions depends in part on which information is old and which is new: If I have been talking about European explorers, then *Christopher Columbus* is the old information and I should choose the active version, but if I have been talking about life on the American continent, then *America* is the old information and the passive version is the better choice.

EXERCISE 7.

a. Find examples of *there*-Insertion in the Hemingway and Lawrence passages in Appendix Section 1. (You will find two in the Hemingway passage and one in the Lawrence passage.) Then (i) return each *there*-sentence to "normal" order, with the logical subject of the sentence in first position, (ii) explain why the author found it necessary to apply *there*-Insertion, and (iii) note whether Locative-Fronting has occurred as well. If it has, indicate what the sentence would look like if the author had applied only *there*-Insertion and not Locative-Fronting.

b. Find four passive clauses in the Stephen Hawking passage in Appendix Section 1. (If you really work at it, you may be able to find five.) Then (i) rewrite the passage, changing the passive clauses to active, and (ii) decide which version—active or passive—is the better choice, and why.

14.4.3 Transformations that Place New, Interesting Information in a Position of Focus.

In *speech,* new information is focused by giving it heaviest stress. Heaviest stress normally falls on the rightmost piece of new information in an intonational phrase:

> *Noam Chomsky teaches linguistics at <u>MIT</u>.*   (Focus on *MIT.*)

But it can also be placed in other positions, as in the examples below:

> *Noam Chomsky teaches <u>linguistics</u> at MIT.*   (Focus on *linguistics*)
> *<u>Noam Chomsky</u> teaches linguistics at MIT.*   (Focus on *Noam Chomsky*)

Written language has no system for marking special stress;[3] instead, a constituent must be focused by moving it to a position where it receives the stress automatically. English has four transformations that can be used to move constituents to stressed positions:

<u>1. Clefting.</u> The constituent in the focal position of a cleft is automatically given *nuclear* (= heaviest) stress. By choosing which constituent to place in this position, the writer can determine which constituent will be stressed:

> *It's <u>Chomsky</u> who teaches linguistics at MIT.*
> *It's <u>at MIT</u> that Chomsky teaches linguistics.*

Read these sentences aloud and notice that nuclear stress falls automatically on the underlined constituent.

<u>2. Moving a Constituent to the End.</u> Because nuclear stress normally occurs on the final piece of new information, a constituent can be focused by moving it to the end of the sentence. Besides Extraposition and Heavy Constituent Shift, which we have already seen, there are two other transformations that move a constituent to the end of the sentence—*WH-Clefting* and *Subject-Complement Reversal:*

---

[3]Of course, it is possible to underline or italize a focused constituent, mimicking what we do in speech. But too much of this gives one's prose style a somewhat breathless feel.

WH-Clefting: *What Chomsky does at MIT is <u>teach linguistics.</u>*
                      (cf. normal word order: *Chomsky teaches linguistics at MIT.*)
Reversal: *Around the corner came <u>Bill</u>.*
                      (cf. normal word order: *Bill came around the corner*)

Read these sentences aloud and notice that nuclear stress automatically falls on the underlined constituent at the end of the sentence.

<u>3. Using Adverbials to Break the Sentence into Intonational Phrases.</u> The subject of the sentence can be given focus by placing an adverbial modifier or parenthetical phrase after it, forcing a pause at the end of the subject. Because the subject now falls at the end of an intonational phrase, it will receive a nuclear stress. In the examples below, intonational boundaries are marked with "/."

  a. *Rachel, / however, / can never be counted on.*
     (focus on *Rachel* and *counted on.*)
  b. *The Bushes, / you know, / have a ranch in Texas.*
     (focus on *the Bushes* and *Texas*)
  c. *P.T. Barnum, / that wily rascal, / knew that a sucker is born every minute.*
     (focus on *P.T. Barnum* and *every minute*)

Read these sentences aloud and notice (i) the pauses at the intonational boundaries, and (ii) the nuclear stress on the underlined constituent at the end of each intonational phrase.

EXERCISE 8. Find a post-subject adverbial modifier in the Hemingway passage in Appendix Section 1. What constituent is put into focus by the presence of the adverbial modifier? Would that focus be lost if the post-subject modifier were omitted?

<u>4. Topicalization.</u> The transformation of Topicalization focuses a constituent by moving it to the front of the sentence, to the subject-of-C position.

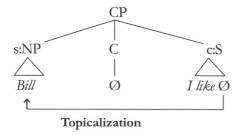

(but I don't think much of his brother Sam).

Topicalization of a negative constituent triggers Subject-AUX Inversion, as well:

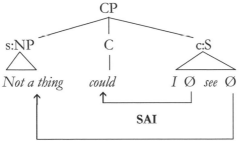

Topicalization

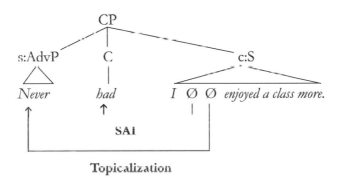

EXERCISE 9. Find instances of Topicalization in the Rachel Carson and James Joyce passages in Appendix Section 1. (You should be able to find one example in each passage.) Which sentence has undergone Subject-AUX Inversion as well as Topicalization, and why?

The transformations that have been introduced in this section allow flexibility in the ordering of information in the sentence. Such transformations are called *stylistic transformations*. A summary of the stylistic transformations of English is provided in table 14.4.

EXERCISE 10. [Summary exercise, adapted from Hudson (1992)] Begin by finding the long, heavy constituent that interferes with the processing of the following sentences. Then try the stylistic transformations—Extraposition, Heavy Complement Shift, *There* Insertion, Locative Fronting, Passive, Clefting, and WH-Clefting—and say, for each sentence, which transformations are possible and whether they help. (You may find it helpful to refer to table 14.4.)

i.   *A long noun phrase that contained two finite relative clauses was near the end of the paragraph.*

ii. *A long noun phrase that contained two finite relative clauses attracted my attention.*

iii. *We found a long noun phrase that contained two finite relative clauses near the end of the paragraph.*

Table 14.4 Stylistic Transformations

Extraposition   [*That you were upset*] *was obvious.* → *It was obvious* [*that you were upset*].

Heavy Complement Shift   *We checked* [*every window and door on the ground floor of the building*] *very carefully.* → *We checked* Ø *very carefully* [*every window and door on the ground floor of the building*].

***There* Insertion**   [*A mouse*] *is under your chair.* → *There is* [*a mouse*] *under your chair.*

Locative Fronting

With *There*-Insertion   [*A mouse with a long tail*] *was* [*under his chair*]. → [*Under his chair*], *there was* [*a mouse with a long tail*].

Without *There*-Insertion   [*A mouse with a long tail*] *was* [*under his chair*]. → [*Under his chair*] *was* [*a mouse with a long tail*].

Passive   [A boy wearing jeans and a red jacket] took [my bicycle]. → [*My bicycle*] *was taken by* [*a boy wearing jeans and a red jacket*].

Cleft   [*A boy wearing jeans and a red jacket*] *took* [*my bicycle*]. → It was [*a boy wearing jeans and a red jacket*] *that took* [*my bicycle*].

WH-Cleft   [*That you were upset*] *was disturbing.* → *What was disturbing was* [*that you were upset*].

14.5 Density of Information

There is an important difference between spoken English and written English in the density with which information is presented. In formal written English, especially academic writing, information is presented in as few words as possible. For example, consider the following sentence from Finegan (1999, 455).

> *In order for different dialects to develop into separate languages, groups of speakers must remain relatively isolated from one another, separated either by physical barriers such as impassable mountains and great bodies of water, or by social and political barriers such as those drawn along tribal, religious, racial or national boundaries.*

A sentence like this is characteristic of written expository English, not spoken English. In speech—even in a formal lecture—the information in this sentence would be parceled out more gradually, perhaps along the following lines.

> *We have already talked about the fact that languages contain variations called "dialects" that are spoken by different groups of people—sometimes because the groups live in different geographical areas like England and the United States, and sometimes because they occupy different social positions, such as working-class and middle-class Americans. Usually, these groups of people have some contact with one another, and they pick up vocabulary and habits of speech from each other, which keeps their speech from becoming too distinct. Consequently, even though they speak different dialects, they continue to be able to talk to one another. But if two groups become completely or almost completely separated over a long period of time, then their speech may become so different that they can no longer communicate. At this point, we would have to say that they speak different languages. This might occur because the two groups are separated by physical boundaries such as impassable mountains or a great body of water. In previous centuries, it was not easy for people to travel across barriers like these. Or it might be that the separation was caused by a political or social boundary—perhaps the two groups belong to hostile tribes or separate nations. Racial or religious boundaries can sometimes create a very sharp separation, as in northern India where adherents of the Hindu religion speak Hindi, but adherents of the Moslem religion speak Urdu.*

You may have noticed this difference between spoken and written English if you have attended a scholarly conference where some participants read their papers aloud. Papers delivered in this way can be very difficult to follow, and for this reason, conference presenters are sometimes advised to "tell" their papers rather than reading them. I have known inexperienced presenters who, lacking confidence in their ability to address a large audience without the support of a written text, have rewritten their papers in the looser, spoken style so that they could *read* their paper but still be understood.

EXERCISE 11. The various genres of written English—and individual writers within each genre—differ in the density of their prose. For example, information is usually presented at a more leisurely pace in stories or narratives than in expository writing; that's why stories can often be read aloud while expository pieces usually cannot. Which of the nonfiction pieces in Appendix Section 1 would you say presents information most/least densely? In answering this question, I would like you to rely simply on your intuition as you read through the passages.

14.5.1 Length of T-Unit. The intuitive notion *density of information* is a related to a more objective difference between spoken and written expository English, namely the length of the sentences. For example, Finegan's written text above contains one 51-word sentence, while my "spoken" translation contains nine sentences with an average of 26.5 words each. However, "words per sentence" may not be exactly the measure we want. In a series of studies sponsored by the National Council of Teachers of English during the 1960s, Kellogg Hunt found problems with simply counting words per sentence. First, the writing of children—as well s some adult prose—may contain idiosyncratic punctuation, so that it is difficult to decide what to count as a sentence. Secondly, it seems intuitively that a compound sentence such as Lawrence's *The morning's post had given the final tap to the family fortunes, and all was over* ought not to count as *more* dense than the two-sentence version, *The morning's post had given the final tap to the family fortunes. All was over.*

To solve this dilemma, Hunt introduced the notion of a *T-unit,* which is defined as one main clause plus any subordinate material that is attached to it or embedded within it. In other words, a T-unit is the smallest unit that *could* be punctuated as a sentence, using standard punctuation. To calculate the number of words per T-unit for a given piece of prose, you should first divide the passage into T-units. Then count the number of T-units and the number of words, and divide. By way of illustration, the T-unit counts for the Thomas and Morison passages from Appendix Section 1 are calculated below, where each T-unit is set out as a separate number:

From the Thomas Passage

Ants are so much like human beings as to be an embarrassment.	1
They farm fungi, raise aphids as livestock, launch armies into wars, use chemical sprays to alarm and confuse enemies, capture slaves.	2
The families of weaver ants engage in child labor, holding their larvae like shuttles to spin out the thread that sews the leaves together for their fungus gardens.	3
They exchange information ceaselessly.	4
They do everything but watch television.	5

From the Morrison Passage

Who discovered America?	1
Or rather, what European discovered America?	2
For we now admit that the people whom Columbus mistakenly named Indians came over from Asia via the Bering Strait, somewhere between 25,000 and 40,000 years ago, and, by the time	3

the Europeans arrived, had spread from Alaska to Tierra del Fuego and had developed several
hundred languages.

In three places at least—Peru, Mexico, and the highlands of Colombia—the Indians developed   4
highly sophisticated societies before Columbus landed;

and if the Spaniards had come a century later, they might have encountered a strong, defensible   5
Aztec empire that would have developed into a powerful nation, like Japan in Asia.

Each of these passages contains five T-units. The third T-unit in the Morison passage contains two *and*s, but the conjoined constituents are not complete sentences and so are counted as a single T-unit. The last sentence, in contrast, contains two T-units. Note that the *and* itself is counted as part of the second T-unit.

Since the Thomas passage contains 71 words, the average T-unit length for this passage is 14.2 (71 ÷ 5). The Morison passage contains a total of 108 words, yielding a T-unit length of 21.6 (108 ÷ 5). This difference corresponds to the intuition of most readers that the Morison passage is considerably *denser* than the Thomas passage. (Be careful not to equate *denser* with *better*; density may be good *or* bad, depending on the author's purposes in a particular piece of writing. T-unit length is simply one property that can be measured as we try to determine what distinguishes the language of one passage or writer from that of another passage or writer.)

EXERCISE 12. Determine the average T-unit length for the other passages in Appendix Section 1. How well does this measure correlate with your intuitive judgment about the density of information in these passages? Do your T-unit counts of the fiction and nonfiction passages in Appendix Section 1 correlate with my statement in Exercise 11 that information is usually presented at a more leisurely pace in stories or narratives than in expository writing?

14.5.2 What makes a T-Unit Long? As we have seen in previous chapters, a statement must contain three elements—Subject, AUX, and VP. But since the AUX can be silent (depending on the choice of tense, modality, and aspect), there are only two elements which must be present overtly—the subject and the VP. How many words the VP contains depends, in part, on the choice of the verb; a statement with the verb *shine* requires only two words, but one with the verb *put* requires at least four words, because *put* requires two complements—a NP and a locative phrase:

    a. *Stars shine.*
    b. *She put it here.*

Thus the length of a T-unit depends, to some extent, on the choice of tense and aspect (which determines whether there will be an overt auxiliary) and the choice of verb (which determines how many complements must be present in the VP). But these are very small differences. Much more important is the presence or absence of optional constituents—of adverbial modifiers that augment the basic subject-AUX-VP sequence, of adjectival modifiers that increase the length of the NPs, and of conjoined constituents below the level of the sentence.

Carson, in her selection, uses all these techniques to create a T-unit of twenty-four words with *shine* as the main verb—twenty-two more than our minimal example of (a.) above. (See figure 14.5 for a structural representation of Carson's sentence.) To the basic core of the sentence (*the waters shine*), she has added two adverbial modifiers—an adverbial clause at the beginning of the sentence (*When darkness falls*) and a long prepositional phrase at the end: *with an eerie glow from the phosphorescent fires of yet more billions and trillions of these same creatures.*

Although Carson uses coordination and adverbial modifiers to expand her sentences, her favorite technique is the use of adjectival modifiers to create long NPs such as the following:

> *such bewildering abundance*
> *the shimmering discs of jellyfish*
> *their gently pulsating bells*
> *a sea of microscopic creatures, each of which contains an orange pigment granule*
> *an orange pigment granule*
> *an eerie glow*
> *the phosphorescent fires of yet more billions and trillions of these same creatures*
> *yet more billions and trillions of these same creatures*

Other writers favor other devices. For example, Hawking uses mostly short, simple NPs:

> *a physical theory*
> *the sense*
> *a hypothesis*
> *how many times*
> *the results of experiments*
> *some theory*
> *the next time*
> *a single observation that disagrees with its predictions*
> etc.

But Hawking makes frequent use of sentential modifiers, some of them long:

> *in the sense that it is only a hypothesis*
> *no matter how many times the results of experiments agree with some theory*
> *never*
> *on the other hand*
> *in principle*

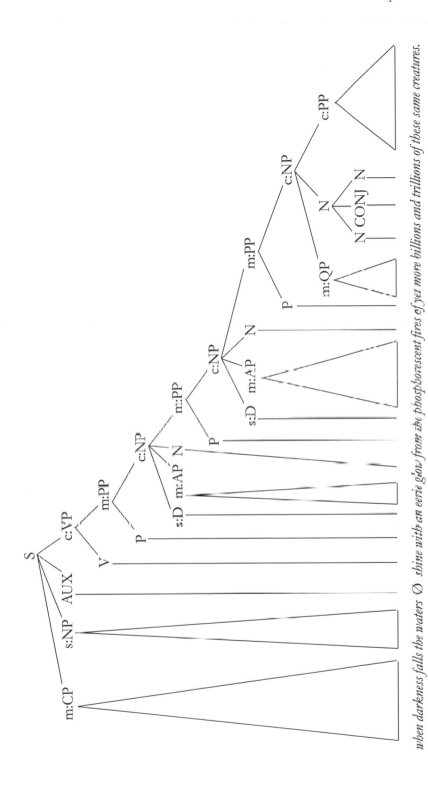

Figure 14.5 Expanding the T-Unit: An example from Rachel Carson.

> *by finding even a single observation that disagrees with its predictions*
> *as philosopher of science Karl Popper has emphasized*
> *each time new experiments are observed to agree with the predictions*
> *if ever a new observation is found to disagree*
> *at least*

Thomas uses one long NP:

> *the thread that sews the leaves together for their fungus gardens*

and two sentential modifiers:

> *ceaselessly holding their larvae like shuttles to spin out the thread that . . .*

But the primary device that lengthens his T-units is coordination:

> Conjoined VPs: *farm fungi, raise aphids as livestock, launch armies into wars, use chemical sprays to alarm and confuse enemies, capture slaves*
> Conjoined Vs: *alarm and confuse*

Again, there is nothing good or bad about the choice of one device over another; however, these preferences are an important part of a writer's style and help to determine the impact of a given piece of writing.

EXERCISE 13. Choose two other passages from Appendix Section 1 (not Carson, Hawking, or Thomas), and discuss the differences in their syntactic structure. Begin by calculating the T-unit length for the two passages, and then describe how this length is created: What devices does the writer use to elaborate the basic structure of the sentences?

Addendum: If the writer uses many adverbial modifiers, you might consider whether they tend to pile up at the beginning or end of the sentence. A sentence with a long adverbial modifier or modifiers at the beginning is called *periodic*:

> *Each time new experiments are observed to agree with the predictions, the theory survives.*

A sentence with adverbial modifiers piled up at the end is called *loose*:

> *A physical theory is always provisional, in the sense that it is only a hypothesis: you can never prove it.*

CHAPTER 15
THE ACQUISITION OF LANGUAGE BY CHILDREN

15.1 Introduction

Human beings are biologically adapted to use language; during the course or our evolutionary history, our vocal tracts, our hearing systems, and our brains have developed in such a way as to make us efficient learners and users of spoken language. Human children, from the very beginning, show their propensity for language. Except in cases of deafness or severe neurological disorders, children learn to speak and understand their language within a few short years; you could no more prevent a child from learning to speak than you could prevent her from learning to walk. Of course, deaf children require special assistance to learn spoken language, but, if given the opportunity, they develop a gestural language such as American Sign Language (ASL), which has all the properties of other human languages except sound. By the age of six or seven, both deaf and hearing children have a solid mastery of the grammar and pronunciation (or gestural system) of their language, and they have also mastered the vocabulary and conversational conventions of everyday communication.

In the first section of this chapter, we will trace the acquisition of spoken language by preschool children. The second section will consider the state of the child's language upon entering school—what do five- or six-year-old children know/not know about their language? The final section of the chapter will discuss the development of written language during the school years and beyond.

15.2 The Acquisition of Spoken Language

Newborn infants do not make speech sounds—their only vocal sound is crying—but they are fascinated by the human voice, and they are already able to make phonetic distinctions that will be important for speech. This has been shown by means of an apparatus that allows the infant to control an audiotape by sucking a nipple. If the same syllable is repeated over and over ([pa], [pa], [pa], . . .), the infant becomes bored and sucks weakly, but when a new syllable is introduced ([ba],[ba],[ba], . . .), the infant's interest is reawakened and it begins to suck more vigorously, thereby demonstrating its ability to distinguish between [p] and [b].

Somewhere around the age of three months, the baby begins making vowel-like noises, called *cooing,* and later, around six months, to *babble,* repeating syllables such as *ba-ba-ba* or *ma-ma-ma.* Babbling often shows intonational (pitch) patterns that are characteristic of the language the child is learning, but babies practice all sorts of consonant and vowel sounds—not just the sounds of the language that surrounds them. Babies have to be able to learn Navaho or Zulu as well as English!

15.2.1 First Words.[1] Children's first words, somewhere around their first birthday, may include names for family members, milk and other favorite foods, bathroom functions, and a few "action" words such as *up, down, out* and *bye-bye*. These words use consonant and vowel sounds that occur in the surrounding language; at this stage, the child is already beginning to suppress his ability to make consonant and vowel sounds that will not be needed in his mother tongue. Early words are often reduplicated (*mama, dada, peepee,* and so on). The *meanings* of the words may be over- or under-extended, as when the child says *milk* only for her bottle, not for milk in a glass, or embarrasses her mother by applying the word *daddy* to strange men she encounters in the grocery store.

The child adds new words gradually at first, and doting family members may be able to recite her entire vocabulary, but at some point around a year and a half, the child realizes that everything has a name and finds a way to ask for it: "Whassat?" "Whassat?" "Whassat?" From this point on, she is in control of her own language acquisition. Her vocabulary doubles and triples within a very short time, and, according to calculations by MIT psycholinguist Steven Pinker (1994), from this point until high school graduation, she will learn a new word approximately every ninety waking minutes.

15.2.2 The Beginnings of Syntax. At first, the child speaks only one word at a time, with that word constituting an entire utterance. This is called the *holophrastic* stage. But somewhere between one-and-a-half and two years of age, the child begins putting words together to form two-word utterances such as the following:

Child's Utterance	Situation
Baby chair	The baby is sitting on the chair.
Doggie bark	The dog is barking.
Ken water	Ken is drinking water.
Hit doggie	I hit the doggie.
Daddy hat	The hat belongs to Daddy.

Two-word utterances express basic semantic relationships such as **<patient>—<location>**, **<agent>—<action>**, **<agent>—<patient>**, **<action>—<patient>**, and **<possessor>—<possessed>**, but they do not necessarily follow adult sentence structure; children at this stage make utterances such as *More swing* (a request to be pushed in the swing) or *Allgone milk*, which are ungrammatical from the adult point of view.

15.2.3 The Telegraphic Stage. Adult syntax begins to show up at the next developmental stage —called the *telegraphic stage* because the content categories (noun, verb, adjective, etc.) are usually present, in the correct order, but inflections and function words are often missing, as in a telegram. Content categories now appear in the correct order and, insofar as these are present, with the correct inflection and functions words:

---

[1]The examples and discussion in sections 15.2.1–15.2.4 are based on Brown (1973).

Chair all broken.
Daddy like this book.
What her name?
Man ride bus today.
Car make noise.
Me wanna show Mommy.
I good boy.
Oh, drop a celery.
No Mommy read. (meaning "Don't read, Mommy.")
Write a pencil.
Kimmy ride bike.
Dolly go to bed now.

EXERCISE 1.

a. Look at the samples of children's speech in Appendix Section 6. Which of the three samples belongs to the telegraphic stage?

b. Children at this stage seem to be aware of the major grammatical categories—noun, verb, adjective, and adverb—and to know which word belongs to each category (though, of course, they could not *say* which category a word belongs to). Give specific evidence for this statement from the examples above.

c. Children in the telegraphic stage already show some understanding of the structure of S, NP, and VP. (i) Judging from the examples above, what do these children know about the structure of S? (ii) Children at this stage are already making NPs with two, or sometimes even three, words. Based on the examples above and the speech of Eve at twenty-seven months (Appendix Section 6), what do children at this stage know about the structure of NPs? (iii) Based on the sentences above and the speech of Eve at twenty-seven months, what VP patterns have children acquired at the telegraphic stage? What patterns have they not acquired? (To answer this question, you may need to review table 12.5 at the end of chapter 12.) (iv) Does Eve at twenty-seven months understand anything about the structure of PPs? If so, what does she know?

15.2.4 Moving Closer to the Adult System: Function Words and Inflection. During the next year, grammatical development takes place primarily on three fronts: (1) the introduction of function words and the inflectional systems for nouns, verbs, and adjectives; (2) the development of questions and negatives (which depends, in English, on the development of the auxiliary system), and (3) the fleshing out of the basic sentence patterns to include modifiers and subordinate clauses. The basic function words and inflectional forms are acquired in the following order (Brown 1973):

a. Present progressive (with or without auxiliary): *(is) playing, (was) singing*
b. Prepositions *in* and *on*
c. Regular plural: *toys, cats, dishes*
d. Some irregular past tense verbs: *came, fell, saw, hurt*
e. Possessive: *Daddy's, doggie's*
f. Uncontracted copula: *Here I am, Who is it?*
g. The articles *a* and *the*
h. Regular past tense: *played, washed, wanted*
i. Third person singular present tense: *sees, wants, washes*
j. Uncontracted auxiliary: *She isn't crying; he was eating.*
k. Contracted copula: *That's mine; What's that?*
l. Contracted auxiliary: *He's crying.*

EXERCISE 2. From the examples of Eve's speech at twenty-seven months (Appendix Section 6), which of these inflections and function words would you say she has/has not yet acquired? What about Julia at age three? *Caution:* As you look at the examples, you will find that children are not absolutely consistent in their development; thus some of the structures in this list may be used correctly in some utterances but not in others.

15.2.5 Pronouns. Young children are (understandably) confused by pronouns such as *I* and *you*, whose reference shifts according to the speaker. Thus, in their earliest utteramces, they often avoid these pronouns and refer to themselves and their listener by name:

> **Julia** *do it.*
> **Mommy** *read.*

For all pronouns, children may have difficulty with case inflection:

> **Her** *do it.*

EXERCISE 3. Judging from the samples in Appendix Section 6, what does the child Eve know about pronouns at age eighteen months and twenty-seven months?

15.2.6 Negatives.[2] From approximately eighteen to twenty-five months, many children form negatives by placing the word *no* at the beginning of the sentence:

> *No the sun shining.*
> *No dog bite you.*
> *No Fraser drink all tea.*

At the next stage (approximately twenty-six to forty-two months), the negative element is placed in the appropriate position inside the sentence, but often without an auxiliary:

> *I no singing song.*
> *Dog no bite you.*
> *We can't talk.*
> *I no want envelope.*

In the final stage, around the age of three or soon thereafter, the particles *not* and *n't* appear sentence-internally, with auxiliary verbs, as in adult speech:

> *I'm **not** singing a song.*
> *The sun isn't shining.*
> *It's **not** cold.*
> *I don't have a book.*

But children at this age still use *some* or *no* rather than the standard *any* inside a negative:

> *I haven't got **some** windows.*   or   *I haven't got **no** windows.*

EXERCISE 4. Describe the use of negatives in the samples from Eve and Julia in Appendix Section 6. What do these children know/not know about forming negative sentences in English?

15.2.7 Questions. In the first stage of development, children signal *yes-no* questions simply by raising the pitch of the voice:

> *See hole?*   *Ball go?*
> *I ride train?*   *Sit chair?*

---

[2]The examples and discussion in sections 15.2.6 and 15.2.7 are based on Klima and Bellugi (1966).

WH-questions are formed with WH-words correctly placed at the beginning of the sentence, but without Subject-AUX Inversion:

> *Where that?*
> *What me think?*
> *Why you smiling?*
> *Why not me drink it?*

As they acquire the auxiliaries, around the age of three, children begin forming *yes/no* questions with Subject-AUX Inversion:

> *Is this a box?*
> *Do it go this side?*
> *Can me put it in like that?*
> *Will you help me?*

However, they sometimes neglect to apply Subject-AUX Inversion in WH-questions:

> *What I did yesterday?*
> *Why kitty can't stand up?*
> *Where I should put it?*
> *Why you are smiling?*

EXERCISE 5. Describe the development of questions at age eighteen, twenty-seven, and thirty-six months, as evidenced by the samples in Appendix Section 6.

15.2.8[3] Passive Voice. Young children do not use passive voice, and even three- and four-year-olds typically misinterpret passive sentences such as the following, where the **\<patient\>** (the undergoer of the even) precedes the **\<agent\>**:

> *The truck was bumped by the car.*

They do better with sentences like the following, which has only one sensible meaning, with the girl as **\<agent\>** of the action:

---

[3] The examples and discussion in section 15.2.8 are based on diVilliers and deVilliers (1979, 76-79) and Perera (1984, 124-127).

The candy was eaten by the girl.

By the age of six, children make well-formed passives and generally understand passives correctly:

The Princess was caught.
All the good ones were alive except the one who was killled by Darth Veda.
My sister, she got cut on her finger by my scissors.

EXERCISE 6. From the samples in Appendix Section 6, what would you say about the development of passives at twenty-seven and thirty-six months?

15.2.9[4] Coordination. Children understand *and* by the age of two and a half and *but* between two and a half and four. However, young children sometimes fail to eliminate repeated material in coordinated sentences, as in the following examples from six-year-olds:

and then we count and then they count.
I done a garden and Chris and Alex done a garden, too.

EXERCISE 7. What conjunctions does Eve use at twenty-seven months? What categories does she conjoin? (NPs? VPs? Ss?) Does she show the tendency mentioned above to repeat material unnecessarily?

15.2.10 Subordination. Children use adverbial clauses, especially clauses of time, from an early age:

When Jack finish this, *Mommy have some.*   (26 months)

And by the time they enter school, they use a wide range of adverbial clauses beginning with *when, until, by the time that, after, before, whenever, every time that, while, because, so* and *if.*
    Clauses also appear early as complements of verbs:

---

[4] The examples and dicussion in sections 15.2.9–15.3 are based on Perera (1984, 105-144).

> *I want* **to take off my hat.**
> *I show you* **what I got.**
> *I think* **it's the wrong way.**

but clauses in subject position are later:

> **Whoever gets the most** *wins.*

Relative clauses (clauses that modify nouns) can be observed by the age of three or four:

I show you the thing **I got.**	(33 months)
Do you have the kind of orange juice **I like?**	(37 months)
There was this cat **called Fred.**	(4 years)
There was a princess **who lived in a golden palace.**	(6 years)

EXERCISE 8. Judging from the examples in Appendix Section 6, does Eve use subordinate clauses at age twenty-seven months? Give examples. What kinds of clauses does she use (adverbial clauses, complement clauses, clauses as subjects, relative clauses)? What about Julia at thirty-six months? Again, give examples and indicate what kinds of clauses she is using.

15.3 The Spoken Language of School-Age Children

By the time they enter school at the age of five or six, native-speaking children speak English that is barely distinguishable from that of the adults around them. One anomaly that remains is a tendency to regularize irregular verbs, using past tense forms such as *shooted, rided, runned, bringed, keeped, digged, comed, keeped, catched, builded,* and *blowed,* and perfect and passive participle forms such as the following:

> *They've* **get** *them.*
> *The airplane has just* **flew** *off.*
> *I haven't* **make** *mine yet.*   (6 yrs)

> *He'd been kidnapped and* **took tooken** *there.*
> *It's just* **drawed** *on the wall.*
> *He got* **blew up.**   (8 yrs)

Pronouns, also, are not quite adult-like. For example, children sometimes fail to move the particle of a phrasal verb to the right of a pronominal complement:

You pick up it. (cf. You pick up your toys.)
He beat up him. (cf. He beat up his younger brother.)

And they characteristically begin a conjoined NP with the object form of the first person pronoun:

*Sometimes **me and my mother** make a house.* (6 yrs)
***Me and Andrea and Jennifer** ... had to write something.* (8 yrs)
***Me and Gareth** will make the house and the garage.* (10 yrs)

Recent research has also exposed some gaps in children's *understanding* of English. For example, children up to the age of seven may think that John is angry in (1) below and not angry in (2).

1. *It is not true that John was angry.*
2. *Mary didn't know that John was angry.*

Similarly, they may not be able to say whether Mary's dress is new in the sentence

Mary's dress was neither new nor pretty.

And up to the age of eleven, children often do not understand that David, in the sentence below, was not really in trouble.

*David pretended **that he was in trouble.***

Children also have difficulty with some types of subordinate clauses. They may misunderstand hypothetical conditional clauses like (1) below, as opposed to (2).

1. *If you had some money, you could buy some.*
2. *If we don't hurry, we'll miss the show.*

And they have not mastered the subordinating conjunction *although*. Only two thirds of a group of eleven-year-olds could pick (1) as the "bad" sentence in the following pair:

1. *The meal was good although the pie was good.*
2. *The meal was good although the pie was bad.*

Nevertheless, despite these occasional deviancies from adult production and comprehension, the conversational English of five- and six-year-old children closely approximates that of the adults around them. Although their vocabulary is still limited, children of this age have full mastery of the sound system of the language and almost all of its syntactic structure.

15.4 The Development of Written Language

Except for cases of serious disability, children are universally successful in learning to speak, but the same is not true of reading and writing. Written language is much less natural to us than spoken language, requiring conscious teaching and learning, and not all children will succeed. Nevertheless, by the time they are five or six, most children are ready to read and write.

15.4.1 The Spelling System. The first task is the spelling system—that is, learning to recognize the letters of the alphabet and the sounds they represent when the spelling is regular. In many cases, the child is aided by knowing the *name* of the letter. Letters like *b, p, t,* and *j* have their sound at the beginning of their name ([pē], [bē], and so on), while for other letters the sound comes at the end of the name: *m, s, l, f* ([ĕm] , [ĕs], and so on). But some letter names do not contain the sound of the letter at all; the child has to simply memorize the sounds for *c, h, w, y* and for the digraphs *ch, sh,* and *th*.

Many children learn to read by a technique called *invented spelling*, which allows them to write words and phrases of their own choosing, sounding out the words as best they can with the knowledge they have. Having gained a foothold into the system by practicing in this way, they can then start to read simple stories and begin to recognize some words in print. This experience, in turn, helps their spelling, because their memory of how the words *look* will help them to learn irregular words such as *the, would, have, one, two,* and so on and will assist them in mastering the more intricate details of the regular system, such as the use of double consonants or of the silent *e* to indicate whether a vowel is long or short.

When they first begin to write words, children concentrate mainly on the consonants, usually the initial and final consonants, like Student 9 in figure 4.9, who spells *camp* as *kp* and *tack* as *tk*. The vowels come later, and details such as the use of the silent *e* and the spelling of [kw] as *qu* are later still.

EXERCISE 9. Return to figure 4.9 in chapter 4, which lists the invented spellings of a group of first graders for the words *camp, zero, hill, tack, five, pickle, muffin, wife, job,* and *quick*. Pick out four of the children who appear to be at different stages in their acquisition of the spelling system. Briefly discuss what each child knows/does not know about the English spelling system. Which children are already fluent readers, and how do you know?

The first-grade author of the story "Mafin," repeated below from Appendix Section 2, has mastered enough of the spelling system to compose simple stories, though she still omits or transposes some letters, especially in irregular words:

Mafin

I hvie a cat. It is named mafin. When my mom washsi mafin. he scashed my mom and it hse (hurts) a lot. My mom gis mad at mafin, and he gis madr at my mom.

This child is also aware of words and sentences. She knows that words should be separated by spaces[5] and that sentences begin with a capital letter and end with a period.

EXERCISE 10. Consider the other first- and second-grade writers in Appendix Section 2 and say what each writer seems to have learned or not learned about spelling and punctuation in English. *Caution:* Remember that these essays have been edited with the help of the teacher; thus they are not completely accurate indicators of the children's own knowledge. If you can obtain samples of unedited writing by first- and second-grade writers, those will be an even better source of data for this exercise.

15.4.2 The Vocabulary and Syntax of Written English.[6] As they gradually master the spelling system, children also begin to acquire some of the vocabulary and sentence constructions of written English. At first, children write very much as they speak. But the first-grade author of "Meanie" (Appendix Section 2) uses the Latinate word *magical*, which he probably learned from a story rather than from conversation, and he begins his story with the written-English expression *once upon a time.* A first-grade teacher of my acquaintance told me that she encourages this development in her children by telling them, "Oh, that's wonderful. It sounds just like a book!"

EXERCISE 11. Look through the writing samples in Appendix Section 2 and find other examples of Latinate vocabulary and grammatical constructions or other expressions that are characteristic of written English rather than conversational English. Does the use of written English constructions increase as children grow older?

A difficult problem for all writers, but especially for young children, is to keep in mind what the reader does and does not know, so that background information can be provided when necessary. In the words of de Villiers and de Villiers (1979, 89):

> *[A] difficult lesson that the child learns over the first ten or more years of life is that others do not have the same privileged access that he does to his thoughts and past experience, and that to be skillful in [the use of language] he must share that knowledge explicitly.*

---

[5] Children who are unable to control spacing consistently in their writing sometimes resort to other devices. For example, I have seen children who carefully inserted hyphens or periods at the boundaries between words.

[6] Except where otherwise indicated, the examples and discussion in this section are based on Perera (1984, 103-105).

One consequence of this difficulty is that children up to age ten or so often fail to establish clear references for NPs. They tend to overuse definite NPs, which *should* be employed only when the referent of the NP is known to both the writer and the audience. Warden (1976) asked children to tell the following story, based on a series of pictures, to a partner sitting on the other side of a screen:

> *A dog is chasing a hen. A cow stops the dog. The hen is hiding behind the cow. The hen has laid an egg.*

Children up to eight years old were likely to say "A dog is chasing *the* hen" even though the partner had been told nothing about the hen. Fawcett and Perkins (1980) found similar errors in children aged eight years old when they were asked to describe the rules of a game to another child:

> Interviewer: *What's Cross Fire?*
> Child: *See, you got a gun and then there's all these. . . marbles on **it** . . . and then you try to get **the one with the blue ring around it** into the box.*
> Interviewer: *What's Willy Wheelers?*
> Child: *It's a game you put some batteries in and you turn **the dial** for **the lap** and little men on motor cycles pedal round.*

Pronouns are a special case. Commenting on children's use of pronouns, Piaget (1926, 102) states that

> *Pronouns . . . are used right and left without any indication of what they refer to. The other person is supposed to understand.*

Fawcett and Perkins (1980) provide some examples:

> Child: *Somebody was going to kill one of the Charlie's Angels, but **it** hit the tire of the Charlie's Angels' car.* (6 yrs)

> Interviewer: *How d'you play chess?*
> Child: *You've got to line **em** up, right?* (8 yrs)

> Interviewer: *How do you play Mouse Trap?*
> Child: *Well you . . . you pick up cards, and you just (um) you carry on from where **it** is.* (12 yrs)

EXERCISE 13. Find inappropriate uses of pronouns and other definite NPs in the following selections from Appendix Section 2: "My Nightmare," "My Favorite Puppy," "My Most Admired Person," and "My Bicycle Ride."

Consistency of tense is another troublesome requirement of written English. As their stories become longer and more complicated, the children find it difficult to hold steadily to past or present tense. For example, the third-grade writer of "My Dog and Me" starts out in past tense, but switches inappropriately to present:

> *One day my dog and me were playing pass. His name is K.C. He likes to play pass with my football. He lives at my grandmother's house. She has a big yard we play in. K.C. is an awesome catcher. He is cute, fluffy and very loveable. He is a good dog and he is a fun dog to be with.*

EXERCISE 14. Find inappropriate changes of tense in the following selections from Appendix Section 2: "My Favorite Puppy," "The Mouse with Tiny Feet," "My Bicycle Ride," and "Respect—What It Means to Me."

15.4.3 The Structure of Sentences. Young children have difficulty identifying the boundaries of sentences. Thus, for example, the first-grade author of "Mafin" punctuates the adverbial clause *When my mom washi mafin* as a complete sentence, and the author of "Meanie" writes two sentences together as one:

> *Once upon a time there was a boy he was mene.*

EXERCISE 15.
a. Find an incomplete sentence (a *fragment*) in "The Seal and the Fish," Appendix Section 2.
b. Find instances of run-on sentences (two sentences written together as one) in the following selections from Appendix Section 2: "The Seal and the Fish," "Your Own Monster" (two examples), "The Mouse With Tiney Feet," and "Respect—What It Means to Me."

In their writing, as in their speech, children rely very heavily on conjoined sentences, often joining sentences that have no logical connection, as in the following sentence from "My Nightmare":

> [*They put me in a space* jail] *but* [*I had a good idea*] *and* [*all I had to do is get that space gun*].

In a study by Rosenberg and Koplin (1968), children and adults were asked to combine simple sentences. The youngest children characteristically coordinated the sentences: *I have a coat and it is red,* but the adults and older children used modification: *I have a red coat.* Kellogg Hunt (1970) found that fourth-graders use conjoined sentences (almost always with the conjunction *and*) three times more frequently than eighth-graders and four times more frequently than twelfth-graders. Furthermore, when they conjoin sentences, children often repeat material that an older writer would not. For example, when asked to combine the following two sentences

> *Bauxite contains aluminum. It contains several other substances.*

fourth-graders tended to write

> *Bauxite contains aluminum and it contains several other substances.*

while twelfth-graders tended to write

> *Bauxite contains aluminum and several other substances.*

EXERCISE 16. Find instances of the overuse of conjoined sentences in the examples of children's writing in Appendix Section 2. Also note instances of unnecessarily repeated words in conjoined sentences.

15.4.4 The Complexity of Sentences. As writers mature and become more skilled, they begin to consolidate their sentences and include more information in each clause. Kellogg Hunt (1965, 1970) developed a measure of syntactic maturity called *words per T-unit*, which we discussed in chapter 14, Ssctions 14.5.1 and 14.5.2. Hunt defines a T-unit as one main clause plus any material that is attached to it or embedded within it; in other words, it is the smallest unit that could be punctuated as a sentence, using standard punctuation. Thus the input sentences

> *Bauxite contains aluminum. It contains several other substances.*

and the fourth-grade rewrite

> *Bauxite contains aluminum and it contains several other substances.*

both contain two T-units. In the fourth-grade rewrite, the first T-unit contains three words and the second (which includes the *and*) contains six. However, as we noted above, twelfth-graders typically rewrote the two sentences using just one T-unit with seven words:

> *Bauxite contains aluminum and several other substances.*

Because older, more mature writers tend to consolidate information in this way, their T-units are longer. In his study of fourth-, eighth-, and twelfth-graders at the Florida State University School, Hunt (1965) found that T-unit scores correlated closely with grade level, as shown in table 15.4.

Table 15.4a Grade Level and T-Unit Scores

Grade level	Average length of T-units
Grade 4	8.6
Grade 8	11.5
Grade 12	14.4

Hunt (1970) later extended this study to a set of eighteen "superior" adult writers who had published articles in the January, February, and March issues of *Harper's Magazine* and *Atlantic* magazines. In the first one thousand words of each article, Hunt found an average of 20.4 words per T-unit.

EXERCISE 17.

a. Choose one first-grade writer, one second-grade writer, and so forth, from the examples in Appendix Section 2. Use the following procedure to calculate a T-unit score for each writer: First, count the number of words in the piece. Then, count the number of T-units. Divide the number of words by the number of T-units to obtain the T-unit score. Does the T-unit score increase as the children grow older? How does your fourth-grade sample compare with Hunt's average for fourth graders?

b. What are the children in your sample doing to increase their T-unit scores as they grow older? In accordance with our discussion of chapter 14, section 14.5.2, look especially for coordination below the sentence level, for the presence of adverbial modifiers, and for the addition of modifiers to NPs.

c. If you or one of your doting parents or grandparents have saved samples of your writing throughout the school years, use these samples to trace the average length of your T-units from your early school years to the present. How does your progress compare with that of Hunt's subjects?

In chapter 14, section 14.5.1, we observed differences in the T-unit scores of adult writers depending on *genre* (the expository pieces tended to have longer T-units than the narratives) and on the writers' individual stylistic choices. This observation raises a question about the results of Hunt (1965): Do the longer T-unit scores of older writers indicate a greater ability to use complex syntactic structures to consolidate information in writing, or do they simply reflect a difference in *genre* and subject matter? Maybe older writers write longer T-units not because they have greater control over the syntactic structures of written English, but because they are dealing with more difficult, more abstract subject matter.

To address this question, Hunt (1970) conducted a follow-up study in which writers of various ages and levels of experience were all given the same task—to rewrite a passage written in extremely short sentences. The passage and the directions for the exercise are set out as follows.

Aluminum

Directions: Read the passage all the way through. You will notice that the sentences are short and choppy. Study the passage, and then rewrite it in a better way. You may combine sentences, change the order of words, and omit words that are repeated too many times. But try not to leave out any of the information.

Aluminum is a metal. It is abundant. It has many uses. It comes from bauxite. Bauxite is an ore. Bauxite looks like clay. Bauxite contains aluminum. It contains several other substances. Workmen extract these other substances from the bauxite. They grind the bauxite. They put it in tanks. Pressure is in the tanks. The other substances form a mass. They remove the mass. They use filters. A liquid remains. They put it through several other processes. It finally yields a chemical. The chemical is powdery. It is white. It is alumina. It is a mixture. It contains aluminum. It contains oxygen. Workmen separate the aluminum from the oxygen. They use electricity. They finally produce a metal. The metal is light. It has a luster. The luster is bright. The luster is silvery. This metal comes in many forms.

EXERCISE 18. Before reading any further, *stop right here* and do Hunt's exercise yourself. Take plenty of time: the children were allowed a whole hour. When you have finished, calculate your T-score, using the procedure described in Exercise 17a.

The results of this follow-up study again showed a steady increase in T-unit length as the children advanced in ages and maturity, though the number of words per T-unit was not as great in this artificial exercise as in the children's free writing. Hunt's (1970) results are listed in table 15.4b.

Table 15.4b T-Unit Results from "Aluminum" Experiment

Grade Level	Average Number of Words per T-Unit
Grade 4	5.42
Grade 6	6.84
Grade 8	9.84
Grade 10	10.44
Grade 12	11.30

To see whether adult writers continue to increase the length of their T-units after they leave school, Hunt tested a group of twenty-five Tallahassee firemen, average age 32, who had completed twelfth grade but who had not attended college. Although their occupation does not require extensive daily reading or writing, they showed a slight improvement over the twelfth-graders, with a T-unit score of 11.85. To obtain a sample of "superior" writers, Hunt sent the "Aluminum" exercise to ninety-five authors who had recently published nonfiction articles in *Harper's Magazine* and the *Atlantic.* For the twenty-five writers who completed the exercise, the average T-unit score was 14.8. Apparently, then, the density of information in written English as measured by counting words per T-unit is a characteristic that continues to develop as we become more experienced as readers and writers. Furthermore, this growth apparently does not stop when we finish school, but continues to develop for writers who continue to hone their skills. Keep in mind, however, that even for skilled, mature writers, the number of words per T-unit varies considerably, depending on *genre* (see chapter 14, section 14.5.1) and depending on the task the writer is given (*cf.* the differences in results for free writing *vs.* rewriting of the "Aluminum" passage, as cited in this section). Clearly there is more to sophisticated writing than simply the length of our T-units!

EXERCISE 19. Calculate the average T-unit length in your own writing sample from Appendix Section 3, using the procedure described in Exercise 17a. If you have included samples of both expository and narrative writing, do this analysis for both samples and describe the differences you find. Include some discussion of the techniques you characteristically use to lengthen your T-units (e.g., coordination below the sentence level, use of adverbial modifiers, and the use of modifiers to increase the length of NPs).

APPENDIX

SAMPLES FOR ANALYSIS

Section 1.
Literary Passages: Narrative

The hills across the valley of the Ebro were long and white. On this side there was no shade and no — 1
trees and the station was between two lines of rails in the sun. Close against the side of the station there was — 2
the warm shadow of the building, and a curtain, made of strings of bamboo beads, hung across the open — 3
door into the bar, to keep out flies. The American and the girl with him sat at a table in the shade, outside — 4
the building. It was very hot and the express from Barcelona would come in forty minutes. It stopped at this — 5
junction for two minutes and went on to Madrid. — 6

—Ernest Hemingway, "Hills Like White Elephants"[1]

The three brothers and the sister sat round the desolate breakfast table, attempting some sort of — 1
desultory consultation. The morning's post had given the final tap to the family fortunes, and all was over. — 2
The dreary dining-room itself, with its heavy mahogany furniture, looked as if it were waiting to be done — 3
away with. — 4
But the consultation amounted to nothing. There was a strange air of ineffectuality about the three — 5
men, as they sprawled at table, smoking and reflecting vaguely on their own condition. — 6

—D. H. Lawrence, "The Horse Dealer's Daughter"

When the short days of winter came dusk fell before we had well eaten our dinners. When we met in — 1
the street the houses had grown sombre. The space of sky above us was the colour of ever-changing violet and — 2
towards it the lamps of the street lifted their feeble lanterns. The cold air stung us and we played till our — 3
bodies glowed. Our shouts echoed in the silent street. — 4

—James Joyce, "Araby"

Accompanied by a plague of robins, Sula came back to Medallion. The little yam-breasted shuddering — 1
birds were everywhere, exciting very small children away from their usual welcome into a vicious stoning. — 2
Nobody knew why or from where they had come. What they did know was that you couldn't go anywhere — 3
without stepping in their pearly shit, and it was hard to hang up clothes, pull weeds or just sit on the front — 4
porch when robins were flying and dying all around you. — 5
Although most of the people remembered the time when the sky was black for two hours with clouds — 6

and clouds of pigeons, and although they were accustomed to excesses in nature—too much heat, too much 7
cold, too little rain, rain to flooding—they still dreaded the way a relatively trivial phenomenon could become 8
sovereign in their lives and bend their minds to its will. 9

—Toni Morrison, *Sula*, "1937"

Literary Passages: Expository Writing

Nowhere in all the sea does life exist in such bewildering abundance as in the surface waters. From the 1
deck of a vessel you may look down, hour after hour, on the shimmering discs of jellyfish, their gently 2
pulsating bells dotting the surface as far as you can see. Or one day you may notice early in the morning that 3
you are passing through a sea of microscopic creatures, each of which contains an orange pigment granule. 4
At noon you are still moving through red seas, and when darkness falls the waters shine with an eerie glow 5
from the phosphorescent fires of yet more billions and trillions of these same creatures. 6

—Rachel Carson, *The Sea Around Us*

Ants are so much like human beings as to be an embarrassment. They farm fungi, raise aphids as 1
livestock, launch armies into wars, use chemical sprays to alarm and confuse enemies, capture slaves. The 2
families of weaver ants engage in child labor, holding their larvae like shuttles to spin out the thread that 3
sews the leaves together for their fungus gardens. They exchange information ceaselessly. They do everything 4
but watch television. 5

—Lewis Thomas, *The Lives of a Cell*

Who discovered America? Or rather, what European discovered America? For we now admit that 1
the people whom Columbus mistakenly named Indians came over from Asia via the Bering Strait, some- 2
where between 25,000 and 40,000 years ago, and, by the time the Europeans arrived, had spread from 3
Alaska to Tierra del Fuego and had developed several hundred languages. In three places at least—Peru, 4
Mexico, and the highlands of Colombia—the Indians developed highly sophisticated societies before Colum- 5
bus landed; and if the Spaniards had come a century later, they might have encountered a strong, defensible 6
Aztec empire that would have developed into a powerful nation, like Japan in Asia. 7

—Samuel Eliot Morison, "Who Really Discovered America?"

A physical theory is always provisional, in the sense that it is only a hypothesis: you can never prove it. 1
No matter how many times the results of experiments agree with some theory, you can never be sure that 2
the next time the result will not contradict the theory. On the other hand, you can disprove a theory by 3
finding even a single observation that disagrees with its predictions. As philosopher of science Karl Popper 4
has emphasized, a good theory is characterized by the fact that it makes a number of predictions that could 5
in principle be disproved or falsified by observation. Each time new experiments are observed to agree with 6
the predictions the theory survives, and our confidence in it is increased; but if ever a new observation is 7
found to disagree, we have to abandon or modify the theory. At least that is what is supposed to happen, but 8
you can always question the competence of the person who carried out the observation. 9

—Stephen Hawking, *A Brief History of Time*

Section 2. Children's Writing[2]

<u>Grade 1</u>:

Mafin

I hvie a cat. It is named mafin. When my mom washsi mafin. he scashed my mom and it hse   1
[hurts] a lot. My mom gis mad at mafin, and he gis madr at my mom.   2

The Seal and the Fish

Once there was a seal. He met a fish, "That looks good said seal. don't eat me" said the fish.   1
One day the seal got caught inside a pece of ice. the fish sucked on the ice, until it turned to water so   2
after that, he always ate ice and snow. but never fish.   3

Meanie

Once upon a time there was a boy he was mene. But he wanted to be remberd as a spashel person.   1
He wanted to be fames. He wanted to go to oter spac. one day somethig majecl hapeind. he was nice   2
agen. He got all of hes friends back. and most of all they thot he was speshel and then he grow up   3
to be a good man a varey good man.   4

<u>Grade 2</u>

My Nightmare

One night I was going to sleep and I had a nightmare about I was going down the walkway and   1
I saw space police walk toward me. They had a long mouth. It could suck up me. They got me. I said,   2
"Help Help." But no one heard me. They took me to their space ship. They put me in a space jail, but   3
I had a good idea and all I had to do is get that space gun. I got loose. When I got out, I saw the alien.   4
I got the space laser and shot a hole through the alien. He melted.   5

Your Own Monster

I have a monster I found him at the park. He enjoys chasing cars and eats rotten goatcheese   1
dunked in green gunk. I don't know where he came from. He likes playing in garbage and scaring   2
people and I have to chain him up so he won't chase any more cars. I like him he's just kind of hard   3
to take care of.   4

My Favorite Puppy

Jessie is my first puppy. She's going to be three years old this year. We got her at the pound. They   1
found her in the middle of the road. One day she ran in front of a car and she got hit on the tail. But   2
it didn't fall off! That's why we are happy, very happy. When Shannon comes over, Jessie jumps on her.   3

---

[2] These examples of children's writing are taken from *Write On!* edited by Cathy Sengel, a supplement to the *Journal Tribune* of Biddeford, ME, which regularly publishes samples of writing from children in the local public schools.

She loves Shannon a lot! She is a beagle puppy. When anyone comes over she is excited. She loves kids   4
very much. She is a hunting dog.   5

Grade 3

Specialness

    Once there was a bird. He was walking with his friend the frog. Then Frog said, "I have more   1
specialness than you, Bird." Bird said quietly, "Why?" "Well I have more camouflage, I hop higher,   2
and I attract people more. You have hardly any specialness," Frog said. They kept on walking. Then   3
Frog said, "I have better eyesight." When Frog turned around Bird was gone.   4
    Sometimes people are not what you think they are.   5

My Dog and Me

    One day my dog and me were playing pass. His name is K.C. He likes to play pass with my   1
football. He lives at my grandmother's house. She has a big yard we play in. K.C. is an awesome   2
catcher. He is cute, fluffy and very loveable. He is a good dog and he is a fun dog to be with.   3

My Most Admired Person

    The person I admire most is my dad. I admire him because he does lots of things with me. He   1
passes a football, fishes, plays catch and chess. These are fun things to do. He also is very nice to me.   2
Sometimes on Friday we go to a place called Federal Jacks and play pool. This is fun, a lot of fun.   3
When we go to my gramma's we go on a paddle boat ride on the lake and fish. We also fish at my   4
house in the creek in the woods. When we catch a fish we eat it. They are good when you put salt on   5
them. So that's why I admire my dad.   6

The Mouse with Tiney Feet

    Once upon a time 100 years ago when mice rould the earth there was a famous mouse known as   1
Theador mouse. Theador was a very interesting mouse he always wanted to know everything.   2
    One day he was walking throu the forest and he saw a mouse factory. So he went inside. He saw   3
tools and a lot of macheans. When he went into the next room he saw a compactor, but Theador did   4
not know what a compactor was. So he asked a werker mouse what a compactor was, and the werker   5
said it makes thing smaller and Theador said can I try it?   6
    Then the mouse said stik your feet in and I'll turn it on. Then the mouse terned it on Theador's   7
feet got smaller and smaller. Then Theador got out and fell down because his feet wor as small as a pea.   8
From now on Theador has to use a wheelchair.   9

Grade 4

My Bicycle Ride

    I press down the dusty button to open the garage. My shiny new bike sits there waiting for me to   1
take it on its first ride. I put on my helmet and I take out my bike into my driveway. I stated pedaling   2
faster and faster, the wind whirling in my face. When I get back I put my bike away and press the   3
dusty button.   4

Respect—What It Means to Me

Respect can be many things. Respect is being nice, saying "excuse me," and not hurting other 1
people's feelings. 2

If you respect someone, they will respect you. If everyone in the entire world respect each other, 3
there would not be any fights or wars or any argument. The world would be nice and kind if everyone 4
respected each other. Everyone would be at peace, and no one will steal and no one will starve. 5

You can do a lot to respect. You could help an elder get around or babysit your little brother and 6
give your parents a break. You could do something small like just listening and not speaking out. You 7
can respect by respecting other people's property, like if you see a jacket on the ground, don't step on it. 8
Pick it up! 9

You don't only respect people, you need to respect the earth by not littering, or the animals by not 10
destroying their homes. They worked hard on them! 11

Don't forget, respect is the best thing you can give a plant or an animal or another person. 12

Billy's Unusual Frog

Once there was an unusual frog. This frog was no ordinary frog. He lived in a pet shop called 1
"Frank's Unusual Pets." The pets there were very unique. The mice did group aerobics. The cat sang 2
jazz, the dogs played tackle football, and the frog talked. He talked to any customer who would listen 3
to him. 4

One day while the frog was talking to the customers, a boy went to the counter and obnoxiously 5
said, "How much is the frog?" 6

Before the clerk could answer, the frog answered loudly, "I'm $20.00. Do you want to buy me?" 7

The boy replied, "Yes I do." He yelled to his mother who was at the other end of the store 8
watching the mice do aerobics, "Mom, can you give me $20.00?" 9

His mother said to her son "Why do you want $20.00?" 10

"I want to buy the talking frog," he replied. His mother gave him the money, and he purchased 11
the frog. 12

On the way home from the pet shop, the frog blurted out, "What's your name, kid?" 13

"My name is Billy," responded the child. The radio was on in the car. Billy's mom was singing 14
along with the song, when she heard a croaking voice. 15

"Billy is your frog singing?" she asked. 16

"Yeah Mom, he is. Isn't he great?" Billy exclaimed. 17

"No he isn't. Make him stop," she ordered. Billy told his new frog to be quiet, and from then on 18
he never talked or sang again. (Not when Billy's mother was around at least!!) 19

Grade 5

The Big Box

In the town of Saco there lived a toy maker. 1

His name was Scot. He had a little girl. Her name was Laura. 2

All Laura wanted was a new doll that danced like a ballerina. The doll had a pink suit with 3
a pink chiffon skirt. Then on Christmas morning Laura and her dad went downstairs. 4

In the middle of the room was a big box. Laura couldn't believe her eyes. She ran to the box and	5
opened it. Inside was a ballerina bigger than her. The doll started to spin and twirl. Her arms went	6
up in the air. Laura's eyes sparkled as she watched the doll. Laura was happy and content.	7

A Ginger Day

One snowy December day a small kitten named Nightmare decided he was bored. He got out his	1
old ball of string and bounced it up and down and up and down and up so high that it landed in the	2
food cupboard. Not wishing to miss any excitement he jumped up as well. He could not see his ball for	3
there was a box, a rather large one at that, blocking his view. High in the air he soared and he was	4
almost over the box when he felt himself plunging through the box cover and falling down and down.	5
He landed on something soft.	6
He soon realized the softness he felt was a marshmallow. In fact he was in a whole world of candy.	7
He walked over to the chocolate sidewalks that had a frosting of ice cream as snow. A doughnut wreath	8
hung from every door and window. Inside the houses were stockings hung from the chocolate brick	9
fireplaces. There were lampposts made of candy canes with little yellow gumdrops as lights.	10
Miles of people (gingerbread people) were roaming the streets. Some were even in the windows of	11
the three-story tall gingerbread houses that were nicely decorated with goodies of all kinds, looking	12
quite nice to eat. A gingerbread mouse dashed across the street in his direction. Nightmare pounced	13
upon it but the mouse just crumbled to a pile of crumbs, frosting, and two little gumdrop eyes. Not	14
wanting to draw attention, he walked off down the street and soon came to a frozen pond. He thought	15
it fun to try and skate and stepped upon the delicate ice. It did not take him long to realize it would	16
not hold his heavy cat weight and he broke through into a whirlpool of milk. Suddenly he opened his	17
eyes. He was in his own room in his own bed. "Here kitty kitty come and eat. Mommy made you a	18
nice gingerbread meal."	19
"Meeooowww," he yelled, and ran off to hide.	20
The End.	21

Shells of the Sea

Here are some similarities of a conch shell and a clam shell. Both shells have a silky-smooth	1
inside. The conch shell could be a home to hermit crabs and other sea creatures. The clam shell is a	2
home to clams. The conch shell and the clam shell are both found in the water, and they are both shells.	3
If you drop either one of these shells, they will break. In both shells you can find white.	4
The conch and the clam shell are both admired, and sold in stores. Many people collect them. Even	5
though the inside is very smooth the outside is very rough.	6
Here are some of the differences of a conch shell and a clam shell. The clam shell is all white, while	7
the conch shell is white and brown. The conch shell is also really spiky.	8
You can curl your finger around the inside of the conch shell, it also has a starlike top. It's difficult	9
to put a clam shell flat down because the clam shell has a little arch. The conch shell holds a hermit	10
crab, while the clam shell holds a clam.	11
Finally if you flip the clam shell upside down it looks like a bowl, and it has a little brown spot	12
at the end.	13

Section 3. A Writing Sample from an Older Student

Here you should insert a brief sample of your own writing. If possible, include *two* samples—one from a piece of narration, and one from a piece of expository writing.

Section 4. Conversational English

Here you should insert a transcription of a conversation you have recorded.

Section 5. The Representation of Conversation in Literature

To an anomalous species of terror I found him a bounden slave. "I shall perish," said he, "I must   1
perish in this deplorable folly. Thus, thus, and not otherwise, shall I be lost. I dread the events of the future,   2
not in themselves, but in their results. I shudder at the thought of any, even the most trivial, incident, which   3
may operate upon this intolerable agitation of soul. I have, indeed, no abhorrence of danger, except in its   4
absolute effect—in terror. In this unnerved—in this pitiable condition, I feel that the period will sooner or   5
later arrive when I must abandon life and reason together, in some struggle with the grim phantasm,   6
FEAR."   7

—Edgar Allan Poe, "The Fall of the House of Usher"

"What should we drink?" the girl asked. She had taken off her hat and put it on the table.   1
"It's pretty hot," the man said.   2
"Let's drink beer."   3
"Dos cervezas," the man said into the curtain.   4
"Big ones?" a woman asked from the doorway.   5
"Yes. Two big ones."   6
The woman brought two glasses of beer and two felt pads. She put the felt pads and the beer glasses   7
on the table and looked at the man and the girl. The girl was looking off at the line of hills. They were   8
white in the sun and the country was brown and dry.   9
"They look like white elephants," she said.   10
"I've never seen one," the man drank his beer.   11
"No, you wouldn't have."   12
"I might have," the man said. "Just because you say I wouldn't have doesn't prove anything."   13
The girl looked at the bead curtain. "They've painted something on it," she said. "What does it say?"   14
"Anis del Toro. It's a drink."   15
"Could we try it?"   16
The man called "Listen" through the curtain. The woman came out from the bar.   17
"Four reales."   18
"We want two Anis del Toro."   19
"With water?"   20
"Do you want it with water?"   21
"I don't know," the girl said. "Is it good with water?"   22
"It's all right."   23
"You want them with water?" asked the woman.   24
"Yes, with water."   25
"It tastes like licorice," the girl said and put the glass down.   26
"That's the way with everything."   27
"Yes," said the girl. "Everything tastes of licorice. Especially all the things you've waited so long for,   28
like absinthe."   29
"Oh, cut it out."   30

"You started it," the girl said. "I was being amused. I was having a fine time."
—Ernest Hemingway, "Hills Like White Elephants"[3]

Section 6. The Speech of Young Children

Eve [4]

Eve at eighteen months	Eve at twenty-seven months
More grapejuice.	*This not better.*
Door.	*See, this one better but this not better.*
Right down.	*There some cream.*
Mommy soup.	*Put in you coffee.*
Eating.	*I go get a pencil 'n write.*
Mommy celery?	*Put my pencil in there.*
No celery.	*Don't stand on my ice cubes!*
Oh drop a celery.	*They was in the refrigerator, cooking.*
Open toy box.	*I put them in the refrigerator to freeze.*
Oh horsie stuck.	*An I want to take off my hat.*
Mommy read.	*That why Jacky comed.*
No Mommy read.	*We're going to make a make a blue house.*
Write a paper.	*You come help us.*
My pencil.	*How 'bout another eggnog instead of cheese sandwich?*
Mommy head?	*I have a fingernail.*
Look at dollie.	*And you have a fingernail.*
What doing, Mommy?	*Just like Mommy has, and David has, and Sara has.*
Drink juice.	*What is that on the table?*

Julia

Julia at thirty-six months

Do you have the kind of orange juice I like? There's no pulp in it.
I like the one that doesn't have pulp best.
The orange juice is for me and the water is for you, Phin [name of dog].
Our refrigerator is good to open [meaning *easy to open*].

[3]From "Hills Like White Elephants." Reprinted with permission of Scribner, a Division of Simon & Schuster, Inc., from THE SHORT STORIES OF ERNEST HEMINGWAY. Copyright 1927 by Charles Scribner's Sons. Copyright renewed 1955 by Ernest Hemingway.
[4]The examples of Eve's speech are taken from de Villiers and de Villiers, p. 55. Reprinted by permission of the publisher from EARLY LANGUAGE by Peter A. deVillers and Jill G. deVillers, p. 55, Cambridge, Mass: Harvard University Press, Copyright © 1979 by Peter A. deVillers and Jill G. deVillers.

Where's me and Daddy and Mama? [in a photograph]

My dad says it's OK if I use the pencils.

This is the muggiest thing I ever had.

Why you can't go inside?

I'm not talking to you.

Does it belong on this part?

Where's the train that goes all by itself? Poof! It disappeared.

Is he too big? No, he's just right.

I came up here and I bet I can be upside down.

That's the way you can do it.

Can you get one of those down for me to play with?

You have to put the little beans in the dirt and that's how it grows. They're not growed yet. They're still seeds. It takes a long time for them to grow.

I'm getting stucker and stucker.

What you can do with this thing?

I have lots of time. I'm very working.

Why a lot of things are closed?

Julia: *I 'rived.* Adult: *You rived?* Julia (scornfully): *"Arrive" means you come.*

BIBLIOGRAPHY

Aitchison, Jean. *Words in the Mind: An Introduction to the Mental Lexicon.* London: Hutchinson, 1987.

American Heritage Dictionary, 2d College ed. Boston, MA: Houghton Mifflin, 1991.

American Heritage Dictionary of the English Language. 4th ed. Boston, MA: Houghton Mifflin, 2000.

Austin, John. *How to Do Things with Words.* New York: Oxford University Press, 1962.

Baldwin, James, "Sonny's Blues." In *Going to Meet the Man.* New York: Vintage Books, 1995.

Barnhart, Robert K., and Sol Steinmetz, with Clarence L. Barnhart. *The Third Barnhart Dictionary of New English.* The Bronx, NY: H. W. Wilson Company, 1990.

Boortien, Harmon S. *Vagueness of Container Nouns and Cognate Verbs.* Diss. University of Texas, Austin, 1975.

Braddock, Richard, Richard Lloyd-Jones, and Lowell Schoer. *Research in Written Composition.* Champaign, IL: National Council of Teachers of English, 1963.

Brengelman, Fred. *The English Language: An Introduction for Teachers.* Englewood Cliffs, NJ: Prentice-Hall, 1970.

Brown, Paul, "The Night I Befriended the Fog," *Points East Magazine* 4.4 (July 2001):55-56.

Brown, Roger W. *A First Language: The Early Stages.* Cambridge, MA: Harvard University Press, 1973.

Carroll, Lewis. *Through the Looking Glass.* New York: MacMillan, 1897.

Carson, Rachael. *The Sea Around Us.* New York: Oxford University Press, 1961.

Chaucer, Geoffrey. *Canterbury Tales.* New York: E. P. Dutton, 1971.

Chomsky, Noam. "The Current Scene in Linguistics: Present Directions." In *Modern Studies in English: Readings in Transformational Grammar,* edited by David A. Reibel and Sanford A. Schane,. Englewood Cliffs, NJ: Prentice-Hall, 1969. 3-12.

Churchill, Winston S. "We Shall Fight on the Beaches." From *The Winston Churchill Home Page,* The Churchill Center, 21 March 2002. www.winstonchurchill.org/beaches.htm.

Cleary, Linda Miller and Michael D. Linn. *Linguistics for Teachers.* New York: McGraw-Hill, 1993.

Cole, Peter, and Jerry L. Morgan, eds. *Syntax and Semantics 3: Speech Acts.* New York: Academic Press, 1975.

Concise Oxford Dictionary of Current English, 9th ed. Oxford: Oxford University Press, 1995.

Connors, Robert, and Andrea Lunsford. "Frequency of Formal Errors in Current College Writing, or Ma and Pa Kettle Do Research." *College Composition and Communication* 39.4 (1988): 395-409.

Crystal, David. *The Cambridge Encyclopedia of Language.* Cambridge: Cambridge University Press, 1987.

Daiker, Donald A., Andrew Kerek, and Max Morenberg. *The Writer's Options: Combining to Composing, 2d ed.* New York: Harper and Row, 1982.

Denning, Keith, and William R. Leben. *English Vocabulary Elements.* New York: Oxford University Press, 1995.

de Villiers, Peter A., and Jill G. de Villiers. *Early Language.* Cambridge, MA: Harvard University Press, 1979.

Dickinson, Emily, "Safe in Their Alabaster Chambers." *In The Complete Poems of Emily Dickinson,* edited by Thomas H. Johnson. Boston: Little, Brown, 1960.

Donnelly, Colleen. *Linguistics for Writers.* Albany, NY: State University of New York Press, 1994.

Farmer, Ann K., and Richard A. Demers. *A Linguistics Workbook.* Cambridge, MA: MIT Press, 2001.

Faulkner, William. *As I Lay Dying.* New York: Random House, 1964.

Fawcett, R. P., and M. R. Perkins. *Child Language Transcripts* 6-12. 4 vols. I-IV. Pontypridd, Wales: Polytechnic of Wales, 1980.

Ferguson, Charles A. and Shirley Brice Heath, eds. *Language in the USA.* Cambridge: Cambridge University Press, 1981.

Finegan, Edward. *Language: Its Structure and Use.* 3d ed. New York: Harcourt Brace College, 1999.

Fodor, Jerry A. *Concepts: Where Cognitive Science Went Wrong.* New York: Oxford University Press, 1998.

Freeman, Mary E. Wilkins, "The Revolt of Mother." In *"The Revolt of 'Mother'" and Other Stories.* Old Westbury, NY: Feminist Press, 1974.

Fromkin, Victoria, and Robert Rodman. *An Introduction to Language,* 6th ed. New York: Harcourt Brace College Publishers, 1998.

Frommer, Paul R., and Edward F. Finegan. *Looking at Languages: A Workbook in Elementary Linguistics.* New York: Harcourt Brace College, 1994.

Frost, Robert, "To the Thawing Wind." In *The Poetry of Robert Frost,* edited by Edward Connery Lathem, New York: Holt, Rinehart, and Winston, 1969.

Greenbaum, Sidney. *A College Grammar of English.* New York: Longman, 1989.

Grice, H. Paul, "Logic and Conversation." In *Syntax and Semantics 3: Speech Acts,* edited by Peter Cole and Jerry L. Morgan, 41-58. New York: Academic Press, 1975.

Hacker, Diana. *Rules for Writers: A Brief Handbook.* 4th ed. New York: Bedford/St. Martin's, 2000.

Harris, Martin, "Demonstrative Adjectives and Pronouns in Devonshire Dialect." *In Dialects in English: Studies in Grammatical Variation,* edited by Peter Trudgill and J. K. Chambers, 20-28. New York: Longman, 1991.

Hawking, Stephen W. *A Brief History of Time: From the Big Bang to Black Holes.* New York: Bantam Books, 1988.

Hemingway, Ernest, "Hills Like White Elephants." In *The Complete Short Stories of Ernest Hemingway, The Finca Vigía Edition.* New York: Charles Scribner's Sons, 1987.

Henderson, Edmund H. *Learning to Read and Spell.* DeKalb, IL: Northern Illinois University Press, 1981.

Hopkins, Gerard Manley, "Spring and Fall." In *Poems: The Poetical Words of Gerard Manley Hopkins,* edited by Norman H. Mackenzie. New York: Oxford University Press, 1990.

Huddleston, Rodney. *English Grammar: An Outline.* Cambridge: Cambridge University Press,1988.

Hudson, Richard. *Teaching Grammar: A Guide for the National Curriculum.* Cambridge, MA: Basil Blackwell, 1992.

Hunt, Kellogg W. *Syntactic Maturity in Schoolchildren and Adults.* Monographs of the Society for Research in Child Development, no. 134. Chicago, IL: University of Chicago Press, 1970.

Hunt, Kellogg W. *Grammatical Structures Written at Three Grade Levels.* Research Report no. 3. Urbana, IL: National Council of Teachers of English, 1965.

Hurston, Zora Neale, *Their Eyes Were Watching God.* New York: Perennial Classics, 1998.

Ihalainen, Ossi, "On Grammatical Diffusion in Somerset Folk Speech." In *Dialects in English: Studies in Grammatical Variation*, edited by Peter Trudgill and J. K. Chambers, 104-119. New York: Longman, 1991.

James, Henry, "The Tree of Knowledge." In *Henry James Complete Stories, 1898-1910.* New York: Library of America (Firm), 1996.

Joyce, James, "Araby." In *Dubliners.* New York: Viking Press, 1965.

Joyce, James, *Dubliners.* New York: Viking Press, 1965.

Joyce, James, "The Dead." In *Dubliners.* New York: Viking Press, 1965.

Klima, Edward, and Ursula Bellugi, "Syntactic Regularities in the Speech of Children." In *Psycholinguistics Papers: The Proceedings of the 1966 Edinburgh Conference*, edited by J. Lyons and R. J. Wales, 183-219. Edinburgh: Edinburgh University Press, 1966.

Kolln, Martha. *Rhetorical Grammar: Grammatical Choices, Rhetorical Effects,* 2d ed. Boston: Allyn and Bacon, 1991.

Labov, William, "Recognizing Black English in the Classroom." In *Black English: Educational Equity and the Law,* edited by John Chambers, Jr., 29-55. Ann Arbor, MI:Karoma Press, 1983.

Labov, William, "Denotational Structure." In *Papers from the Parasession on the Lexicon*, edited by Donka Farkas, Wesley M. Jacobsen, and Karol W. Todrys, 220-260. Chicago, IL: University of Chicago Chicago Linguistic Society, 1978.

Lawrence, D. H. "The Horse Dealer's Daughter." In *The Complete Short Stories of D. H. Lawrence*, vol. 2. London: Heinemann, 1955.

Lewis, Thomas, *The Lives of a Cell: Notes of a Biology Watcher.* New York: Penguin Books, 1978.

Loban, Walter D. *Language Development: Kindergarten Through Grade Twelve.* Research Report no.18. Urbana, IL: National Council of Teachers of English, 1976.

Lodwig, Richard R., and Eugene F. Barrett. *Word, Words, Words: Vocabularies and Dictionaries.* Montclair, NJ: Boynton/Cook Publishers, 1981.

Longman Dictionary of American English: Your Complete Guide to American English. Addison Wesley Longman, 1997.

Lunsford, Andrea, and Robert Connors. *The St. Martin's Handbook,* 3d ed. New York: St. Martin's Press, 1995.

Malmstrom, Jean. *Understanding Language: A Primer for the Language Arts Teacher.* New York: St. Martin's Press, 1977.

Marckwardt, Albert H. *American English.* Revised by J. L. Dillard. New York: Oxford University Press, 1980.

Marlowe, Christopher, "The Passionate Shepherd to his Love." In *The Poems of Christopher Marlowe*, edited by Millar MacLure. London: Methuen and Co., 1968.

Merriam Webster's Collegiate Dictionary, 10th ed.. Springfield, MA: Merriam-Webster, 1995.

Mitchell, Joseph, "Rats on the Waterfront." In *Up In the Old Hotel and Other Stories*. New York: Vintage Books, 1993.

Morison, Samuel Eliot, "Who Really Discovered America?" In *Sailor Historian: The Best of Samuel Eliot Morison*, edited by Emily Morison Beck, 14-31. Boston: Houghton Mifflin, 1977.

Morrison, Toni. *Sula*. New York: Knopf, 1998.

Nichols, Patricia C., "Creoles of the USA." In *Language in the USA,* edited by Charles Ferguson and Shirley Brice Heath, 69-91. New York: Cambridge University Press, 1981.

Noguchi, Rei R. *Grammar and the Teaching of Writing*. Urbana, IL: National Council of Teachers of English, 1991.

O'Donnell, Roy C., William J. Griffin, and Raymond C. Norris. *Syntax of Kindergarten and Elementary School Children: A Transformational Analysis*. Research Report no. 8. Urbana, IL: National Council of Teachers of English, 1967.

O'Grady, William, Michael Dobrovolsky, and Mark Aronoff. *Contemporary Linguistics: An Introduction*, 4th ed. Boston: Bedford/St. Martin's, 2001.

Okrand, Marc. *Star Trek: The Official Guide to Klingon Words and Phrases*. New York: Pocket Books, 1985.

Olsen, Tillie, *Tell Me a Riddle*. New York: Dell, 1984.

Oxford Advanced Learner's Dictionary of Current English, 4th ed., edited by A. S. Hornby, with the assistance of A. P. Cowie. Oxford: Oxford U Press, 1989.

Penfield, Joyce, and Jacob L. Ornstein-Galicia. *Chicano English: An Ethnic Contact Dialect*. Philadelphia, PA: John Benjamins, 1985.

Perera, Katharine. *Children's Writing and Reading: Analysing Classroom Language*. Oxford: Basil Blackwell,1984.

Piaget, Jean, *The Language and Thought of the Child*. London: Kegan Paul, Trench, Trubner, 1926.

Pinker, Steven. *The Language Instinct: How the Mind Creates Language*. New York: William Morrow, Inc., 1994.

Poe, Edgar Allan, "The Fall of the House of Usher." In *The Complete Tales and Poems of Edgar Allan Poe*. New York: Vintage Books, 1975.

Pooley, Robert C. *The Teaching of English Usage*. Urbana, IL: National Council of Teachers of English, 1974.

Quirk, Randolph, Sidney Greenbaum, Geoffrey Leech, and Jan Svartvik. *A Comprehensive Grammar of the English Language*. London: Longman, 1985.

Random House Webster's College Dictionary. New York: Random House, 1991.

Read, Charles. *Children's Categorization of Speech Sounds in English*. Research Report no. 17. Urbana, IL: National Council of Teachers of English, 1975.

Reibel, David A. and Sanford A. Schane, eds. *Modern Studies in English: Readings in Transformational Grammar*. Englewood Cliffs, N.J.: Prentice-Hall, 1969.

Roberts, Paul. *Understanding English*. New York: Harper and Brothers, 1958.

Roberts, Paul. *Understanding Grammar*. New York: Harper and Brothers, 1954.

Rosenberg, S., and J.H. Koplin. *Developments in Applied Psycholinguistics Research*. New York: Macmillan, 1968.

Sengel, Cathy, ed. *Write On! A Journal of Writing by Elementary Students in Arundel, Biddeford, Dayton, Kennebunkport, Old Orchard Beach, Saco, SAD 57, Sanford, Springvale, Wells: A Supplement to the Journal Tribune*, Biddeford, ME, 1995 -1996.

Searle, John R. "Indirect Speech Acts." In *Syntax and Semantics 3: Speech Acts,* edited by Peter Cole and Jerry L. Morgan, 59-82. New York: Academic Press, 1974.

Shakespeare, William, "Hamlet, Prince of Denmark." In *The Complete Signet Classic Shakespeare,* New York: Harcourt, Brace, Jovanovich, 1972.

Shakespeare, William, "My Mistress' Eyes Are Nothing Like the Sun." In *The Complete Signet Classic Shakespeare,* New York: Harcourt, Brace, Jovanovich, 1972.

Strunk. William, Jr., and E. B. White. *The Elements of Style,* 3d ed. New York: MacMillan, 1979.

Tan, Amy. *The Hundred Secret Senses*. New York: G. P. Putnam's Sons, 1995.

Thomas, Lewis. *The Lives of a Cell: Notes of a Biology Watcher*. New York: Penguin Books, 1978.

Todd, Loreto. *Modern Englishes: Pidgins and Creoles*. Oxford: Blackwell, 1984.

Traugott, Elizabeth C. and Mary Louise Pratt. *Linguistics for Students of Literature*. New York: Harcourt, Brace, Jovanovich, 1980.

Troupe, Quincy. *Take It to the Hoop, "Magic" Johnson*. New York: Jump at the Sun Hyperion Books for Children, 2000.

Trudgill, Peter. *The Dialects of England,* 2d ed. Oxford: Blackwell, 1999.

Trudgill, Peter, and J. K. Chambers, eds. *Dialects of English: Studies in Grammatical Variation*. New York: Longman, 1991.

Tufte, Virginia. *Grammar as Style*. New York: Holt, Rinehart and Winston, 1971.

Twain, Mark. *The Adventures of Huckleberry Finn*. New York: The Heritage Press, 1940.

Scholar, Mina Shaughnessy. *Errors and Expectations: A Guide for the Teacher of Basic Writing*. New York: Oxford University Press, 1977.

Sedley, Dorothy. *Anatomy of English: An Introduction to the Structure of Standard American English*. New York: St. Martin's Press, 1990.

Warden, D. A. "The Influence of Context on Children's Use of Identifying Expressions and References." *British Journal of Psychology* 67 (1976): 101-112.

Weaver, Constance. *Teaching Grammar in Context*. Portsmouth, NH: Boynton/Cook Publishers, Heinemann, 1996.

Weaver, Constance. *Grammar for Teachers: Perspectives and Definitions*. Urbana, IL: National Council of Teachers of English, 1979.

Webster's New World College Dictionary, 3rd ed. New York: Simon Schuster Macmillan, 1996.

Welty, Eudora, "A Worn Path." In *Thirteen Stories by Eudora Welty*. New York: Harcourt, Brace, Jovanovich, 1977.

Whately, Elizabeth, "Language Among Black Americans." In *Language in the USA*, edited by Charles Ferguson and Shirley Brice Heath, 92-107. New York: Cambridge University Press, 1981.

Williams, Joseph M., "The Phenomenology of Error." *College Composition and Communication* 32 (1981):152-168.

Williams, Joseph M. *Style: Ten Lessons in Clarity and Grace,* 4ᵗʰ edition. New York: HarperCollins College Publishers, 1994.

Wolfram, Walt, "Varieties of American English." In *Language in the USA*, edited by Charles Ferguson and Shirley Brice Heath, 44-68. New York: Cambridge University Press, 1981.

Wright, Richard, "The Man Who Was Almost a Man." In *Eight Men*. New York: Avon Books, 1961.

Zipes, Jack, trans. *The Complete Fairy Tales of the Brothers Grimm*. New York: Bantam Books, 1987.

INDEX